Speaking from the Body

Speaking from the Body

LATINAS ON HEALTH AND CULTURE

edited by
Angie Chabram-Dernersesian
and Adela de la Torre

Jessica M. Núñez de Ybarra, MD, MPH

the university of arizona press   tucson

The University of Arizona Press
© 2008 The Arizona Board of Regents
All rights reserved

www.uapress.arizona.edu

Library of Congress Cataloging-in-Publication Data

Speaking from the body : latinas on health and
culture / edited by Angie Chabram-Dernersesian and
Adela de la Torre.
    p. cm.
  Includes bibliographical references.
  ISBN 978-0-8165-2664-2 (pbk. : alk. paper)
  1. Hispanic American women---Health and hygiene.
2. Hispanic American women---Biography.
I. Chabram-Dernersesian, Angie. II. Torre, Adela de la.
RA778.4.H57S64   2008
613.089'968073—dc22   2008025273

We would like to acknowledge the Dean's Book Fund at
the University of California, Davis, for assistance in the
production of this book.

Publication of this book is made possible in part by the
proceeds of a permanent endowment created with the
assistance of a Challenge Grant from the National Endowment for the Humanities, a federal agency.

Manufactured in the United States of America on acid-
free, archival-quality paper containing a minimum of 30%
post-consumer waste and processed chlorine free.

13   12   11   10   09   08   6   5   4   3   2   1

To Angie González Chabram, Herminia de la Torre, and Yolanda Butler

Contents

Speaking from the Body

Introduction

Narratives of Latina Health

Angie Chabram-Dernersesian

Within contemporary health literature, the voices of Latinas who are living with illness and engaged in extensive health work often appear as excerpts illustrating important trends, health disparities, and treatment modalities (see, for example, Espín 1997, 2003; de la Torre and Estrada 2001; de la Torre 2002; Delgado 2002). This volume, however, incorporates a substantially different approach. The thirteen essays vividly illustrate that Latina cultural narratives and narrative actions are themselves important venues for accessing crucial information about diverse health states, constructions of illness, illness experiences, and the web of sociocultural relationships and practices that shape Latinas' worldviews *and* health status. The idea for anthologizing Latina cultural health narratives surfaced as a result of a series of conversations that led to new transdisciplinary perspectives bridging health and culture.

One day amid the hustle and bustle of teaching, service, and the work of diversity and gender-based Latina research, my coeditor, Adela de la Torre, and I paused for a moment and made plans to catch up with each other after a hard day's work. When I entered her office for our promised meeting, we quickly took care of business in order to get down to the real issues at hand, which involved our all-important personhood: "How are *you?*" As daughters of aging mothers who had reared us as single parents, we both knew that another question would follow on the heels of the first: "How's *your mother?*" Like many Latinas, we were raised in close-knit families, and we maintained that connection to family by regular, lengthy phone calls to our mothers all our adult lives. As our mothers aged, however, our pláticas became increasingly focused on their "health rituals" and commitment to la salud—to maintaining health and independence in spite of a variety of health challenges, some routine, others chronic.

Adela and I have continued sharing our mothers' stories, and our answers to *the* question get richer and richer, more and more detailed. Yes, we are involved in academic bridgework and long-distance caregiving and community building. Part of this work involves repeating the contents of the "latest phone call," naming complex health ailments, and offering the best possible advice. As the ritual repeats itself, we become acutely aware that the daily telephone calls to or from our beloved mamás (Angie González Chabram and Herminia de la Torre) are the basis for passionate as well as thought-provoking conversations about Latina health and, more generally, the importance of speaking about illness in order to negotiate its place within our lives. Here, as elsewhere, aspects of Latina/o culture place high value on the power of conversations in building community and braving the challenges life places before us.

As privileged listeners, we learn firsthand about aches and pains, fears and hopes, cultural rituals and productions, illnesses and remedies, health care, home care, and barrio care. In the course of our conversations, we familiarize ourselves with aging bodies, the names and costs of prescription medicines, the specialties of various health-care practitioners, and the obstacles and challenges confronted by aging Latinas. Yet we see so much more than our mothers' doctors would ever imagine: how illness impacts the full context of our mothers' lives, the changes in family roles, the ways our mothers integrate the clinical treatments prescribed by their physicians with the traditional means of healing they have always used within their communities, and how, despite commonalities, their illness experiences are unique. We take note of uncelebrated victories, instances of empowerment, and the expressions our mothers use to speak about health and experiences with illness.

Our roles are complex and require critical reflection as well as action. We witness and intervene in the processes by which our path-breaking Latina mothers attend to their bodies, families, and communities and negotiate medical institutions, health-care providers, and health states. Although we enjoy privileges our mothers do not have, we are not in any sense disinterested observers. Apart from the fact that we are daughters and family members, we are also community members (Latinas) who do advocacy research. In this capacity, we identify, process, and catalog information, and we create health discourses as well as practices of Latina cultural representation.

We also clearly recognize that our health dialogues with our mothers are not unidirectional. Our mothers also listen to us when we are sick, must confront new bodily states or health challenges, or require a proactive stance. At these moments, their expertise and sabiduría (wisdom) kick in to such a degree that we switch roles. At these key moments, they translate our bodies and health states back to us, asserting their medical and experiential knowledges and providing insights from other community members who offer more instances of long-distance wisdom about health.

In the intervals between our conversations about our mothers' specific health narratives, Adela and I reflect on new threads in scholarship. We note that books such as *Latina Health in the United States: A Public Health Reader* (Aguirre-Molina and Molina 2003), *Salud! A Latina's Guide to Total Health—Body, Mind, and Spirit* (Delgado 2002), *Latina Realities: Essays on Healing, Migration, and Sexuality* (Espín 1997), *Woman Who Glows in the Dark* (Avila 1999), and *Latina Healers: Lives of Power and Tradition* (Espín 2003) are placing Latinas at the heart of the healing and health studies policy agenda. Outside of this domain, in the ever-growing field of expressive cultures (the Internet, motion pictures, CDs, poems, and novels/testimonials), we also detect increased attention to the issue of Latina health. For instance, M. Cecilia Wendler's online article "Frida Kahlo: Wounded Woman" directs virtual audiences to the art of Frida Kahlo, which "opens up a subjective experience of one person's pain through the medium of painting" (2005). Yet other depictions of Latina health can be found in the music of the bold-spirited Chicano El Vez (Robert López), who translates Elvis Presley's song "Kentucky Rain" into a memorable account of Kahlo's suffering that he calls "Frida's Life of Pain." The acclaimed motion picture *Frida* (2002) captures Frida's intimate struggles with chronic pain; affirmation of her disability; efforts to achieve a full, productive life; and triumphant movement from the domestic to the public space, sick bed and all.

In turn, Latina-centered productions such as the movie *Real Women Have Curves* (2002) capture the role of young Latina caregivers in the family as well as a variety of issues concerning body image, mental health, and health education. Print culture offers other vivid illustrations of Latina health issues. For instance, Chicana feminist testimonials such as *Forged under the Sun* (Lucas 1993) and detective novels such as *Cactus Blood* (Corpi 1995) represent in graphic detail the health consequences of pesticide poisoning among Latina fieldworkers who have restricted access to social and health services. Theatrical works such as *The Fat-Free Chicana and the Snow Cap Queen* (Romero 1999) stage the threats of diabetes, obesity, and heart disease—the three top causes of death among contemporary Latinas—in the context of a Mexican restaurant whose female owner is faced with the question of how to change artery-clogging, fat-filled menus into healthier dishes while satisfying the demands of business and traditional palates. Contemporary Latina testimonial literature such as *Medicine Stories* (Levins Morales 1998) and *Borderlands / La frontera* (Anzaldúa 1987) draws from health and bodily discourses in order to illuminate the effects of the trauma of colonialism, and Latina autoethnographies such as *The Vulnerable Observer* (Behar 1997) target the complex dynamics of "insiders" who write about themselves and others and exhibit a variety of vulnerabilities, including their own infirmities.[1]

These cultural productions are increasingly interpreted within Chicana/o, Latina/o, and cultural studies frameworks arguing that "[n]othing stands outside of representation" (Denzin and Lincoln 2005) and that "representations are inscribed within the forms and practices of culture" (Fregoso and Chabram 1990, 206). This broader perspective on Chicana/o and Latina/o cultural studies allows us to deconstruct stereotypes about Latina/o culture and opens up new possibilities for re-viewing the multifaceted and "constructed" nature of culture, society, and community. These frameworks also encourage a closer look at "how our [Latina] bodies express carnal and creative influences and create venues for bringing to life forms of social and cultural expression that normally remain tucked away, hidden from inquiring eyes" (Latina Feminist Group 2001, 1–2).

Motivated by the desire to engage our personal conversations about our mothers with this growing field of Latina/o cultural studies and representation, Adela and I resolved to bring Latina health narratives out of the shadows and the family to foreground Latina expressive speech, cultural representations, *and* health stories. As we pushed forward with our endeavor, we discovered within the academic literature narrative inquiries into the illness experience. Although these inquiries provide a much-needed perspective on the social construction of illness, they lack in-depth attention to the experiences and analytical frameworks of minority groups. In addition, seminal investigations have largely been written in case study form—the dominant narrative genre in medicine (for example, Kleinman 1988)—and initially by male physicians and academics (see Kleinman 1988; Frank 1995), who, no matter how empathetic, inevitably impose an external interpretation on the patient's experience.[2] As Chicana feminists, we recognized that such an approach doubly silences those patients who are both Latina and women and wish to tell their own stories. And the new body of health literature featuring women's illness experiences and narratives, though groundbreaking (such as DasGupta and Hurst 2007), in many respects may not include Latinas as subjects of narrative speech or inquiry and certainly does not foreground their experiences.

Cognizant of this silence, we invited Latinas living an illness experience—whether directly themselves or indirectly as caregivers and friends of ailing women—to share their stories, uncensored by us. By not directing them to "write Latina" or "write feminist" or indeed write anything other than their illness/wellness experience, we gained diverse visions of Latina health, illness, community, and identity. We found that although Latina/o culture mediates Latinas' representational landscapes and health practices, these women are *more* than their health status or their Latinidad: they partake in multiple identities that overlap and relate to one another. In addition, their ailments are not isolated events; they form part of the larger whole of Latina lives that encompass family, community, the medical profession, and society. Indeed, the multicultural influences in these narratives cannot be ignored. For this reason, aspects of these stories will resonate with the illness experiences of members of other social groups, including minorities whose heath states are also affected by race, class, gender, and transnationality. The result, we hope, is a book that will have wide-ranging relevance not only to scholars in Chicana/o studies and women's/gender studies, but also to those in medical ethics, narrative medicine, public policy, literature, and cultural studies in general. In fact, some of the contributors to this book decided to share with their physicians what they wrote, which had amazing results in terms of the sensitivity of care they have received since then.

In addition, this collection was ultimately motivated by the shocking and untimely death of leading Chicana feminist, writer, lesbian, and cultural practitioner Gloria Anzaldúa from the complications of diabetes and by the many health narratives that were told in the wake of her death.[3] Armed with the recognition that contemporary Latinas have many stories of health and ailments to tell, we proceeded from informal telephone and office exchanges to this book. Within a traditional academic context that encourages individualism and the monodisciplinary research, this collaboration is not business as usual. My coeditor is a health-policy researcher, and I am a cultural studies/literature researcher. It might appear that our disciplinary affiliations are at odds with each other or that our commonalities are confined to the arena of Latina/o culture, but they are not. In fact, a number of recent works point to the "increasing propensity" toward interdisciplinarity (Lupton 2003, 5) in scholarship at large.

Recent theoretical perspectives on medicine and society also foreground the fact that medicine is part of culture, that "people construct their understandings of the world, including their beliefs about medicine and disease, from their interaction with cultural products as well as personal experience and discussion with others" (Lupton 2003, 19). In addition, "medicine," "health care, and the doctor-patient relationship" are increasingly interpreted as social, "cultural activities and experiences" and as "appropriate areas of study for sociologists of culture and scholars in the field of cultural studies" (Lupton 2003, 19). In turn, linkages between literature and health are also prominent in scholarly works that emphasize the importance of narrative and storytelling in recognizing that "illnesses . . . are socially constructed events, reproduced and perpetuated through talk, and most specifically, narrative" (Elwyn and Gwyn 1998, 166; see also Espín 1997, xi).

We believe that this collection is an important development in Latina/o studies and health studies proper because it does not emulate other studies that limit Latina voices to "excerpts" or confine narrative inquiry to the doctor-patient relationship or the traditional case study. Our realignment of the scholarly landscape affirms that Latinas "experience illness within a narrative, or story, that shapes and gives meaning to what they are feeling, moment to moment" (Donald 1998, 17). Our collection promotes this idea in the context of the need for a greater appreciation of the sociocultural knowledges and contexts that Latinas themselves produce *outside* of clinical settings—in places where subject-producing discourses, social relations, and treatment modalities thrive—and *within* the context of the underrepresentation of Latinas in the health literature (Aguirre-Molina and Molina 2003, 4), illness narratives, and health institutions.[4]

This book comes on the heels of published works warning that "as the nation's minority population continues to grow, the lack of minority trained health professionals and general ignorance of cultural issues will continue to create health care barriers for [the minority] population" (de la Torre and Estrada 2001, 104), compounding the barriers posed by socioeconomic status, low educational attainment, and poverty.[5] Scholars of Latina/o health suggest that in order to be culturally competent, healthcare practitioners require more than familiarity with the Spanish language and with significant cultural differences.[6] They also must be familiar with cultural interpretations of illness and traditional treatments and be cognizant of the fact that many gender stereotypes associated with Latinas are contestable (de la Torre and Estrada 2001, 101, 108).

Irrespective of the fact that many common themes can be found in the narratives that compose this volume, the Latina contributors are individuals with unique stories to tell. To foreground their distinctive voices and approaches, we have chosen to allow the Latina narratives to stand alone, without annotation or interpretation from us. Not until chapter 13 and the conclusion do we insert our editorial voices, discussing some of the key cultural features and health-policy implications that are woven, sometimes subtly, through the particular narratives. Rather than one overarching conclusion, we offer two separate analyses, one of narrative retrospective and the other of the broader health context for U.S. Latinas, focusing on the particular conditions addressed in this volume.

The narratives in this collection can play an important role in supporting the formation of broad-based sociocultural literacy in relation to Latinas. They offer a number of Latina cultural interpretations of illnesses that have important implications for health-care providers and the public at large—and that, we hope, debunk stereotypes that all Latinas are culturally "the same" and that their experiences are necessarily "different" from those of women of other cultural backgrounds. These narratives also have embedded within them an important female culture of orality: the plática. As de la Torre explains in chapter 3, "Pláticas are at the core of how many Latinas cope with illness and disease. They are the symbolic mechanisms though which these women address the challenges of maintaining their physical and emotional health." Throughout these collected narratives, pláticas are at work—in the whispered confidences between cousins; in the consejos (counsels) among mothers, daughters, and granddaughters; in the exchanges between sisters; and in the female epistemologies by which Latinas teach each other. Pláticas come to us through the mediums of language, culture, tradition, experience, and bodily revelations in describing how to navigate challenging physical and social ills that often feed off one another.

If this collection demonstrates how the fluid categories of (Latina) gender and culture intersect within health narratives, it also illustrates how selected Latinas negotiate complex gender roles in different individual circumstances and periods of the life cycle. At times they break with patriarchal and traditional gender roles, but at others they conform to them, yet nevertheless become respected community leaders. At times they forge egalitarian partnerships with the men in their lives, but at others they opt for independent lives or sidestep normative heterosexuality. And all exhibit a strong sense of self-determination and personal agency in their quest for their own or family members' well-being.

Another unique aspect of this book is that it brings together the experiences of Latinas working in the factories, fields, and domestic sector with the experiences of Latina academics working in history, literature, public health, epidemiology, education, political science, and Chicana/o or Latina/o studies. This collection also includes Latina health-care professionals (two doctors and one psychologist) who write from the perspective of recipients rather than practitioners of health care. In addition, most contributors are from working-class backgrounds and are either immigrants or first- or second-generation Latina "Americans."[7] In many instances, they are the first in their families to attend college.

Of equal significance, many of these contributors form part of a larger informal social network of Latinas who collaborate across academic departments, universities, families, and professional and service organizations. These contributors consider Latina health narratives important not only for academics and health professionals, but also for community members who may be living with similar ailments and wish to find resources beyond the traditional health literature, seek to follow the example of this book and write their own health narratives for personal healing, or educate their comadres or health providers. For that reason, the contributors share important medical information that can be useful to those living with particular ailments, but these narratives do not and are not intended to reproduce generic clinical descriptions of disease profiles. In this sense, the book is geared to a diverse readership that includes health-care professionals, academics, students, Latinas, and others from many walks of life.

In addition, this volume rejects strict divisions between the worlds of the Latina researcher, the Latina clinician and health-care provider, and the Latina patient and research subject. As medical professionals, academics, advocates, immigrant and domestic workers, and family members, the contributors to this collection emphasize overlaps and mixtures; social networks and community interactions; and the importance of speech, culture, and social change for community building and healing. These narratives also capture the multiple roles of Latinas as agents of representation of diverse health states. In this collection, Latinas articulate, witness, analyze, report, and practice health; they "write self" (Gabriela Arredondo, Concha Delgado Gaitan, Lorena García, Adaljiza Sosa-Riddell, "Christi," and Clara Lomas), and they "write other" Latinas (Jessica Núñez de Ybarra, Enriqueta Valdez-Curiel, Adela de la Torre, Yvette Flores, AnaLouise Keating, and Angie Chabram-Dernersesian). The contributors also embed their diverse illness experiences and definitions in a variety of cultural forms and productions that are important in Latina/o expressive culture: the personal letter, the dependent testimonial that speaks when the Latina subject cannot, the biographical account of another Latina's life, the redacted interview, and the autobiography.

Without a doubt, these narratives collectively illustrate the complex intersubjective contexts and expressions of Latina health. Here, Latinas not only "speak" through different venues of Latina culture and states of subjectivity, but also are listeners-receptors and producers of meaning, health messages, and narratives. In this sense, they participate in fluid health dialogues that are multivoiced as well as multisited. These narratives capture the hopes, aspirations, agencies, cultures, struggles, languages, knowledge systems, social milieus, and healing practices of selected Latinas in the twenty-first century.

Our decision to highlight this rich discursive, communicative, and narrative context of Latina health is guided by the idea that the story of Latinas and their health remains only a partial one if Latina agents and forms of cultural production are not included in the story's construction and if Latinas do not actively participate in general discussions about health policy. In addition, we agree with Dr. Rafael Campo, who suggests that "no greater expertise can be achieved than that which actually comes from living with an illness" (2003, 96). Latina health narratives "harness this wisdom and expertise" in different manners, "asserting the authority of the afflicted in the most persuasive and incontrovertible of terms, in an idiom which shares its power instead of wielding it like a weapon" (Campo 2003, 96). Yet as Dr. Campo warns in *The Healing Art*, this power can be wrested from patients by "torrents of medicalese" and by "appropriated, preconceived versions of what is happening to them" (26).[8]

In putting together this book, we offered selected Latinas the opportunity to claim their discursive and representational space and to "luxuriate" across the page in great depth and detail. This opportunity is particularly important given the obstacles to Latina discourse that are evident within clinical settings, where Latinas are expected to adopt normative, English-language clinical discourses (in describing their symptoms and in completing health questionnaires and fill-in-the-blank medical histories) that do not allow for in-depth understanding of the multiple ways in which Latinas live, experience, document, speak, heal, identify, and negotiate particular health states.[9] Yet, as we have seen, Latinas view the sharing of pláticas and the telling of stories as integral to diagnosis, wellness, and healing.[10] We contend that it is important to recognize and engage the cultural, narrative, and experiential dimensions of Latina health rather than suppress them, especially if the goal is to understand and identify the serious health challenges facing an increasingly ascendant population group that has made significant contributions to culture, society, and economy.[11]

For the most part, the Latinas whose narratives are captured in this collection are of Mexican descent and reside within the western United States, although one is a Panamanian migrant who has returned to her homeland and another is a Mexican national who has immigrated from Mexico to the United States several times. We adopt the designation *Latinas* as a way to highlight pan-ethnic solidarity—here, meaning a strategic set of health alliances among underrepresented Latinas. In addition, this book expresses lived experiences of a number of ailments that have important implications for Latina health: hypertension, breast cancer, obesity, diabetes, depression, osteoarthritis, rheumatoid arthritis, dementia, Parkinson's disease, lupus, and hyper/hypothyroidism. (See the conclusion for demographic and health-policy information on these ailments within the Latina community.) The fact that U.S. Latinas/os have disproportionately high rates of diabetes—higher than either white Americans or Mexicans resident in Mexico (Aguirre-Molina and Molina 2003, 25, 44)—is reflected in four narratives relating to different forms of diabetes: types 1 and 2, gestational, and prediabetes. Although four chapters on this subject may seem overkill, each narrative articulates a very different perspective on and approach to the disease. In particular, AnaLouise Keating's interview with Gloria Anzaldúa focuses not on the manifestations of diabetes, but on Anzaldúa's quest to understand the lessons inherent in a lifetime of illness.

Aside from recounting diverse illness experiences, these narratives illustrate important aspects of the social contexts and real-world family relationships that writers and psychiatrists such as Dr. Arthur Kleinman (1988) argue are crucial for understanding the "experience" and "interpretations" of illness. In addition, these narratives alert us to the important ways that personal identity and community intersect to affect interpretation of illnesses, compliance with treatment, and utilization of mainstream Western medicine, alternative therapies, and traditional healing practices. From the perspective of a (Latina) patient-centered process, the chapters offer health-care providers, caregivers, and educators some insights into how Latinas blend medical diagnostic and narrative elements of their disease and incorporate healing practices that include listening to their bodies and articulating communal and social legacies and spiritualities, many of which have persisted despite conquest and colonization.

These Latina narratives are important because they illustrate the overarching influence of cultural mediations in health that must be considered in the treatment of any disease. In the final analysis, these women not only produce cultural narratives, but utilize culture as a way of healing, speaking, protesting, setting the record straight, making sense of their illness experiences, and empowering themselves and their communities. Through their examples, they show us that the "public" Latina health narrative can be "a tool of advocacy in itself, a methodology by which otherwise marginalized voices can be heard" (DasGupta and Hurst 2007, 269). As Sayantani DasGupta and Marsha Hurst note, "Advocacy is fuelled by life stories, stories that transform illness from an individual experience to a collective phenomenon" (2007, 271). Through narrative, important "connections" can be made that resist the separation of the ill from the healthy (and the ill from their bodies) and that enable the creation of larger "communities of caring" (Stanley 2007, 23) that go beyond empathetic witnessing to empathetic action.

As the editors of this collection, we are well aware of the larger social inequities (including classism, racism, sexism, ageism, xenophobia, homophobia, limited educational access) that society and the medical community must address in tandem with Latina health issues. We agree with Rita Charon (2006, 230) and others who suggest that the goals of achieving fair and decent health care should be subsumed under the goals of social justice. In this spirit, we deliver a text that we hope will generate further research and a blossoming of narratives in which Latinas make their private health stories public and advocate for themselves and one another.[12]

1

Of Breasts and Baldness

My Life with Cancer

Gabriela F. Arredondo

There are a few moments in my life that haunt me. For the past thirteen years, one has been the memory of Abuelita Tencha in her warm kitchen, opening her thin cotton bathrobe and showing me how the radiation had cooked the skin where her breast was removed. "Parezco un chicharrón, m'ija!" (I look like a fried pork skin, my dear!). There in the one place I most associated with my grandmother and with wonderful food always on the stove . . . "sí, m'ija, vente, siéntate, comete algo, m'ija, aquí tengo unos tamalitos y salsa" (Yes, my dear, come, sit down. Eat a little something, my dear. Here I have some tamales and salsa). Her gentle face and determined though usually laughing eyes held so much sadness that afternoon. . . . "Mira lo que me hicieron." (Look what they've done to me.)

"Si, mira lo que me hicieron," I think to myself as I'm waking up from surgery, realizing that, like my abuelita, I no longer had a left breast. The radical mastectomy had meant taking off the whole breast and what turned out to be twenty-seven lymph nodes. I'd always wanted to be more like mi 'uelita, but not this way, not fighting breast cancer a slice at a time. This disease whose treatments and protocols have been developed to treat the "average breast cancer patient"—a white, postmenopausal woman in her early sixties—had now hit me too. And now I know firsthand that it also strikes young Latina women.[1]

I know I have a very different relationship to my doctors, to medical knowledge, to my own body than did my 'uelita. Tencha was filled with a fatalism toward and distance from her medical care common among those of her generation. Doctors didn't always know best (and the curandero could always be counted on instead), but they were persons with much education, so we'd best do as they say. Thus, "mira lo que me hicieron" for her carried much of the hurt and lack of understanding that came of not knowing much about cancer or the world of advanced oncology, or even about her own body: "Pues, fíjate, ni supe que viejitas como yo tuvieron cáncer del pecho" (Well, imagine that! I didn't even know little old women like me could get breast cancer). Part of the pain about my 'uelita's short, fierce struggle with breast cancer is my own guilt. After all, *I* knew older women could get breast cancer, that it wasn't just a disease of women in their fifties and sixties. Somehow, though, I never talked with her about breast cancer before it came into our lives. (And where was her doctor? Why didn't she or he talk to her, insist on mammograms?) I could have told her that she, too, was at risk and should keep getting her mammograms, but I didn't. Neither did her doctor—Did she or he write her off as an old Mexican woman who would most likely die of something else soon anyway? I'll never know whether, if I had talked with her about breast cancer, the cancer would have been caught early enough to have her live through her seventies and into her eighties and nineties, as many people had in her family. Life is like that sometimes—you don't think to talk to those closest to you about issues that don't seem to be directly relevant . . . and when they are relevant, it's often too late to talk about them.

Niña Que No Llora, No Mama

March 10. My birthday and the day I got my diagnosis: invasive ductal carcinoma that had already spread out of the breast and into the lymph glands. I remember feeling waves of heat and cold as I sat in the comfortable little room at the medical clinic with my husband, trying to process that we were talking about me, my body, my cancer. Of course, I asked if they were sure they hadn't mixed up my biopsy samples with someone else's. After all, I had no symptoms, no lumps, faithfully did my monthly self-exams, and only had pain *after* the mammogram. My first mammogram ever, and it showed some worrisome calcifications and inflamed lymph nodes.[2] Ultimately, the doctors decided to biopsy not the breast, but the lymph nodes (yes, it hurts). When I got the diagnosis, I was shocked because there hadn't been much evidence in the breast tissue. I thought about the other mujeres (women) before me who had been through this: my abuelita and my mami, and I wondered how they had felt when they found out.

Mi mamá was diagnosed with ductal carcinoma in situ (DCIS) about seven years ago, and after a lumpectomy and radiation she has recovered well and officially is considered cured (that is, she has lived five years with no cancer recurrence).[3] Of course, I'm betting that after cancer, few people really feel cured or shake the knowledge that it could come back at any time. Ironically, I discovered after genetic testing (BRACA 1 and BRACA 2) that I have no known genetic predisposition for breast cancer.[4] So I find myself not allowing people to get comfortable with my cancer by linking it to my mother's or my grandmother's. People somehow don't feel themselves to be at risk if they can mentally link cancer to genetics. I, however, am one of the more than 80 percent of women who get breast cancer but have no known genetic link for it. The National Cancer Institute, part of the U.S. National Institutes of Health, estimated that 178,480 women and 2,030 men were diagnosed with breast cancer in 2007. Among them, 40,460 women and 450 men died of the disease (National Cancer Institute n.d.).

Breast cancer develops first in the milk ducts of the breast (DCIS, or stage one), then it breaks out of the ducts into the breast tissue itself (stage two). From there, it moves most commonly into the lymph glands under your arm (stage three), where you run the highest risk of its becoming systemic cancer that metastasizes in other parts of the body (stage four). People can live with stage four cancers for a long time, but at stage four the doctors don't talk about curing you, only about controlling the cancer in a terminal condition. The many permutations of and variations on staging depend on tumor size and number of nodes involved, but this rough description helps to describe the protocols for each step. With stages one and two, women usually undergo a lumpectomy followed by radiation. With a few stage-two and most stage-three breast cancers, the recommended treatment is modified radical mastectomy (removal of the whole breast), chemotherapy, and radiation. With locally advanced stage-three cancers that involve the lymph nodes (my situation), there is also surgical dissection of the nodes.[5] Removal of any lymph nodes opens up possibilities for yet more side effects and a lifelong transformation of one's body. The lymph nodes under your arm, the ones most usually involved in locally advanced breast cancers, help to circulate and drain the lymph fluids from your arm. Without all your lymph nodes, you run the risk of developing lymphedema, a potentially very dangerous condition that involves swelling, pain, and even the loss of the use of your arm.[6]

I have been guarding against the threat of lymphedema since the evening I woke up in that surgical recovery room and wondered, "¿Que me hicieron?" After healing from the surgery, I have been in physical therapy for months to learn how to massage my arm to help the fluids move properly through it, to bandage my arm (with five layers!) at night to prevent swelling, and to do daily exercises to improve my range of motion. And I'm learning how to make all this a part of my life forever, even as I try to accept that I have to use a specialized pump an hour a day, wear compression sleeves at night, and don a special sleeve when I fly or travel to high elevations.

After I got the diagnosis of aggressive, locally advanced breast cancer, my husband and I immersed ourselves in research, taking some comfort in the power of knowledge. We spent hours and hours surfing the Web (with mixed results) and talking with family and friends who are doctors. We read medical journals, research trials, and protocols in both the United States and Europe. Then we read more medical journals and even got the librarians at the Stanford Cancer Center to copy articles in the more obscure oncology journals we couldn't find ourselves. We tried to find out what the state of the field was in treating breast cancers in premenopausal women and to learn as much as possible about issues of survival, fertility, neoadjuvant chemotherapy (chemo before surgery to shrink big tumors and try to preserve breast tissue), and even reconstruction. At the same time, we worked to get diagnostic tests to try to figure out how widespread the cancer really was.

As I look back on those few frenzied weeks between diagnosis and surgery, on the monumental and life-changing decisions we had to make in a ridiculously short time, I am overwhelmed by how much we had to become advocates for me within a medical care "system" that was incredibly opaque, even to such educated people as ourselves. We interviewed several doctors—from surgeons to oncologists to radiation oncologists— at leading research medical centers such as Stanford University and the University of California, San Francisco. We attended lectures and talked with cancer "buddies" at wonderful breast cancer resource centers such as the Community Breast Health Project in Palo Alto, California, and WomanCARE in Santa Cruz, California.[7] We even researched the medical training and backgrounds of all my potential physicians. When choosing the surgeon for my mastectomy, for example, we realized that a close friend did his own medical internship at the same institution as this surgeon (though at different times). So we asked our friend to see what he could find out about the surgeon through colleagues. When the word came back that he was the best surgeon this institution had trained in more than a decade and that they had even tried to hire him there, we made our decision. We had no qualms about pursuing these kinds of networks and were keenly aware of our privilege in being able to do so. We often came home from long days at libraries or in doctors' offices and medical centers feeling frustrated and no closer to answers for our difficult questions. And we wondered how people with less education or fewer resources or less ganas[8] could ever navigate the medical system or even make truly informed decisions. And, of course, I thought often about my abuelita—a determined woman for sure, but one who would have been stymied by the maze my husband and I crawled through in those four weeks.

Ultimately, we were blessed in our surgeon. Despite his own harried schedule, he and his assistant worked with us to time the surgery to a particular day in my menstrual cycle to take advantage of both recent research indicating higher cancer survival rates and critical timing in egg harvesting for what would probably be our last opportunity to have our own biological child.[9] And all of this was based on research my husband and I did on our own and then discussed with the surgeon! In fact, repeatedly throughout this cancer process, we have e-mailed, faxed, and taken hard copies of relevant medical journal articles to my doctors for them to read and discuss with us at our next appointment. We don't pretend to be physicians ourselves, but we do take full advantage of our privileged position as educated people to keep up with relevant research. Moreover, we understand the challenges of keeping up with developments in one's field, and we are committed to making sure my doctors don't miss any new research that might impact our treatment decisions. Again, I am awed at how others with less access, less resources, and simply less ganas or means to direct their ganas navigate the complexities of an overburdened medical system that is geared to lowest-common-denominator care.

And it does take ganas to be willing to be the squeaky wheel, to be constantly vigilant in following up with everyone involved in your medical care. At every stage of this process, we have pushed for more tests to confirm the status of my cancer and my body's condition during and after chemo. And at every point we have hit the wall of "standard of care": the standards for treatment for specific medical conditions that dictate what tests get done when. Although understandably useful, this method erases the particulars of your own individual case—not to mention your own sense of self.

It took ganas and an unflinching willingness to be annoying if necessary to get follow-up tests, to get "wet reads" (same-day readings of films), to make my case a priority not simply for doctors, but also for all the medical personnel and support staff who are the real engines of the medical superstructure. We developed all sorts of strategies from simple smiles and thank yous to baking cookies and filling out "above and beyond" forms for particular staff people who went out of their way to help us. We even figured out how to suggest to my physicians the efficacy of questioning standard protocols and of considering nonstandard medications, procedures, and diagnostic tests.[10] This process involved sending them current research papers, discussing the results with them, and then a week or two later suggesting I have this or that test based on the suggestive findings of the latest research. For instance, we learned about Lupron, a drug that suppresses ovarian function through monthly shots. Standard protocol recommends it only for women in their twenties—presupposing that older women won't be interested in preserving fertility after chemotherapy. But we are. We convinced my oncologist to let me take Lupron and noted the added benefit that it would suppress the production of estrogen, a hormone that feeds my cancer (the cancer is considered estrogen and progesterone positive, which means it thrives on these hormones). After six months of these shots, we convinced the oncologist to test my estrogen levels to see how well the Lupron was working.

Pushing the system also took other forms. After completing nearly six months of chemotherapy, for example, I had an appointment with my radiation oncologist to tattoo markers for radiation on my skin. This was to be followed immediately by a CT scan to confirm the boundaries of the field on my chest. These procedures had to be done before we could start the radiation therapy that is critical to treating locally advanced breast cancer. Both appointments had to be on the same day, though at different facilities, creating a scheduling challenge. Unfortunately, the day before my appointments, the office called to reschedule for a week later because one of the machines was being serviced. A week later, again the day before I was supposed to go in, the office called once more to reschedule. I told them how critical it was that these delays not impact my radiation treatments, and I was assured they wouldn't. I couldn't shake my overwhelming sense of urgency. It took ganas, though, to call back and insist that they reserve a daily block of time for my radiation treatments and indicate that I needed the radiation to start on October 9. I could tell the staff preferred to wait until after the tattooing and CT scan even to think about scheduling the radiation, which would mean a week's or even two or three weeks' delay in treatment. Because I had just finished what I thought then would be my last chemotherapy treatment, any delay in the radiation would possibly open a window for any remaining cancer to get going again. So I pushed, they pushed back, I pushed again, and I got my times and dates reserved.

It turned out my sense of urgency was well founded. New lymph nodes lit up on the CT scan. This could merely have meant they were infected, but a core-needle biopsy of each (yes, again, it hurts) confirmed more cancer, leading to many more tests, doctor consults, and a review of my now-unusual case by the "tumor board." Several leading medical centers have tumor boards that meet once a week to study and discuss particularly unusual cancer cases. After meeting the patient, conducting examinations, reviewing all previous information on the case, and discussing it, this board of usually five to ten doctors makes a recommendation regarding further treatment. In one morning, I met with eight specialists, all leaders in their fields. They ultimately recommended six more months of chemotherapy and concurrent radiation.

Dancing with one's diagnosis of cancer is difficult enough, but having to do this constant kind of thinking ahead, pushing, and advocating for oneself on top of it is exhausting. So is sharing the news of cancer with people around you. The day we got the diagnosis, we picked up our son from childcare and took him home to explain, as best we could, that Mami was sick with cancer, that she was going to take lots of medicines that would make her bald, but that would help her get better, and that he and Papa would be helping by taking care of her when she needed it. Then we packed the car and drove several hours to my parents' house to tell them in person. It was a difficult conversation, but we approached it directly and discussed openly what we then knew about my treatment to come. I spent the better part of that weekend on the phone with family, friends, and colleagues. I really wanted to be sure people heard the news directly from me. There were many times when I found myself in the bizarre role of com-forter (Wasn't I the one who was sick?), giving assurances that everything was going to be fine, frequently repeating that it would be a long struggle, but I'd come out of it strong and healthy. Those few days were long but ultimately rewarding.

My next task was telling my students. It was the last day of the college quarter. Near the end of class, I sat on the desk and began to outline the now-optional final exam. Then I explained why the final was optional: I had locally advanced breast cancer and was going into treatment immedi-ately. Despite my resolve not to cry, I broke down as I talked. Several of my students also cried, but they rallied and asked many questions. I gave as many answers as I could, and we left feeling some closure.

People have all kinds of reactions when they find out you have cancer.

Most are empathetic and supportive, but most also feel compelled to share stories of someone they know who had cancer ("my friend . . ."; "my Great-Aunt So-and-so . . .") or of someone they read about who beat cancer (e.g., Melissa Ethridge, Lance Armstrong). Although people mean these stories to be encouraging and are obviously trying to convey some familiarity with your circumstances, I have found that the stories ultimately end up being annoying. If I've learned anything about cancer and its treatments so far, it's that it is a very individualized disease—from the actual biology of tumors to treatments to side effects. I find myself thinking about Magritte's famous painting *Ce si n'est pas une pipe* and repainting it in my mind's eye as *Ce si n'est pas un cancer*. No two cancers are the same.

Similarly, as family and friends see you going through treatment, they all remark, "Wow, you look great!" I want to give them my perplexed response, "Pues, y que? Did I look like crap the last time you saw me, or what?" Of course, I catch myself (mostly) and remind myself that they are very well meaning. I find that people's comments really say more about their own fears and expectations than the reality of my condition. People often seem to expect those of us with cancer to look like famine victims, and in my experience very few of us do. Instead of the "wow, you look great" line, I wish people would explicitly own their expectations and fears by saying something like, "Wow, you look great—I somehow thought you'd look worse because of chemo" or "Hey, your baldness really brings out how beautiful your cheekbones are." But I was also amazed to discover how many cancer survivors surround us all, and I have really connected with several newfound friends. In many ways, they have become the only people besides my husband with whom I share all the pains, discomforts, and feelings of the cancer journey. They've been there, they understand, they just listen and do not feel compelled to say anything comforting.

Peluda y Pelona

There's something very anonymous about being bald—not just bald, but having no body hair at all. I look in the mirror—before the makeup—and I don't see myself at all. I look like all those classic cancer patients I see on posters for fund-raisers: smiling faces with no hair, no eyebrows, no eyelashes. Perhaps it is this look that friends and family expect to see? Who knew that hair could be such an integral part of personalizing oneself?

"Bald is the new sexy, or so I've been telling myself for the past fifteen years," wrote my balding friend Ben. And I am instantly struck by the gendering of baldness itself. Bald heads on men somehow make them more "manly."

They carry connotations of fitness and freedom and professional sports and hipsters. On women—despite Demi Moore and Sinead O'Connor—baldness is too much about loss and defeminization. Although short hair on women, especially in Latina/o cultures, is a statement of being free and bucking cultural norms, baldness for women is still inseparable from illness and loss—perhaps because it is accompanied by a lack of eyelashes and eyebrows. I've gotten pretty good at drawing on eyebrows and lining my eyes to minimize my lack of lashes. I even have human hair eyebrows, just in case I ever decide I don't want painted eyebrows. Yes, human hair eyebrows! Who knew? Cancer consumer culture is vast, and there are multiple ways to dress up the basic pelona (bald woman) into an approximation of a peluda (hairy or shaggy woman, or "La Pintada"?). Of course, drawing one's eyebrows can be a lot of fun—picture the big arches of the early 1960s or the deer-in-the-headlights look if done wrong or Frida's lush unibrow!

The oncology nurses who initially gave me the IV chemo warned me that on day fourteen of treatment, my hair would start to fall out. At the time, I had nearly waist-length, thick, curly black hair, and I knew losing that would be a mess. So with my husband and son, I went to a hairstylist's home to have my hair cut really short. We brought my son so that he could be part of the transformation and help me pack the cut hair to donate to Locks of Love, an organization that makes human-hair wigs for children with cancer.[11]

Once I started shopping for wigs, however, I yearned for my own long locks. Despite hours of searching and telephoning, I couldn't find wigs that were even similar to my hair. And I discovered that race permeates the wig world too. I found a few Web sites featuring "Latin" looks that left me laughing and shaking my head in sadness. These "Latin" looks were either the long, straight braid of the China Poblana or the two-tone bleached blonde of the telenovelas. ¡Imagínate! I explored the few sites for African American women and finally found the curly hair absent in what I by then had realized were Anglo-only Web sites. One day I even went to a wig store specializing in wigs for cancer patients, but I found the wigs so expensive that I couldn't indulge my fantasy of several different wigs. After all, I thought, this could be my chance to be a redhead, a blonde, have long straight hair, short hair—pero, no. I did end up with a wig that wasn't too bad, but it looks nothing like my hair. I haul it out when I want to be really anonymous. I've resorted mostly to scarves and hats and baldness.

I did have some fun as my short hair started to fall out in chunks. One sunny day, my husband, son, and I shaved it into a Mohawk! Yes, for four lovely days I sported a Mohawk. We discovered that curly hair unfortunately doesn't spike very well, no matter how much gel gets glopped into it. My son was in charge of the gel, and, needless to say, he had a blast gooping it on. He even got a few spikes on his own head with it! We went out to dinner that night to celebrate my new do. I'd been hoping someone would notice, or at least give me a second glance—I felt so transgressive! Apparently, however, lefty, hippie, vaguely progressive Santa Cruz, California, is not the place to be noticed for a funky hairdo. No one batted an eyelid, even as we strolled downtown and window shopped.

June 24. Woodies on the Wharf—a quintessential Santa Cruz event with lots of old cars and old-car/surf buffs. . . . Unlike in my Mohawk days, that day I was tired of people staring at my now-complete baldness, so I wore my wig. No stares at all, but I looked at some photos from the afternoon and didn't recognize myself.

Bizarre as it is to shop for wigs (or in insurance company jargon, "head prostheses"), eyebrows, even eyelashes, it is nothing compared to shopping for a breast. The whole notion was so surreal I still find it hysterical. For weeks while I awaited official approval from the insurance company to buy my "breast prosthesis," I shopped for boobs, online and in brick-and-mortar stores. I never imagined there were so many varieties, from perky to round to oval. There were even different weights within the same size. And as I navigated the many skin tones available, I realized race was integral to this experience as well. The ones labeled "white" turned out to be shades of pink; others were labeled "mauve," and the list went all the way to "chocolate." I never did get the right skin tone, but given how artificial most of the hues looked, probably no one did. The woman at what I affectionately call the "boob store" (our local specialized pharmacy) had years of experience helping women with mastectomies select breasts, and she guided me to a great boob that almost matches the other side. Gone are the days of cleavage—at least until reconstructive surgery—but at least for now I'm not so lopsided in clothes. And whenever I get frustrated at having a fake boob, all I have to do is remember my son running around the house with it on his head, yelling "boob head," to make me smile and be content.

Tequila y Chorizo

It should come as no surprise to me, I suppose, that food is the primary lens through which I experience chemotherapy. My abuelita Tencha spoke best through her food, and even during her own cancer ordeal she continued her expressions of culinary love.

May 9. First chemo. Early on, the chemo hangover is like a tequila hangover—a hard and empty headache centered right above and around your eyes, and a mouth filled with a metallic taste. Your hair—while you still have it—hurts, like when your pigtails were tied too tight, but you didn't know it until you took out the rubber bands at the end of the day. The nausea is something else. On the worst days, you almost fear eating because it'll make you feel as if you really did drink too much tequila. The medications keep you from actually upchucking, even though your body is aching to. Your body occasionally wins out.

May 19. Lunch at a restaurant with a friend and colleague. We talked and talked, two mujeres enjoying time together, chismiando (gossiping) about life and work and kids.[12] Surprisingly, it was refreshing to talk about work and what was happening on campus—it seemed a world away and yet now also a new world as I gazed through much older eyes. A wonderful time. Yum, teriyaki—which later that afternoon, while I played blocks with Noé on the living-room floor, became teriyuki. I had felt very nauseated all afternoon, and beside us was the white bucket, my familiar companion. "Por si acaso" (just in case), I told myself.

In the midst of building a giant city of blocks, the nausea won, and I threw up in the bucket, over and over. For my son's sake, I tried to be quiet and to minimize what was going on.

"Mama, what are you doing?"

"Querido, I'm throwing up . . . all the food in my stomach is coming out through my mouth . . . because my tummy is . . . can't handle the food being in there."

He watched me for a moment, then smiled and said, "Oh, OK. Here's a blue block to build with, Mama!"

We quietly created imaginary cities until Papa came home. Noé excitedly told Papa about the city we built and about getting to flush the potty when Mama poured the bucket of yuck into it. Nothing like a three-year-old to refresh one's perspective! Even my ongoing fever was fun for him because it required regular monitoring with the thermometer that beeped.

May 29. Two chemo treatments down, pelona and nauseous. My mouth sometimes felt itchy and kind of fibrous, like when you eat too many mangos. On chemo day, they gave me a steroid that made me hungry for eggs and chorizo every time. I also knew I'd be nauseated for many days and wouldn't be able to eat more than rice, tortillas, and avena (oatmeal)—which somehow made chowing down eggs and chorizo even sweeter. Sometimes I tried to be healthy about it and cook up eggs and soyrizo—I knew Tencha wouldn't approve, but it often kept my gastrointestinal tract happier later.

To soy or not to soy: of course, dietary questions are constant with cancer and in treatment. What should you eat? Avoid? Cut down on or eat more of? The questions are endless. I'm discovering the real question for a cancer patient is, What *can* you eat? One of the frequent side effects of some chemo drugs is mouth sores. They are often tied to specific foods such as citrus and tomatoes. Other times, your taste buds get really swollen and raised—like a cat's tongue, only very sore! I had several of these experiences as my treatments progressed through the summer. Some special mouthwashes helped (over the counter and prescription), but my body mostly just had to heal itself, however slowly.[13] By the end of the summer, I experienced peripheral neuropathy around my mouth that felt a bit like having Novocain at the dentist's. I found myself frequently biting my lips or the insides of my cheeks because I couldn't really feel them getting in the way of my teeth! Fortunately, this side effect lasted only a few weeks. The neuropathy in my fingers and toes has taken much longer to heal. There's a chance I'll never recover all feeling, but I won't know until almost a year after chemo ends.

In mid-June, in the midst of chemo treatments, I found out I received tenure, a giant step in the career of a college professor. Somehow, though, while fighting for my life, this news was very anticlimactic. All I could think was, "Ah well, now I have to live long enough to enjoy it." I tried to roll this off my tongue with humor—or at least a bit of levity—but it somehow came out hard-edged and much too sharp.

Tish Hinojosa Trumps Taxol

July 18. I went in for my second round of Taxol, and within twenty minutes of it entering my bloodstream, my heart started racing, my muscles seized, my throat constricted.[14] Fortunately, the nurses were right there. As this reaction was starting, I called out to them that I felt very weird, and I thought I was having an allergic reaction. They rushed over, turned off the Taxol drip on my IV, and immediately pumped me full of Benadryl. Bill, my husband, and Kendra, one of the oncology nurses, held my hands and rubbed my knees to comfort me. About ten minutes later, I was feeling significantly better, though still a bit shaken. Only then did the tears came, and I confessed to them that my eyes must have sprung a leak. My blood pressure was still through the roof, but they monitored it for half an hour while I rested in the Barcalounger (I love that they have these chairs in the chemo room!). We consulted with the oncologist, who decided to try a different chemo drug, Taxotere, because I was clearly allergic to

Taxol. Fortunately, Taxotere is just as effective, although it meant getting IV chemo every week and extending the treatment an extra month. So I went back the next day for the new infusion and had no troubles. A day after the successful chemo, we went to a lovely outdoor music concert— Tish Hinojosa. I was mesmerized by her beautiful voice and guitar play- ing, accompanied by a couple of great musicians. My son danced with the abandon of a totally unself-conscious youngster, the evening sun filtered through the redwoods . . . great peace.

I wanted to keep that peace with me, but as the days progressed, staying happy and content became ever harder. Emotions kept crowding in—fears of dying and not seeing Noé grow up, of what life would be like for him without his mami, the chemotherapy road feeling so long, too long. . . . And then Joe died.

Joe, our very close friend, was thirty-three years old, very healthy, no previous medical conditions. He died of a heart attack in his sleep early one Wednesday morning. He had kissed his wonderful wife good night, they had fallen asleep, and in the morning she woke up, but he did not. Joe's death hit many of us hard, but he gave me an incredible gift: he shook me completely out of the mild depression I'd been in for three days. I couldn't be depressed—at least I was alive! This gift of life from Joe continues to offer me strength even now. As we celebrated Día de los Muertos in early November and fondly recalled him and all he was about, we discovered he had given us another gift. His death has begun to allow our son, who dearly loved him, to deal with death—its permanency, its unpredictability, the beauty of memory, and how people live on in our hearts.

Booty over Booby

August 8. I went swimming with my husband and son for the first time that summer. Getting into a bathing suit used to be such an ordeal—finding the right one that minimized my Latina butt and childbearing hips, trying to ignore the cellulite on my thighs. . . . And even when I found a flattering suit, I always felt self-conscious at how not-perfect my body was. Well, no more. Somehow when you're missing a breast—and it wasn't a small one either, so the remaining one looks very definitely alone—it's hard to get worked up over a big behind and too much fat. The icing, of course, is being totally, completely devoid of body hair. For some odd reason, being bald and knowing that my painted-on eyebrows and eyeliner would wash off in the water overshadowed my otherwise very obvious lack of a breast! People seem to be so aware of my baldness that they don't notice I have one headlight out. All this has been very liberating in a weird way. Now I find myself happily walking along poolside without worrying about how I look in a bathing suit. I actually don't care because now it's about being thankful I'm even *able* to play in the water with my wonderful son and loving partner. I am alive! And I have to admit some pride, particularly at the largess of my booty and my newfound freedom to enjoy it!

Chicharrones y Más Tequila

I woke up one night in late November hearing my 'uelita's words again: "Mira lo que me hicieron; parezco chicharrón." Eight weeks of daily radiation therapy had burned a large patch of skin measuring about ten inches by ten inches from my breastbone to my armpit. The burn was like no other I've ever had. After about four weeks, the skin started to blister, reminding me of the time I badly blistered my face from snow burn as I climbed Mt. Hood. But unlike other burns, the exposure to the source—that is, radiation therapy—continued to char this skin. It was strange, going in to get more burned when I was already charred. By the end of the radiation treatments, my skin had evolved from blistered to charred to black to peeling to gone, exposing bleeding and oozing tissue below.[15]

It's odd to get such a burn from something you can't even feel. The radiation itself is painless and not even warm. Treatments involve lying on a long metal bed that moves you into place under a big armlike structure that looks a bit like a giant—albeit very fancy—desk lamp. The radiation specialists move you under the head of the "lamp" and check with lasers to align you exactly where the radiation beams need to go (i.e., to avoid radiating your heart or lungs or trachea!). Then they leave, y te quedas allí solita. Lying there all alone, looking into the face of that "lamp," constantly transported me to a science-fiction world of machines with personalities of their own, who move like robotic cats and rule over humans. Inside the clear faceplate were corrugated lead plates that moved and buzzed while they got into place. Too often, they simply looked like big gray teeth, lined up in a sneering smile.

Throughout the treatments, the radiation oncologist prescribed all kinds of great creams. I managed to find surgical pads that wouldn't stick to the burn and held them all in place with giant ace bandages wrapped around my torso. In the list of unexpected side effects: if my other breast wasn't already pointing south, it is now after being bandaged this way for going on three months! I'm looking forward to the nip and tuck it'll get during the reconstruction of my left breast. After inhabiting this medical world for nearly a year, however, I expect to delay reconstruction for several years. Time to heal and get strong.

We went on a family vacation to Lake Tahoe in early December to celebrate the end of radiation. A week before we were to leave, a routine ultrasound revealed a blood clot in my right arm, a deep vein thrombosis (DVT). Although potentially life-threatening, DVTs in one's arms are much less serious than in the legs (this is the reason doctors warn you to get up and move around during long airplane flights).[16] Treatment for DVT is blood thinners, so I continue weekly blood checks to monitor the thickness of my blood—another delicate dance between too thin and too thick. Then, two days before leaving for Lake Tahoe, I had a gallbladder attack: "very common in Mexicans and Native Americans," the doctors informed me. It feels like an incredible stomachache or like giving birth through your stomach. Despite all these bumps in the road to Tahoe, we did make it and had a wonderful time. In between sledding and making snow angels, I gave myself shots of blood thinners twice a day and changed my radiation burn bandages, also twice a day. The pain of that much-burned skin required serious painkillers, but they really helped to allow us a terrific holiday. Several friends joined us later in the week, and we played Legos, went sledding, drank hot chocolate, and generally cavorted.

I continued chemotherapy throughout the radiation, which meant I carried around that tequila-hangover feeling most days. Radiation supposedly can be very exhausting after a few weeks, but in combination with the chemo, I'm not sure what created what effect. I do know that having to do another six months of chemo was a hard reality to swallow—kind of like ingesting más tequila for breakfast after a long night of drinking too much. But I found it less traumatic than the previous news of having to extend the chemo because of my allergic reaction to Taxol. I take this response as a measure of how much stronger this whole experience is making me. When I finish, I will have completed a full year of chemo, having taken Adriamiacin, Cytoxin, Taxol, Taxotere, Methatrexate, 5Fu, and more Cytoxin (not to mention the cornucopia of drugs to battle side effects!).[17] Weirdly enough, I've gotten fairly used to feeling hung over and still functioning at a high level (kind of like some college days, que no?). And I have absolutely no desire to touch alcohol of any kind.

A critical component of current breast cancer therapy is the hormonal therapy following chemotherapy. This therapy typically involves taking Tamoxifen for five years (though there are some new drugs on the market for specific kinds of breast cancers and for postmenopausal women). Fortunately, this drug has few side effects, so most women can resume an active life. That was the course I expected to take. However, new clinical information about the even better effectiveness of aromatase inhibitors (AIs), along with other factors (including the aggressiveness of my cancer, its sensitivity to estrogen, and its tendency to recur), convinced us to put me on AIs.[18] These drugs are available only to postmenopausal women, so, again, we faced an incredibly painful, heart-rending decision: Do we surgically remove my ovaries to send me immediately into menopause and cut my body's production of estrogen while rendering me permanently infertile? We decided that my—and our—life depended on doing so.

After completing twelve months of chemotherapy and more than eight weeks of intensive radiation, I underwent another surgery. I like to call it the three-in-one special: three surgeries, two surgeons, one day. They removed my ovaries, my gallbladder (thanks to a second major attack), and my port catheter. Fortunately, I had to take only a week off of work. My colleagues covered two classes, and I was able to be back in the classroom the following week. The physical scars are healing more quickly than the emotional ones, but I now look forward to recovering fully and becoming healthy again.

Mangled Time, Alma Viejo

Going through cancer, however harrowing, has been very empowering for me. It has come to mean speaking frankly, not taking any day for granted, being grounded in the present rather than always living for the future, and being an advocate for myself and those close to me. Cancer has brought clarity and perspective on what really matters in life; it has helped me cut out the dead wood, cobwebs, and unnecessary clutter that we all live with but would thrive without. In short, cancer has given me insights into my body and soul that I imagined would come only with advanced age. Cancer has made me muy viejita.

I feel incredibly privileged to be developing such an old soul in such a relatively young, if scarred, body. Perhaps it is in part the legacy of my abuelita, and she is still very much with me in this newly old soul. This disease has completely broken the linearity of my personal worldview and physical reality as a historian who is rooted in time and in change over time. Time is fast-forwarded in my soul and even in my body. I am physically marked by a disease I shouldn't have—statistically less than 20 percent of women with breast cancer are premenopausal (Buzdar et al. 2006). The majority of women with breast cancers are older than fifty-five, don't have young children as I do, and aren't in the process of trying to have another child, as I was. Even as surgery has carved my body into that of an older woman, so too did chemotherapy and surgery age my body. I am sterile; bifocals are in my near future because my eyes don't seem to be recovering from the chemotherapy; my joints hurt from the Arimidex (an AI); and I still have peripheral neuropathy in my fingers and toes. I find, however, that this chemically and prematurely aged body is more appropriate housing for the aged soul that has grown within.

The mangling of time parallels that of my body. The past continues to have a strong hold on me in ways that bring it out of the past and into the present. As a Mexicana, I've always appreciated the constructedness of linear time and how problematic that can be for telling people's lives and experiences, but my training and the methods historians use cut against that grain. As I face my own mortality, the future becomes the present, the now, the immediate. The future is diminished because I no longer plan for it at the expense of appreciating and living in the present. In this way, I find myself much more like my three-year-old son, who has a strong concept of *today* and *now* and only vaguely understands—or cares about—tomorrow. I'm realigning my priorities and goals and am much more likely to embrace the beauty of moments as I live them. I know now more than most people my age, I suppose, that there's no telling what the future holds. I plan as though there is a future, and yet I live confident in and revel in today.

As I write this narrative (in 2007), I am not finished with my cancer treatments, but I am grateful already for the incredible love and support of family and friends, for the lessons learned, and for the perspective carved. I know that much of my success thus far has been because of the wide web of generosity, support, love, and friendship that has sustained me. I have been blessed with an amazing family who are willing and able to talk directly about all things—the fun and the scary. My friends and colleagues have made meals for us (and continue to!), written cards and e-mails, sent presents, and had long phone chats. One wonderful friend who was just finishing chemo herself even sent me a "chemo care package" full of the items that helped her—from those special mouthwashes to an extra soft and vivid purple blanket. And I'll never forget a terrific oncology nurse, herself a cancer survivor, who happily lifted her shirt and bra to show off her two breast reconstructions! With all my family, friends, and colleagues, I am covered by a truly exceptional cloak of protection.

I look forward to sharing a long life with my son, watching and helping him to grow into a wonderful citizen, a strong feminist, and a truly happy and caring human being. And I look forward to growing into a very old woman alongside my amazing partner. ¡La lucha sigue! The fight continues!

2

Embodying Dementia

Remembrances of Memory Loss

Yvette G. Flores

When I introduced my mother to Carlos Fuentes in the mid-1990s, he kissed her hand and autographed her first edition copy of *Cambio de piel*: "Para Aura, a quien conocí en un sueño" (for Aura, whom I met in a dream). He, of course, was referring to the book he wrote that carries her name. Nonetheless, the dedication was fitting. My mother had lived her life as if in a dream, trying to forget the abuse she had lived through as a child, the heartbreak of her youth, and the pain of her marriages. She sought refuge in books and in loving her only daughter.

Loving my mother was akin to breathing in deep waters. She was there in body, but absent emotionally. In my childhood, she would see me only when I spoke of books or schoolwork. So we loved each other by reading, by sharing ideas, by visiting faraway places in our imagination. She never spoke of feelings and rarely showed the depth of her emotions. Even as a small child, I knew Mother was sad, yet I could not understand why because I was ignorant of what she had lived through. She gave only vignettes of her childhood and youth, emphasizing her upper-class origins and her good breeding. "We were once French," she would say, referring to her French Panamanian father who died of alcoholism when she was seven; "we were once wealthy," remembering her petit bourgeois upbringing. "We became poor when Father died," she stated once. "Mother had to take in other people's sewing to make ends meet." "Mom had to send me to boarding school to protect me," she added, but I did not know from what or whom. All she would say was that her mother sent her to a convent school, where she was educated to become a teacher by Spanish and criolla (New World–born) nuns. She saw her mother only on long holidays and spent most of her free time—when other girls went home—either alone at school or with a favorite aunt in a small seaside town. What little she said of her childhood was positive, especially when she spoke about her literature professors. My mother's first love was poetry; her second was Spanish literature of the Golden Age. She once told me she married her first husband because he was a decent poet—and also to get him to stop bothering her. Indeed, Mother saw marriage and women's household obligations as impediments to her intellectual development. "But what was a woman to do?" she would ask, not expecting an answer. When the poet, her first husband, did not assume the responsibility of supporting his wife and children as culture and custom mandated, she left him and went to work.

Looking at photographs of Mother as a child, a young woman, and later a young single mother of two boys, I was always drawn to the sadness in her eyes, a faraway look that seemed to be gazing inward, not at the camera or the world around her. She always seemed detached, absent, as if dreaming or imagining something else.

Above all, Mother was smart, brilliant, and insightful. She was known as the intelligent woman in the family. She could speak eloquently and passionately and did not hesitate to do so in defense of her values or her loved ones. Despite limited English ability, she charged into my high school in Los Angeles to demand I be placed in college-preparatory courses when I was tracked into a basic curriculum because of my surname rather than my academic record.

Throughout my childhood and adolescence, I could count on my mother to defend me when I was wronged. She even stood up to my father, who towered over her in height and overt power, when he treated me unfairly. My mother did everything within her means to teach me that no man had a right to rule over me, mistreat me, or betray me—early lessons in feminism I came later to "relearn" in college. As I grew up, I realized that Mother was an informal counselor, consulted by all the young women in the family and community who had man problems, whose parents did not understand them, or whose children were difficult. She was respected because she was brilliant, did not gossip, and was fair. She could be trusted with one's problems because she never divulged anything she heard. "Tu mamá es una tumba," her friends would later tell me. She was like a tomb, never disclosing anything she was told. Mother held other people's secrets as well as she guarded her own.

So I never heard about her father's violence and her own mother's sorrow; I didn't find out about her losses, sacrifices, and desires, her longings for her homeland through multiple migrations. I did not get to know the real woman who was my mother until dementia grabbed hold of her.

Diagnosing Dementia: The Early Days

When I was a young parent of two small children and my father had retired, my parents left southern California and the family members who lived there and moved within a few miles of me in the Bay Area to help me parent and to be close to the grandchildren, as culture and tradition dictated. Before my children were nine years old, Mother had taught them both, without my knowledge, to read and write in Spanish. Their school was making sure they were bilingual in French and English; she would ensure they knew proper Spanish. My father picked up the children every day after school; Mom would feed them and get them started on their homework, as she had done with me decades earlier. Because of their loving presence and support, I could have my career, time to read and write. I had become a professor, a therapist, a successful woman. I had done Mother proud. I had accomplished all the things she had dreamed of doing. Quietly, without taking any credit, she could help me be a good mother by filling the spaces created through my absence and by giving my children the nurturing and love they needed when I was not there.

Mother was always thought of as absent-minded, a trait everyone attributed to her intelligence; my aunts would laugh and say, "Oh, Aura, she burns the rice because her nose is in a book and she forgets the world exists." So no one really noticed her deteriorating memory—except the kids. But as children often do, they said little about it. She had never been good at finding her keys or her purse or remembering whether she had turned off the stove, so no one really noticed how much more frequent her preoccupation with these things had become.

I was too busy pursuing tenure, commuting to work, helping others in distress, and fighting my long, silent war against patriarchy as embodied in my father and husband to notice her decreasing activity level, her occasional disorientation, or her disinterest in things—until the day she got lost. As happened at least once a year, my parents' apartment was full of relatives; the patriarch of a large extended family, my father always hosted visiting relatives from his native Costa Rica. Never mind that I had a three-bedroom home with a den and lots of room to spare; relatives always stayed with Dad, even if they had to sleep on the floor. Engrossed in conversations and loud exchanges of the latest news from home, no one noticed Mother had slipped away to do some shopping at the Mexican market around the corner. More than an hour later she returned full of consternation: she had been unable to find the store. Later, she told me that she knew she had to turn right at the corner but had continued walking straight ahead for several miles. She could not figure out why she was unable to find the market; she eventually became frightened, retraced her steps, and came home. At this precise moment, the entire family went into absolute, impenetrable denial. We did not mention this incident for years. Like many families facing the tragedy of dementia, we chose denial over acceptance that something was wrong with Mother, and we collectively "forgot" this incident. I ignored the knot in my stomach and the dawning realization that Mother was getting old; although she was in her seventies, she had not, until that moment, appeared or "acted her age."

Then one day when I came to pick up the children, Mother was lying down. Mother never sat (unless to read) and, it seemed, never slept. She was always doing something, a whirlwind of energy from sunup to sundown, always attentive to the needs of others. But that day she was lying down, appearing to be asleep. I said nothing, but I worried. A few days later, I invited a girlfriend to spend the weekend with the kids, Mom, and me at a resort. I said nothing to my friend—a geriatric psychologist—about my concerns. I wanted her expert opinion after a weekend of observation. But even before my friend arrived, I knew. The first morning Mom awoke, sat at the kitchenette table, and asked: "¿Hija, que tengo que hacer?" My heart broke. Mom never asked what she had to do. She was the omniscient woman who knew it all, anticipated it all, and made coffee before anyone else got up. I made coffee for us, fighting back tears and a pain in the pit of my stomach. We spent the day together; she in silence, I in observation. She whispered to herself or to others I could not see; she grimaced; she argued alone in the bathroom. Mother was clearly hallucinating. The lack of energy, the disorientation—I knew they were symptoms of dementia, not normal aging. Moreover, I realized that visual hallucinations and confusion were possible signs of early Alzheimer's.

When I would ask her what she had said, pretending that I had not heard or that I was unaware she spoke to unseen others, she would cover up by laughing, "Ay tu sabes nosotras las Perigault siempre hablamos solas" (Oh, you know us Perigaults, we always talk to ourselves).

On the way home, Mother stated that she did not want to go back. She said she was afraid and began to cry. I asked her what frightened her; she said the nuns did. They were going to get mad and hit her if she returned late from the weekend. The pain-rage-horror that engulfed me was overwhelming. I held her and for the first time heard the story of the childhood abuse she had suffered from the nuns. In the following weeks and months, repressed childhood memories began to flow as the censors in her frontal lobe began to falter. I could no longer deny that Mother was suffering from a dementing illness; the behavioral and cognitive changes were there: her tiredness, disorientation, uncontrollable episodes of crying, and confusion between past and present.

After the weekend, I asked my friend what she thought about Mom, without naming the concern that filled my mind and heart. She answered gravely, "It's not good, Yvette." So I went home and spoke to Father, who had not spoken to me in three years. I asked how long she had been that way, still without naming what I suspected. He responded that she was suffering from menopausal depression; he had heard about it on *Oprah*. I gently reminded him that Mother had gone through menopause nearly fifteen years earlier. He persisted that menopausal women get depressed, both Oprah and Cristina had said so; besides, he argued, Mom had always been a depressed, difficult woman. Nothing had really changed; things had only gotten worse. We argued again, the silence rebuilding between us. Latino family members commonly attribute the behavioral changes brought about by dementia to normal aging or to personality traits. Given the difficult relationship Dad and I had, I chose not to challenge his denial of Mother's illness until I had medical support for my diagnosis.

The Search for Answers

I am a scholar, and my mother taught me well. I searched for answers in books, I talked to colleagues, and I consulted experts. All roads led to Alzheimer's disease. The denial began to break. We were not unfamiliar with Alzheimer's in the family. Mom's only (legitimate) brother had spent years under its hold. It had started like Mom's, with memory difficulties, repetitive questions, preoccupations about money and the children, an exacerbation of all the things that as a good husband, father, and provider he had worried about all his adult life. Then Tío Chevo began to show subtle personality changes; a religious man, he had become somewhat inappropriate with the maids. He eventually became incontinent, loud, and difficult to manage, and then gradually transformed back into a quiet, sad, unresponsive, and sweet man until his death. Before reading a single page on the subject, I knew what lay ahead for Mom, for us. All I could do was cry—until I got angry.

Dementia describes a group of brain disorders, most related to aging, that involve problems with memory, behavior, learning, and communication. In the early stages, the disorders are characterized by difficulties carrying out daily tasks. The problems are progressive, worsening over time. Although memory loss and other symptoms of dementia are present in elderly people without dementia, the cognitive and behavioral changes associated with dementia are beyond what is expected in normal aging. Moreover, the risk of being affected by a dementing illness increases with increased longevity. In the world, one percent of people from sixty to sixty-five years old, 6 percent of those from seventy-five to seventy-nine, and 45 percent of those ninety-five or older are affected by dementia. In Mother's case, the personality changes, hallucinations, and other psychiatric symptoms suggested she had Alzheimer's disease, the most common form of dementia (Hinton et al. 2003).

Although the specific causes of dementia are not completely known, genetic factors are involved, and research studies point to a history of depression as a risk factor. Likewise, diabetes appears related to the development of dementia. My mother had enjoyed excellent health throughout her life, but she did have a history of depression. I began to suspect Alzheimer's because this particular form of dementia involves the parts of the brain that control thought, memory, and language. Moreover, the disease affects the brain in different ways. One known effect is that a key brain chemical, acetylcholine, is lost.

I suspected Alzheimer's as well because Mother showed significant memory loss; she began to repeat herself, telling the same stories over and over. She became obsessed with losing her purse and her keys; she spent hours looking for items she believed had been stolen. With each symptom I observed, my anger and sadness grew. My search for answers was fueled by the injustice that someone who loved words so much found herself unable to name things that were commonplace to her (Graham 2006). Alzheimer's also is characterized by behavioral changes that often are painful and frightening to family members (Hinton et al. 2003). My mother, who had always acted like a lady, began to swear and accuse my father of multiple infidelities.

I insisted that Mother see her physician. A Spaniard impatiently awaiting his retirement, he agreed to see Mom at Dad's urging. He then minimized all of her symptoms and agreed with Father that Mother was depressed. He prescribed an antidepressant, which Mother refused to take because she was convinced my father was trying to poison her. I called the doctor, using my professional title of "doctor" (without specifying that I was a PhD, not an MD), and spoke to him about my concerns. He was furious that I had contacted him directly and hung up on me, after insisting that I was not qualified to diagnose my mother. I thus began a decade-long battle with her health maintenance organization (HMO) and multiple physicians therein. Three physicians and ten years later, after I myself had already diagnosed Mother and sought support from the Alzheimer's Association and my professional contacts, her physician agreed that she had Alzheimer's. By then, she was eighty years old. Because of her age, her physician recommended that we merely medicate her symptoms of psychosis and depression. Had she been diagnosed earlier, perhaps she could have received some of the cognitive enhancers (for example, Aricept) then coming on the market, which might have slowed down her cognitive decline. But by the time she was finally officially diagnosed, her neuropsychiatric symptoms were severe; she saw men in the house who were not there, and she believed Father had a mistress who came in and stole her clothes. She was delusional and paranoid, the doctor said.

Dementia as Metaphor

During this time, my children became my informants. "Grandma talks to herself all the time; she fights with people in the bathroom," they said. She no longer left the house alone, had Father pay all the bills, refused to handle money, and "rested" more and more in the afternoons. And then the phone calls began. Using the speed-dial function on the phone, Mom would phone me early in the morning or late at night to tell me Father was abusing her. The first few times I ran to my car and drove frantically to their apartment, only to discover them both fast asleep or peaceably having breakfast. She always seemed surprised and happy to see me at such unexpected times. Forced to break his silence and confronted with the need for support, Father began to speak to me again. He told me she was sleeping poorly; he would find her up and about at night, looking for things or afraid that the front door was unlocked or the stove left on. He was exhausted, unable to sleep well. A few times I came to visit and found them both asleep—with the stove left on.

Then Mother began to tell me Father would leave her alone for long periods to go see his Mexican mistress. "La Mexicana" became a code for Mother and a source of amusement for the entire extended family, who teased Mom for being jealous about my father, whose own health was rapidly declining.

As Mother's paranoia and delusional thinking increased, the family denial system strengthened proportionately. Her progressing illness was explained as "nerves"; others believed she had finally succumbed to madness. (Attributing early signs of dementia to nerves or personality attributes is common among Latinos; see Hinton et al. 2003.) I tried to explain that she was suffering from dementia. However, I only made matters worse because the Spanish word *demencia* means "madness." In a sense, the extended family was more comfortable with the idea of Mother being crazy than with the idea that she was suffering from Alzheimer's. Madness is curable, at least, argued one of my aunts; dementia was too cruel, too final, too difficult to accept.

Yet even without naming the illness that robbed my mother of her intelligence, her quick wit, and her role as family healer, the women in our family rallied around to support her, help her maintain her dignity, and facilitate the tasks of daily living. When the aunts visited, they stayed up until Mother fell asleep. Then they would take the clothes she had worn and wash and dry them so that Mom could wear them again day after day.

Cultural and medical anthropologists speak of symptoms as idioms of distress and suggest understanding illness from the perspective of the patient, not the physician or the illness (Kleinman 1988; Hinton et al. 2003; Kaufman 2006). Mother's neuropsychiatric symptoms—her hallucinations, delusions, and fears—gave voice to the memories and experiences that her culture, her gender, and her loyalty had silenced. Dementia freed her to speak her truth. When she accused my father of having an affair with "the Mexican woman," she was disclosing the details of his long-term affair with a family maid in Costa Rica, an affair that produced two daughters, younger sisters I had not known existed. Father understood her verbal assaults, her recriminations, and her rage as payback for his betrayal, as punishment for his misdeeds. I finally understood why we had left Costa Rica and come to the United States. He had fled an untenable situation and, in doing so, had chosen Mother and me over his other woman and "her" children. He had borne the pain of this decision in silence; Mother never spoke of his affair until dementia weakened her repression.

As the present evaporated with Mother's inability to remember day-to-day events, the day of the week, or how to cook rice, her past came rushing forward. I heard about her parents' violent relationship as she relived the pain and sorrow of hiding and crying as a child when her father would come home drunk and beat her mother. She told me stories of Colón, the city of my birth, during the time the "Americano sailors" came onshore and decent women had to hide because the sailors mistook all Panamanian women for whores. Mother would sometimes forget that I had not yet been born when her best friend died, saying, "Acuérdate, hija, de Berta Irene." I did not have the heart to tell her that I did not remember her friend. She would bring me into her past and make me a co-conspirator in her remembered story. When Mother could no longer read new books because she would forget the sentence she had just read, she began to reread old favorites. She knew the stories well; it did not matter what page she read, she could always find "her place" in the book.

As Mother's judgment deteriorated, she began to speak out of turn; her wild tongue became untamed.[1] Riding along with me one day, she said, "¿Hija, tu sabes no, que a mi siempre me han gustado los negritos?" (You know, daughter, don't you, that I have always liked black men?). I repressed my laughter and responded, "No, Mamá, no sabía, pero me alegro" (No, Mom, I didn't know, but I'm glad). Mother would flirt with the young mariachis at church and tell everyone to go to hell when they upset her. My mother, the perfect lady who had never used profanity (unless she was really, really angry), now resorted to colorful Caribbean obscenities with great ease and at the slightest provocation.

My mother had loved to entertain, so I often brought my women friends to visit. She would tell us outrageous stories of her youth, while handing out advice that we should not let men try to control us. But as we laughed at her stories and mischievous ways, and as I got to know better the woman my mother had been, I wept internally for the mother I had lost.

Aura[2]

Te pienso Viejita[3]
Y me llamas
Sales de la nube gris
De tu demencia
Y respondes al llamado
Silencioso de mi alma
Te extrañaré cuando te vayas
Añoraré tus caricias
Las que tampoco pudiste darme
Cuando yo era niña
Porque ya no extraño
Tu inteligencia perdida
Ya me acostumbré a tus obsesiones

A tus miedos antiguos
Al espacio perdido de tu mirada
Ya no eres quien tu fuiste
Pero tu instinto maternal
No le extingue nada
Todavía percibes
Lo que no te digo
Todavía anticipas
Los peligros que no veo
Todavía lees mis deseos
Invisibles hasta a mi
Te extrañaré viejita
Cuando al fin te vayas

—*Yvette Flores*, México, February 9, 1998

Desconsuelo

For several years, Mother continued to retreat from the present deep into her past, protected by my father and surrounded by the love and respect of her grandchildren, my friends, and me. My mother's second son, Julio, who lived in Panama, retired and began to spend half of the year helping to take care of Mother as Father's health worsened. He became the day-to-day caregiver as I gradually took over my parents' financial and medical affairs. My father was the firstborn; everyone had catered to him and reported to him. One day I realized those phone calls were coming to me instead. I was no longer the daughter. I was quickly becoming the matriarch of my extended family in the United States. I felt thrown into maturity almost overnight. I could no longer be the spoiled "only" daughter, treated almost like an only child; adult decisions were left up to me now.

My parents' home was filled with Father's sisters and my favorite cousin, who came to help. That is how things are done in Latino families that adhere to familismo (Flores et al. 2008). The women left their homes, country, spouses, and children to support me in taking care of both my ailing parents. They would phone, saying they wanted to visit. They came, cooked, cleaned, drove Father to the doctor, entertained Mom, and gave me strength. Their love was expressed through food, jokes, and new carpeting or curtains. I was not allowed to thank them: "Somos familia" (We are family) was all they would say.

As my father's health worsened, I became once again the interpreter for the family, as I had been for my mother upon our migration to the

United States. I was a bridge between the family and the medical estab-lishment. I became an interpreter of my father's unspoken needs and my mother's silent fears. I became a bridge between my mother's estados de conciencia, her different degrees of consciousness, and my father's tenuous hold on life.

Then my father died. Mother's secure world collapsed overnight. As he lay dying, she begged him not to leave her. "You promised never to leave me," she cried. They spent an entire day saying good-bye. That night, my father told me he could no longer hold on. He did not want to leave her, he said. He had promised always to take care of her. He was fourteen years Mom's junior, and neither he nor Mom ever expected he would die first. None of us was ready for his passing. I assured my father that my brother, my children, and I would take care of her; we would never put her in a home. She would always be with family. We said our good-byes; the following morning he died.

Living with Alzheimer's

After my father's death, I became the authority figure in my mother's life. It was up to me now to decide her care, where she should live, and with whom. For elders, particularly those affected with dementing illnesses, stability, predictability, and peace are essential (Valle 1998), so I hesitated to move her into my home, but it was the most practical thing to do, and she repeatedly stated she did not want to stay in the apartment without Dad. She came to live with my nuclear family and me. Although she loved my house, she could not get accustomed to it. She was totally disoriented and ungrounded in the house's peculiar design. There were too many steps and too many angles for her to negotiate; she became totally dependent on her son. She could not be apart from him. He and I were now her parental figures. I was challenged to be the comforting, caring, and loving mother she had not had. My brother was challenged to become the present, stead-fast, nonabusive father she had dreamed of having. My children in their adolescence and young adulthood were challenged to be more considerate, involved, and present—more Latino and less Americanized.

We filled the house with flowers, music, and her familiar things. Photos of family members in Panama, whose names she could no longer remember, surrounded her. She wanted her husband and longed for him. She began to rewrite the story of their life together. As I was growing up, all I heard about my father was how authoritarian, rigid, cold, and cabrón he was. She also emphasized that because men were so weak emotionally, we needed to keep him in the dark about most things in order not to upset him. Now, however, she spoke of his integrity and his dedication to her and her sons when they first met. After his death, my mother created a multidimensional view of my father. Through her waning cognitive abilities, I gained a clearer sense of the man we both had loved, albeit ambivalently.

A year after Father's death, Mother announced at breakfast that although it was customary for widows to die soon after their husbands, she had no intention of doing so. Nevertheless, she refused to wear anything but black because of "el que dirán," what people would say if she wore colors. She was a widow and must act with dignity.

When Mother chose to continue living despite her grief over her husband's death, I stopped running away to Mexico to pursue my research and became a more responsible adult, but being my mother's daughter was not enough. I began to study Latino/a caregivers of elderly people with dementia. I began to collect stories of other women's pain and sorrow so that I could give voice to my own (see Flores et al. 2008).

Ethics of Care

How should elders with dementia be cared for? What is right, what is best? Who has the right to choose how they spend the rest of their lives? How does one preserve their dignity in the face of irreversible deterioration? Caregivers face these ethical dilemmas daily. My mother spent her life in the United States longing for her homeland, for the warmth of Caribbean ocean breezes, for the sound of Spanish and the smell of arroz con guandules y ropa vieja.[4] She missed the sounds, sight, and smell of the sea. She had spent her entire life divided: longing for home and family while at school, longing for Panama while in Costa Rica, longing for Panama and Costa Rica while in the United States, longing for her sons while in my company, longing for me while with them.

I wanted to create a beautiful, peaceful home where she could spend the rest of her days or years. But I could not give her the warmth of her country; I could not create a Caribbean climate during cold northern California winters. With each passing year, the winters became colder for her; she retreated to her room, no longer interested in pretending to read her books. She wanted to spend more and more time in bed. It was too cold here, she would say. So I let her go home to her sons.

Mother now spends her days looking out the window at the city she loves, at the emerald blue Caribbean Sea, remembering her youth, meeting her new great-grandchildren. She no longer remembers having lived in the

United States. She is still surrounded by her lifelong companions—fear, loneliness, and sadness.

And I, her daughter, long for her presence and her companionship. I remember the woman she was while missing the woman she is. When I was born, my mother chose to stay with me and leave her young adult sons so that I could be raised with a father. Now I choose for her the comfort of her homeland and the love of her family there over my need for her presence, and I find comfort in the memory of the mother that she was.

3

Countering the Pain That Never Heals

Pláticas That Mend the Soul

Adela de la Torre

Pláticas—conversations that allow us to self-discover who we are in relationship to ourselves and others—are embedded within Latino culture. Pláticas, charlas, chisme:[1] we Latinas are immersed in an oral tradition from childhood. Our abuelas, tías, madres, primas, and compañeras surround us with the syncopated sounds of carcajadas, gritos, and murmuras, cloaking us in a cocoon of our cultural traditions.

Yet as we rely on these voices to place us within our community, we soon recognize certain familial voices that have a relatively more powerful influence. These voices stand out, nurturing us through adulthood and soothing us during times of crisis. Just as a newborn infant immediately responds to its mother's voice, so do Latinas respond to the voices of those closest to their souls: their mothers' voices from birth and, later in life, their comadres' comforting voices. These voices often linger in their souls, soothing the pain and enhancing the joy they experience along life's course. Our comadres maintain important confianzas (confidences), listen intently, and reflect deeply before providing the guidance we so desperately need as we reach each important milestone.

As we move into adulthood, pláticas are transformed, perhaps, only by the gravity of the issues discussed. Pláticas are powerful spiritual and, by extension, physical healing processes because they provide the empathetic balm that heals new and old wounds. Pláticas are the glue that maintains the cohesion, resiliency, and protection of Latina culture, social networks, and identity and that sustains the individual and family during periods of distress. Thus, it is no surprise that whether one looks at folk healing practices used by curanderas/os or self-help by individuals, pláticas are at the core of how many Latinas cope with illness and disease. They are the symbolic mechanisms through which these women address the challenges of maintaining their physical and emotional health. Pláticas allow Latinas to approach illness holistically by using words and language to cope with ailments and disease (Avila 1999).

The physical and emotional challenges of aging often increase the need for pláticas to fill the emotional void created when loved ones die or are no longer present in the home. This emotional pain is heightened when physical pain, sometimes chronic, enters into the aging process. Chronic pain resulting from arthritis and other illnesses emerges as a daily threat to many older Latinas' independence and perception of social cohesion, increasing both their psychological and their physical vulnerability to illness.

The physical and emotional effects of chronic pain are not fully understood, particularly among older Latinas. Although chronic pain has many causes, arthritis in its many forms is a major source of it for many older Latinas. A lifetime of physical trauma through working physically demanding jobs as farm, domestic, and manufacturing workers or a family history of arthritis makes this disease an important medical concern. Compared with whites, Latinos have a lower prevalence of doctor-diagnosed arthritis (21.9 percent versus 15.8 percent). However, among respondents age eighteen to sixty-four years, Latinos had a higher proportion of work limitations due to arthritis (38.8 percent versus 28.0 percent of whites) (CDC 2002b). With regard to both effective treatment and pain management for this chronic condition, Latina elders' voices are missing from the medical narratives. Moreover, the arthritis rubric as captured in the medical literature covers more than one hundred specific musculoskeletal conditions that cause inflammation of the joints, including bursitis, gout, and fibromyalgia (Lefers 2004). Thus, arthritis is a disease with enormous complexity and diversity, requiring sophisticated diagnostic and pain-management skills from medical practitioners. These combined factors make it a compelling area for further investigation.

Within the broad arthritis rubric, the more common and debilitating forms of the disease—osteoarthritis and rheumatoid arthritis—are most likely to be diagnosed in a medical practitioner's office. Osteoarthritis, or degenerative joint disease, is the most common form of arthritis, oftentimes linked to age- and trauma-related breakdown of the cartilage between joints (American College of Rheumatology 2004; CDC NCHS 2004b). The symptoms are localized pain, stiffness, redness, and decreased mobility in the involved joints. A higher proportion of Latinos with doctor-diagnosed arthritis report severe joint pain, compared with whites (32.5 percent versus 22.6 percent) (CDC 2002b). One of the more debilitating manifestations of arthritis is rheumatoid arthritis, which often results in crippling disfigurement of the joints. Rheumatoid arthritis is a chronic autoimmune disorder affecting the synovial lining of the joints, which, if left untreated, can lead to permanent disability (Arthritis Society 2005). Symptoms include low-grade fever, dry eyes and mouth, and the involvement of other internal organs. Its peak incidence is among younger adults (usually between twenty and forty-five years of age), and it occurs three times more frequently among women than among men (American College of Rheumatology 2004).

These sterile medical definitions of arthritis may explain the physiological processes that create pain in the body, but they do not describe how women respond psychologically and physically to this pain. For some women, the disease process may inflict constant or piercing pain that attacks the joints, spine, and limbs with a sharp throbbing that has been compared to being jabbed with a hot poker (CDC NCHS 2004b). Rheumatoid arthritis likewise shows no mercy. Like the torturers of the Spanish Inquisition, it commands respect and compliance as it eats away at its victims' mobility, vitality, and optimism by relentlessly piercing and destroying the cartilage and joints of the body, creating a sea of disfigured sufferers begging for remission.

Metaphorically describing our pain allows us to visualize a process that has no obvious markers to either casual observers or medical professionals, who are often unwilling to see beyond physical reality. Schooled in Descartes' scientific description of pain, the latter especially often ignore the emotional and spiritual components involved in the perception of pain.[2]

Only recently have Latinas begun to voice their narratives of chronic pain and disease. Rooted in social networks imbued with strong familial and religious bonds, Latinas not surprisingly face this disease with distinct narratives that go beyond physical descriptions of their pain (Avila 1999). Their family role and relationships may define the ways they articulate the disease, the pain process, and their coping patterns. This is why traditional healers, curanderas, may provide insights that help us more fully understand how chronic pain may manifest in Latinas. The curandera Elena Avila describes chronic pain in terms that would sound very foreign to mainstream medical practitioners: "Co-dependent people can develop *empacho* of the heart from 'loving too much.' Women are especially susceptible to this form of empacho. When we lose ourselves in another person, an energy block develops that prevents us from growing emotionally. We can also get *empacho* from being around someone else's toxic energy. A common saying is 'Me tiene empachado' ('He has me *empachado*,' meaning 'blocked')" (Avila 1999, 47).

Empacho creates both physical and emotional pain, which often causes Latinas to seek healing processes that go beyond traditional medicine. To understand health problems such as empacho, we must unfold the individual narrative that precedes the actual onset of the physical disease to make a diagnosis that brings together the spiritual, mental, and physical components of a woman's health. By understanding these elements in Latinas' lives, we can better understand their outward responses to the chronic pain and physical disability created by arthritis.

A Family Narrative

My own family has lived with arthritis for decades. It has touched every woman on my maternal grandmother's side and preys on my own joints today. As a child, I witnessed my grandmother's struggle with the disease. Her gnarled, arthritic hands would daily brush my long black hair and gently fold the locks into two neat trensas (braids). In the innocence of youth, I would rub her bumpy knuckles, transfixed with the comfort her worn hands would give as she rubbed my head to help me sleep on those nights when I felt a sudden chill of fear as darkness entered the room. We never talked of her pain when foggy winter days made those hands struggle with her normal chores of mending a torn sock or rolling out flour tortillas for the hot comal. Not until adulthood did I realize that the disease that had crippled her body was arthritis. In her silence, she protected me from the unknown but also denied me the knowledge that could have prepared me for this dreadful disease.

Even though arthritis touched every woman in my family as we grew into adulthood, we experienced it in different ways. Perhaps the youngest victim of our family curse was my mother's cousin Guadalupe "Lupe" Juana Salcedo Grace, who by the age of thirty-three developed the most damaging form: rheumatoid arthritis. Yet Lupe was not forewarned of a life of pain. As young women, my mother and she would play tennis on weekends on the Oakdale High courts, exchanging quick volleys and smashing backhands. Long before Serena Williams became a household name, Lupe's athleticism made her shine on the courts and later in the glittery ballrooms of Los Angeles. With her soft green eyes and golden hair, Lupe would move her hips to the latest samba beat, twirling circles in her stiletto heels as young men on the sidelines beckoned for her attention. Her carefree and fun-loving demeanor never revealed the ticking time bomb that would engulf her youth and steal her body. Yet all too soon she was forced to trade her stilettos for flat orthopedic shoes and throw her prized wooden racket in the trash when the searing pain in her joints held her firmly in its clutches.

According to her daughter, Ana Maria, Lupe never really complained about her disease, even though she endured several surgeries—one to fuse her hip, another to straighten her feet, and a third to improve the mobility in her legs—so that she could move with a little more ease and less pain. Lupe always placed mind over matter and sought out the latest medical therapies, both conventional and nontraditional, to combat her disease. Her positive attitude masked her pain so as never to inflict her physical burden on others. Lupe would not let suffering define her identity or her social condition. Her own intrinsic personality and cultural values kept her from elevating her pain to the same plane as her familial responsibilities as a wife and mother.

In hearing my cousin's interpretation of her mother's illness, I wondered to what extent empacho might have played a role in how her illness had manifested. How did Lupe's response to the disease intersect with her early emotional life experiences? According to my mother, she and Lupe shared similar experiences as young girls growing up in California's Central Valley. Both fended off negative experiences with grace and humor. They also shared an enormous capacity to give emotional support to those around them. In addition, their support systems were closely tied to family members, and they maintained tremendous loyalty and commitment to these kinship networks, often sacrificing their own immediate needs for a family member's well-being. Moreover, my mother and Lupe viewed themselves as kindred spirits; since childhood, they had been best friends, so close that neither would let family disputes or disagreements interfere with their relationship.

Lupe and my mother, Herminia ("Mimi"), were atypical Mexican American girls of their generation—both married men who had been married previously, and they quietly rebelled against the prescribed roles of the earlier generation of Mexican women. They shared a maternal grandmother,

Demetria Escamilla, who was known as a great healer by her neighbors in Zacatecas and who died tragically from cancer shortly after the birth of her last child, Adela, my own grandmother. Demetria, through blood and spirit, joined these women, bringing together my mother's innate psychic skills with Lupe's keen analytical skills to create a force to be reckoned with when the two women plotted together. Over time, each created her own spiritual reality; neither was compelled to embrace the stifling structure and discipline required of "good Catholic girls," yet both still respected and understood these traditions. Thus, they lived their lives challenging the parameters of their culture on one level, while at the same time strictly adhering to the familial loyalty and obligations that defined Mexican social structure.

The fact that Lupe and Mimi were "soul sisters," closer to each other than to their own biological sisters, allowed them to share important pláticas as they went through the different experiences of the life cycle. Avila describes a plática as a "deep heart-to-heart talk that continues in installments for as long as it needs to" (1999, 143). For as long as I can remember, whenever I heard a hushed voice in my mother's bedroom, I knew my mother was talking to Lupe; sometimes I would hear a quick chuckle, but when she hung up the phone, I could tell from the look in her eyes that she had cleansed her mind through deep conversation. Even though distance separated the two cousins physically—Lupe lived in San Bernardino and my mother in Berkeley—it altered little their intimate relationship. My mother always told me that she and Lupe found in each other a safe refuge where shared secrets were never repeated to probing relatives or friends and wounds inflicted by other family members were quickly healed by a sympathetic ear. They intuitively knew when pláticas were needed during the crisis points in each other's lives. For example, when Lupe lost her only son, Frank, from a sudden heart attack, my mother consoled her over the phone. Lupe shared her grief freely with my mother so that other family members would not be burdened by her deep sorrow. My mother knew how profoundly Lupe loved Frank, who was larger than life itself, and how his death had created a bottomless chasm in Lupe's soul. Mother, knowing that her support was needed more than ever, would keep tabs on her beloved Lupe, calling her often in fear that the emotional and physical pain of his death might strip the life from her fragile bones. It was clear from my mother's narrative that without these pláticas, neither Lupe nor she could have coped with the pain they shared.

My mother and I were fortunate to visit Lupe three years ago, shortly before she passed on. What struck me when I saw my mother and Lupe together was how beautiful they became when their eyes met. Lupe, like my mom, had made sure her hair was nicely combed and that her well-formed lips were painted to highlight her milky smooth, pale skin. Both were fastidious about how they dressed and looked, lest it appear that age and infirmity had robbed them of their dignity. Despite Lupe's limited mobility, she insisted that we go to her favorite Mexican restaurant. My cousin Ana Maria was quite skilled at handling her mother, and she adeptly but carefully maneuvered her into the car, aware that after thirty years of Prednisone and other anti-inflammatory drugs, her mother's bones had become as fragile as fine vintage china. (Prednisone has been found to increase the risk of osteoporosis and to cause muscle weakness, steroid myopathy, and loss of muscle mass [Medlineplus 2006].)

Although neither my mom nor Lupe finished their meals, they left with a fullness that made the journey complete. My mother knew in her heart that this would be the last time she would see her soul mate, her closest friend and "sister," but in her mind everything was as it always was, on their terms and with their shared memories, dreams, and secrets. The image of Lupe's face on that day, she says, is etched in her mind; she knew that Lupe was emotionally and physically ready to meet Frank on that long journey to the next world.

Even though my mother knew almost instinctively when Lupe died and understood intellectually that her time had come, emotionally she was not ready to let her go. Her grief so overwhelmed her that at the risk of appearing insensitive, I avoided any mention of Lupe's name to prevent the inevitable torrent of tears.

My mother claims her chronic arthritis pain became almost unbearable a little more than two years ago, not coincidentally soon after Lupe's death. Although noticeable arthritis had begun to plague Mother's fingers, knees, and one shoulder when she was in her midseventies, she could control the pain using over-the-counter remedies. She rarely complained to me about her arthritis except when the dampness of winter rains or summertime Bay Area fog would send a chill through her bones. Then the pain, particularly in her knees, would put a grimace on her face and make her reach for her stash of pain medications.

Her repertoire of favored medicines includes an ointment made of chili powder called Capsaicin, which Lupe had told her about; her favorite old lady's perfume, Ben Gay; and a good dose of Tylenol. If she is really "going to battle against the pain monster," she pulls out her stronger meds, such as lidocaine patches, but given her hypersensitivity to drugs, she prefers to keep her wits and balance about her and uses these meds only as a last resort. Her experience with prescription pain medications over the years has been quite negative because even low doses of them cause dizziness and sometimes shortness of breath or heart palpitations, which as a result has deterred her from pursuing aggressive pharmaceutical pain treatment.

My mother has recently begun to fear she is losing her battle against the pain monster. Her doctor has diagnosed her condition as trauma arthritis resulting from multiple physical traumas, such as bone fractures in her youth as well as misguided and inept surgical mistakes. These traumas have created multiple stress points within her body. In addition, the lingering effects of the chickenpox virus manifest in her body as sharp nerve pains similar to shingles. (Chickenpox is an infectious disease caused by the varicella-zoster virus, which results in a blisterlike rash, itching, tiredness, and fever [CDC NIP 2001].) As a result of this chronic pain and the recent emotional and physical stress of having surgery to implant a pacemaker, my mother has become so emotionally frazzled that tears erupt suddenly whenever a stressful event occurs. Today, she is struggling to rebuild a life of independence, which requires her to cope with an even higher emotional and physical pain threshold.

The fact that my mother continues to be as sharp as a tack mentally, even though her emotional and physical states are rapidly declining, creates conflict for family members as we attempt to balance our growing frustration over her deteriorating health with greater empathy toward her new physical and emotional plight. Compounding these issues, my mother has always prided herself on her self-sufficiency, even during the most stressful times in her life. She does not appreciate family members' gentle guidance, seeing it as an attempt to direct her choices or actions. In many respects, she clings fiercely to her independence, continuing to live alone in the rambling Berkeley home where she has lived most of her eighty-five years. She refuses to give in to "the monster" (or to anyone else, for that matter), relinquish her freedom, and leave the place where her neighbors adore her and regard her as the resident matriarch of the neighborhood. Moreover, she perceives that living with either of her two daughters would further intrude her taxing illness into their private lives. She prefers the solitary confinement of her home over listening to the muttered commentary of spouses or other family members when tears become her best coping mechanism during her bouts of chronic pain. No, for her, it is either her own home or a rest home; she will not even consider enduring the humiliation of being dismissed or treated like a child by her own relatives. Besides, she has saved religiously for a retirement home, so that when the time comes she will be ready. My mother is somewhat unusual in that

respect. Latinos are less likely than other ethnic groups to institutional-
ize their elders, so elderly Latinos generally live with spouses or familial
caregivers (Cox and Monk 1993; Harwood et al. 2000).

Mother's mind rationally discerns what she wants, but, according to
her, the wounds in her heart still have not healed. Underlying my mother's
most recent litany of physical and emotional complaints about her pain is
her most recent traumatic experience, which she describes as something
akin to near death. For at least two years, my mother had complained of
dizziness and physical weakness, but the heart problem these symptoms
signaled had remained undiagnosed until she collapsed on her front porch
and was rushed to the hospital. (More than 20 percent of Latinas have high
blood pressure. Nearly 60 percent say they get no leisure-time physical
activity, and nearly 60 percent of Latinas are overweight or obese. All of
these conditions can lead to heart disease, the number one cause of death
among Latinas [Aetna 2006].) During her first night in the hospital, her
heartbeat suddenly dropped to thirty beats per minute, setting off immediate concern that she was dying. The next morning, without hesitation,
the cardiologist recommended a pacemaker to regulate her heartbeat and
completed the implantation surgery that very day.

My mother claims that a week prior to having her pacemaker implanted,
she was warned of her possible death through two very distinct out-of-
body experiences. These experiences terrified her even as they warned her
of an undiagnosed health problem. In many respects, they fit within the
context of what curanderos refer to as *susto*. Susto occurs when the body
and soul are not in harmony with each other: "The spiritual self, the aura
that surrounds us, is the most vulnerable to trauma. . . . [I]f we experience
a frightening or traumatic event, this can result in soul loss, a state in which
we do not feel fully present or as if we are really ourselves. We experience
a feeling that 'something is missing' because our spirit, the energetic aura
that surrounds us, has been violated" (Avila 1999, 64).

My mother said that she had had two horrible dreams the previous
week. The first was about having dinner with Lupe's sisters and mother, all
of whom are deceased, at the Fairmont Hotel in San Francisco. They were
trying desperately to convince her to stay longer, despite her protests that
she must return home. The following night brought an even more startling
dream. In it, my mother was taking a bath when, suddenly, Lupe's mother,
Maria, and sister Tita showed up and pushed her head under the water.
She struggled as they tried to drown her, telling her that she must die. My
mother woke up in a chilled sweat, gasping for breath and terrified of what
she described as an out-of-body experience. Lupe was in neither of these

dreams, and, to my mother, her struggle for life was linked to this vision of death that was not harmonious, but could only be described as "susto."

My mother's near-death experiences in her dreams are compelling not only because they warned her of her impending health crisis, but also because they triggered memories of the past traumas that defined her present physical and emotional pain. They prevented her from coping with her physical pain as she had previously done—with her self-prescribed treatments and doctor's visits. Instead, she was in great need of a serious plática in order to identify a new strategy for tackling her physical, spiritual, and emotional pain.

A Major Turning Point

Mother's fragile emotional state as a result of these physical and emotional traumas made it impossible for her family members or even her physician to intervene and effectively lessen the pain in her life. As we family members pondered how we could provide more focused oversight of her care, she pulled back into her own world, viewing each suggestion from us as an attempt to rob her of her independence and dignity. Yet even she knew she needed help in focusing her life away from her now-daily torrent of tears. Finally, she began to realize, with support from her doctor and family, that it was time to seek some type of counseling.

We all were surprised at how quickly my mother recognized her need to find someone who, like Lupe, could once again listen to her with an uncritical ear and help her manage her pain in a way that would give her the emotional resources to tackle her latest problems. Through self-analysis, she recognized that her immediate family members, given their busy lives, were not in the best position to help her address the emotional pain that plagued her. In her eyes, family members were better at giving commands than respecting her wishes, a dynamic that only aggravated her physical pain because her muscles would tense up during the verbal skirmishes when she disagreed with one of us.

In addition, my mother realized that she had not fully addressed the feelings of failure and sorrow in her own life. She needed time to revisit her own past so that she could begin to move forward once again. A single mother, she regretted that she had never had the luxury of playing the role of the "typical self-sacrificing Mexican mother" who cared for the home and children. As a young divorcée in the 1950s, she learned quickly that her family's survival relied on her working, and she relinquished the role of mother to my grandmother. My mother would often say to me that she "envied those mothers who were the 'real Mexican mothers,'" those who earned their families' respect and protection by staying at home. Instead, "for those of us who had to work outside the home, we must now face the pains of old age alone and know the only respite from this pain is death." Of course, this pain is not physical but emotional—it is the pain of not meeting expectations, which many Mexican American working women may feel when they do not fulfill their traditional familial roles.

Despite my mother's regret over not meeting traditional role expectations, in many respects she went beyond what most women—Latina or non-Latina—of her generation accomplished. At the tender age of nine, she lost her beloved father to cancer during the middle of the Great Depression. Her mother, Adela, a young single mother with three children, needed to work, and my mother early on began to recognize her role as a key economic provider. During high school, she worked in the local doctor's office, not only doing office work but also assisting the doctor with his patients. This early experience created a passion to pursue medicine, so she enrolled in the local community college, graduating in two years and later pursuing a bachelor of arts degree at the University of California at Berkeley—no minor feat for a Mexican American woman of her generation.

Although she was never able to fulfill her dream of becoming a doctor, she did become a master teacher in the public elementary education system and served in that capacity for forty years before she retired. Her compassion, intelligence, and generosity of spirit endeared her to all her students. Over the years, my mother received countless cards and notes from students she taught, acknowledging and thanking her for her positive presence in their lives. And she treasures each card with the dignity and respect that, in her opinion, every student deserves.

Despite the many triumphs in her life, her courage in raising and supporting a family alone and giving her unselfish attention to her students, she could no longer sustain her battle against the chronic pain monster she faced in her daily life. She needed help to begin the important process of not just medicating her pain, but speaking about it. Acknowledging the pain through pláticas with the right person could make an important difference to her quality of life. In her case, it was not a traditional healer who helped her heal her emotional wounds, but a trained therapist experienced with geriatric counseling.

Feelings of hopelessness and perceived stress—such as what my mother was experiencing—are strongly linked with depression. It also seems that Latinas are at high risk for depression. In a study examining ethnic differences in depressive symptoms, Latinas were rated as significantly more depressed than African American or Caucasian women, which the researchers attributed to their facing a disproportionate amount of psychological distress due to their family structures, environment, and tendency to remain silent and not seek treatment (Myers et al. 2002). Moreover, geriatric psychiatrists are in short supply, a major problem facing the psychiatric workforce (Colenda, Wilk, and West 2002), and geriatric psychiatrists sensitive to minority cultures are particularly difficult to find. With medical advancements, life spans have increased, presenting new challenges to meet the social, environmental, psychological, economic, and health-care requirements of increasing numbers of elderly individuals (Colenda, Wilk, and West 2002), so the need for geriatric counselors will only increase.

My mother was fortunate in that with little effort she found an excellent therapist. Although not a Latina, the therapist was empathetic and nonjudgmental of Mother's unique experiences and, more important, validated the courage she had exhibited throughout her life. Mother began to realize that she did not have to forget the emotional pain in her life but instead could learn to use it in a more constructive way. When I would take my mother to her appointments, I would marvel at how in order to meet with her therapist, she would struggle up three flights of stairs with a walker—something that was beyond her normal daily living activities. She was determined to have her "plática" and move toward healing the emotional pain that was hindering her ability to cope with her physical pain.

As I write this story, my mother has successfully fought off the ghosts of death and has begun to focus on handling her pain more proactively. She is now exploring hypnosis with her therapist, as well as the use of acupuncture in her healing process. She has invested in a motorized easy chair that allows her to rest in alternative positions when the pain in her back prevents her from sleeping in bed. She is also beginning to normalize her living patterns with her family and friends once again. The physical pain is still there, and oftentimes it is still almost overwhelming, but her emotional and spiritual pain is beginning to subside as she heals her many old wounds. According to my mother, this process makes sense because "when you have a near-death experience, all the memories from the past surface as your spirit leaves your body, and oftentimes, the most painful memories linger."

For many indigenous cultures, the type of trauma, or susto, my mother experienced requires a limpia (cleansing) or plática to be healed (Avila 1999). Curanderas believe that it is not sufficient merely to diagnosis a health problem. Instead, it is important to understand what is going on in the patient's heart and soul. Moreover, the patient needs to tell the story of the pain so that the soul can be healed (Avila 1999). Although my mother did not use a traditional healer, she did seek healing in the context of traditional concepts that for centuries were part of indigenous cultures. That is, she recognized early on in her illness that the mind and the body are organically linked both spiritually and physically, and that to cope with her chronic pain, she would need to work on healing them simultaneously.

Concluding Thoughts

My mother's narrative of her pain provides an important backdrop to understanding how Latinas may articulate chronic pain as they move into their golden years. The physical pain associated with illnesses such as arthritis may be clearly present. However, the broader psychological response to the pain associated with illness is equally significant in providing comprehensive and sensitive treatment.

Culture and past emotional traumas create an emotional space that constrains how Latinas respond to clinical pain therapies. Moreover, because most Latinas operate within the context of extended family networks, Latino families need culturally sensitive and responsive primary-care providers who incorporate emotional support of the elder and the family into compassionate models for pain treatment, which may help alleviate miscommunication and resentment between primary caregivers and the elder parent.

It is critical that health-care providers and geriatric counselors account for both the structural and the cultural contexts of elderly Latinos, responding to their bicultural realities and integrating them into treatment (Flores et al. 2008). Recognition of these cultural nuances will ultimately increase caregiver agency and lessen patient distress.

Latinas and their families can learn to accept their physical and emotional vulnerability with the support of comadres, curanderas, or culturally sensitive therapists. Pláticas to address current and past emotional traumas as well as spiritual needs should be part of the healing repertoire available to our Latina elders. This combination will provide more holistic pain management and, I hope, bridge the divide between the clinical diagnosis and treatment of a disease, on the one hand, and the patient's emotional response, on the other, thus enhancing the overall palliative care needed to improve the quality of life for women who live their daily lives in chronic pain.

4

Letters to Ceci

A Journey from Hyperthyroidism to Hypothyroidism

Clara Lomas

Metabolic roller coaster
Towering, dipping energy levels
zenith efficiency shooting toward overload, lethargy, numbness,
un cansancio infinito . . .
Forgotten deep breaths turned winded gasps,
Marathon-throbbing heart pushed in with sweaty hands,
brain flooded with a million racing thoughts
shooting off in all directions at warp speed
swiftly fleeing,
unintelligible,
an effervescence of brilliant stars
slowly dimming into abyss.

—*Clara Lomas*

January 30, 1981[1]
Santa Cruz, CA

Querida Ceci,

It's been five months since Luis Alberto was born, and my life has been transformed forever. Somehow, however, I don't feel this transformation has to do with motherhood alone. Although my life is close to perfect (after all, I feel great about where I'm at: ABD with three chapters of my dissertation done, a wonderful and supportive husband, a healthy and gorgeous baby, and a new teaching job at a great University of California campus), I feel completely frustrated and unsatisfied. The doctor says I have postpartum blues, but what I feel isn't at all like blue. I feel an incredibly hot, burning rush—as if I'm speeding—there aren't enough hours in the day to do everything I feel driven to accomplish. I'm usually irritable, anxiety ridden. I don't understand what's going on.

By the way, the thyroid test was borderline high. Doc says we have to keep an eye on it.

I hope you're doing well. I miss you, my friends, and family down south very much!

June 30, 1984
Santa Cruz, CA

Dearest Ceci,

¿Cómo has estado, m'ija? Remember the unfathomable speed, the superwoman syndrome of my life? Well, it's getting worse! I'm sleeping only about three hours a night, teaching myself pedagogical techniques of language instruction, carrying an overload of courses, directing the program, getting the required articles and conference presentations out—just under the wire—while working as housing preceptor for the Latina/o wing of the college. Although I completed the master's program and the PhD program up to the candidacy exams in four years, I haven't been able to finish my dissertation in the following three and a half years . . . and, of course, I feel awful. The anxiety and irritability are unbearable. I want out desperately. I never thought I would accept a spousal scholarship in order to finish my dissertation. But that's what I'm doing now that we're moving to Austin. I hope I'll be able to finish this last, obnoxious academic "incomplete" and also get rid of the debilitating, shooting pain caused by these nasty ovarian cysts. I'll let you know.

November 30, 1989
Colorado Springs, CO

Dearest Sis,

My life keeps moving too fast since I completed the PhD four years ago. The three years as a visiting scholar and professor at UT Austin, were very productive nonetheless. If only I could catch up with my own mind. It's like I'm on fast-forward and everything outside me is moving in slow motion. We went shopping together yesterday, and Luis and Luis Alberto kept complaining that they couldn't keep up with me, literally. They tell me I walk too fast, talk too fast, think too fast. But the way I see it, they, and everyone else for that matter, are moving too slowly. It's surreal. At any rate, I decided to take the job at UCLA.

The doctors here in the Springs continue to tell me that my thyroid hormone level is borderline high . . . that we should continue to keep close tabs on it. Pero, nada. They don't offer me anything I can DO about it.

Y como si fuera poco, I slipped on the ice outside my office and gave myself quite a goose egg on the back of my head—another argument for relocating from Colorado to the warmth of LA, I guess. Luis joked that he'd finally found a way to make me stop for a minute, but he insisted on taking me to the emergency room. A waste of time, as usual. The physician's assistant who saw me said I just had a minor concussion, nothing to worry about, and no need for X rays. I don't know . . . the pain throbs against the back of my head and vibrates all the way down my vertebrae. Wish you were here.

December 30, 1991
Los Angeles, CA

Querida Ceci,

I caused quite a sensation among the faculty when I waddled into my new job at UCLA eight months pregnant. One of my colleagues said that they had been waiting two years for me to get there, and what was I doing, arriving in this condition? I told him that some of our gender are not only into knowledge production, but into species reproduction as well. He wasn't very amused. Neither was the department chair. He said UCLA did not offer maternity leave for faculty, that I should have planned my delivery for the summer! I wasn't about to put up with that kind of discrimination—even in a brand-new position. I had to fight the administration all the way up to the vice chancellor, but I won the right to keep my hard-bargained-for research quarter off *and* get maternity leave. And I've gotten a surprising amount of support from my colleagues and even from several of the administrators.

But, you know, it's ironic—it's my own body that's fighting me: I have terrifying heart palpitations; I feel as if I'm perspiring all the time (I know, but it wasn't just the pregnancy, it's still going on). My muscles feel weak and shaky. I can barely keep my legs under me anymore when I climb the stairs to my office. My thoughts are racing, I see double, and I'm losing weight without even trying to (I suppose there's always something to be thankful for). I'm sure my body is trying to tell me something, but no one knows what. The frequent headaches in the back of my head, the nausea, and the fatigue persist. Could head trauma be causing all of this?

I've started back on the medical merry-go-round, trying to get answers. I've been seeing four doctors at the medical center (my obstetrician referred me to an endocrinologist, who sent me to a cardiologist, who recommended a neurologist). Not one has given me any answers. The last one I saw recommended I see a psychiatrist! They think it's all in my head. Between you and me, they're the ones driving me crazy! And listen to this one, m'ija: the psychiatrist maintains that I need to relearn *how to breathe*—in LA!

I've decided to return to Colorado Springs for various reasons. I hate to leave the wonderful students, exceptional colleagues, and extraordinary libraries of the UC system. I'll try hard to live my life at a slower pace. ¿Qué sé yo? . . . the doctors consistently recommend it.

I wish you could come with me. You don't seem to be doing all that well either, Ceci. Are you all right? I worry sometimes.

August 30, 1992
Colorado Springs, CO

Dearest Sis,

Unavoidable collisions! As my marriage is imploding due to (among other things) my stubborn, unconscious drive to continue at full speed, I am also physically "crashing" with thyrotoxicosis.

I ended up in the emergency room again a couple of days ago. Thank goodness this time I was seen by a *real* doctor, not some assistant . . . and he finally put a name to what's been going on with me for more than a decade. This Dr. Steinhour said I have GRAVES' DISEASE. Hearing the "grave" part, I immediately said, "I'm sorry, doctor, but I can't go to the grave yet!

I have a nine-month-old baby to raise!" He laughed, "No, no. You've just been going at a hundred miles per hour, probably for years. All we have to do now is to get you down to the speed limit." He explained that Graves' disease has been treated quite successfully for the past fifty years or so. "¡Qué chistoso!" is all I had to say at that revealing and shocking moment. I guess the disease explains how last week I ate an entire apple pie à la mode in two sittings and still lost five pounds.[2]

Pues, fíjate, how many doctors does it take to get an answer? It took a physician with the same ailment to diagnose it! He tells me that many people go untreated because the condition is so difficult to diagnose—especially when doctors work individually within their own areas of expertise. You see, lab results don't always reveal the abnormal hormone levels. I was one of the lucky ones. No te digo. But at least the disease is getting a flurry of attention recently after George and Barbara Bush were diagnosed with it.[3]

Pero, en todo caso, the good news is that there are effective treatments, according to Dr. Steinhour, who has had it for forty years and has been treating it, quite safely, with synthetic thyroid hormone—not that I much like the idea of pumping my body full of artificial chemicals for the rest of my life. Yet he reassures me that the treatments are quite effective and that I should have no long-term health consequences if we can get the condition under control. He outlined the three basic choices, and I am mulling them over. I'd love to know your opinion. And, who knows, maybe this is why you haven't been feeling great either. Doc says there does seem to be a hereditary link.

The basic problem seems to be that, just as I told you, my own body has betrayed me with this autoimmune disease. It's kicking out antibodies that act like thyroid-stimulating hormone. So they're busily telling my thyroid to crank out more thyroid hormones, keeping my metabolism in permanent overdrive (and my body out of control). One way or another, we have to get those hormones under control.

1. Beta-blockers. These immediately counteract the symptoms of overactive metabolism—those scary heart palpitations—but they do nothing to lower the levels of thyroid hormones in my blood. There can be some pretty serious side effects on the immune system, so Dr. Steinhour wouldn't recommend doing this for more than three months. I guess sometimes the condition can more or less go into remission, so if I go this route, I'd basically be banking on short-term treatment.

2. Radioactive iodine. One dose of radioactive iodine is given orally (either by pill or liquid) to destroy the active cells in the thyroid gland.

Again, the doc reassured me that the iodine is picked up only by thyroid cells, and the destruction is local. Thus, there are no widespread side effects—nothing like the things you usually associate with radiation therapy for cancer. Radioactive iodine ablation has been safely used for more than fifty years, and the only major reasons for not using it are pregnancy and breastfeeding. Baby Ceci is already eating solids, so I could start weaning her soon anyway, whatever I decide. This form of therapy is the treatment of choice for recurring Graves' disease. Only thing is, because the radiation wipes out most or all of the thyroid gland, my body would swing the other direction—into permanent hypothyroidism. To get my metabolism back into a normal balance, I'd have to go on permanent synthetic thyroid-replacement therapy, probably within a few months after the radiation.

3. Surgery to remove part of the thyroid gland. Apparently, this isn't as common a treatment for hyperthyroidism as it used to be. The objective is to remove just enough of the thyroid tissue that is producing the excessive hormone to get my metabolism to a normal level. If they take out too much tissue, however, I could end up with hypothyroidism and still need thyroid-replacement therapy. I guess the surgery has to be done carefully, too, so as not to damage the nerves supplying the vocal cords or the four tiny glands in the neck that regulate calcium levels in the body. If the doctors accidentally remove or damage those glands, I might need calcium-replacement therapy, too. Can you imagine me with complications that leave me unable to talk normally? ¡Claro que no, mujer![4]

I don't really like my choices, and I'm still reeling a bit. I'd almost come to believe my problems were all in my mind. I couldn't sleep anyway, so I spent hours last night surfing the Internet, looking for alternative, less-invasive treatments. I even found a chat room for people who have thyroid problems (four out of five are women).

I have asked Mami if she can suggest any herbal or other natural, alternative remedies for my condition. But she says that as far as she knows, no one in our immediate or extended family has been afflicted with these health issues. In the meantime, I'm starting on some "live" juice and herbal therapy. I found a book at the health-food store that recommends certain fresh ("live") vegetable and fruit juices—in particular broccoli, brussels sprouts, cabbage, kale, spinach, turnips, pears, and peaches. They are considered specific "healing juices" for hyperthyroid disorders. Just put them through the juicer and voilà! They're pretty tasty. The book also recommends herbs, including bayberry, black cohosh, golden seal, skullcap, and white oak bark.[5] I've bought them all! But they're not likely to offer a quick fix for my very advanced condition, and I don't have a lot of time. I'm already struggling to keep up with teaching and my kids, and I cannot take more than a six-month medical leave. Needless to say, I'm torn. I'm afraid I'll have to go the invasive route and choose between the lesser of two evils: radiation or surgery! I wish you were here. I need a hug.

P.S. I'm enclosing some information I downloaded from the Mayo Clinic Web site on hyperthyroidism and hypothyroidism. There is also a useful bibliography and list of Web sites and support groups.[6] Some things to watch for in family members are underactive thyroid, premature graying (beginning in the twenties), or a history of related immune problems, such as juvenile diabetes, pernicious anemia (due to lack of vitamin B12), or vitiligo (painless white patches on the skin). We've seen all of these conditions in the family. But what we've seen the most, I suspect, are symptoms of hypothyroidism.[7]

April 19, 1993

Queridísima Ceci,

I am so very sorry to hear that the first surgery didn't work, and you needed more surgery to get out those ovarian cysts. Please, please take good care of yourself. I can tell you from experience that the recovery takes much longer than anticipated. But what am I talking about? You know that much better than I do, given the other surgeries you've had for endometriosis.

I think you and the rest of the family helped me make the right decision. I can't believe it's been six months since I took the radioactive iodine, RAI, a.k.a. "radioactive cocktail." You know, I still think the worst part was the seventy-two-hour isolation period. I'm so thankful that Mami could be there to support me because I couldn't even touch baby Ceci due to the chance of radiation contamination. ¡Te imaginas!

As the RAI has been wiping out my thyroid, I've been feeling the inevitable onslaught of the dreaded hypothyroidism. From living on fast-forward, I now feel as if I'm moving in slow motion. I often feel like I'm trying to climb out of a hole of lethargy and depression. It is now quite evident that my health condition was the last straw in what had become a very strained relationship with Luis. He was offered a job in Illinois, and he took it. Luis, of course, could see the roller coaster I was on. I not only could not understand the changes in my body and behavior, but at times didn't even notice them.

Although I had no help during the medical leave, at least I had the luxury of sleeping all day. I would get up at 6:00 A.M., get Ceci and Luis

Alberto ready for school and daycare, drop them off, and go home to sleep. I'd set the alarm clock for 3:00 P.M., pick up the kids, feed them, do homework, play a bit with them, get ready for the following day, and go to sleep by 9:00 P.M. I'm back at work full time, and, unfortunately, the thyroid-replacement therapy hasn't had any noticeable effect yet.[8] So I keep crawling.

I've had to cancel my scheduled research trips, conference presentations, and everything except what I absolutely have to do. I'm grounded at a snail's pace. I keep my hopes up that this lifelong therapy will eventually level my metabolism, and I'll finally have the normalcy I've been struggling to find for more than a decade. On an upbeat note, though, I've managed to continue working with the Recovering the U.S. Hispanic Literary Heritage Project and published *The Rebel*.[9]

Please let me know how you are doing.

May 30, 1995

Dear Ceci,

I'm glad I pressured everyone in the family to get thyroid tests. I just heard from Nena. She's gotten a diagnosis of Hashimoto's disease.[10] That means all of us have some sort of autoimmune thyroid condition: Nena, you, Rosa, Joe, and Alma with hypothyroidism; Beto and I with alternating hyperthyroidism and hypothyroidism. And along with these, other endocrine system problems: your hypoglycemia; the two of us with our ovarian cysts; your and Joe's adrenal issues, etc. Hmm . . . Isn't it strange that our parents don't seem to have any problems and can't remember any of our grandparents having any symptoms? I'm beginning to think that, for us, there's an environmental cause. Growing up in the Imperial Valley next to all those agricultural fields in the days when they were still spraying DDT and God only knows what else couldn't have been good for us.[11]

November 30, 1997

Querida hermanita,

I'm now directing our Mexico Program in Guanajuato, and unfortunately I can't travel with our students as I had planned. My autoimmune system continues to control my life. These past four years—what with the headaches, dizziness, nausea, fatigue, lethargy, memory loss, and lack of concentration, not to mention the disintegration of my marriage—have been quite unbearable. Now I've been diagnosed with a severe case of anemia, and I've been hemorrhaging almost every day. I'll need surgery (God willing, only a partial hysterectomy) as soon as I return to the States.

In general, everyone here, even the students, has been very understanding and supportive; but, I tell you, two of the students in the program have been unforgiving about the fact that I have not been able to work with them every day of the week. Being ill is simply a luxury I cannot afford. I fondly remember las mujeres of the Latina Feminist Group at our weeklong summer institutes over the past few summers who were "al pie del cañón" [ready to step in] when I couldn't continue to assume all the responsibilities of running the institute. Those seventeen mujeres collaborated to make these institutes some of the most productive and successful any of us has ever attended. The level of solidarity, trust, and friendship we developed is like nothing I've ever experienced elsewhere. In fact, I'm happy to say that we made the collaborative process itself a major thematic component of the book we produced out of those institutes.[12]

At any rate, I'll be in touch as soon as I return. Thanks so much for offering to come to Colorado Springs to help me during my recovery. Mom is insisting on coming to help with the kids. What would I do without my extended family now that I'm a single parent? In fact, I feel truly blessed to have such a supportive community of family, friends, and comadres.

December 17, 2000

Estimada Ceci,

Brindis time! I'm glad that la doctora Italia in Mexico was able to help you. Isn't it unfortunate that now most of our conversations are about health? As for me, I've been working hard to raise my energy level. You know, it seems as if the past few years have been all about medical treatments. First came all the tests at the Mayo Clinic, then the visits to the Santa Barbara facilities. I'm glad that at least there are some explanations for my overwhelming fatigue: the interdependency of the hypothalamus-pituitary-thyroid axis, which further slows down my entire endocrine system. The neurologists point out that my advanced disc degenerative disease is further aggravating the musculoskeletal issues I've been addressing through frequent physical therapy sessions. What has been difficult to determine is whether all of these disorders originate with the endocrine problems or with the head injury I suffered about a decade ago.[13] Nonetheless, adding to the fatigue, cognitive deficits are slowly but surely surfacing. I am not a "happy camper" as little Ceci would say.

Can you believe it? I have the energy level of an eighty-year-old woman! No wonder I have to rest so much throughout the day, something I used to think was such a waste of time. I continue working, but I have to pace myself and take breaks to meditate as often as I can. I even come home for a few hours during the day when I am extremely fatigued and become nauseated. I am so lucky to have such a supportive department. During my partial medical leave, I was able to take good care of myself, learn yoga to increase my energy level, and work with the doctor to taper down my medications. Just the slightest change to my dosage can throw me off-kilter! I go from being slow and tired to being hyperactive if the dosage is increased too much! Sometimes when I really need to produce, I'll take a bit more, but I really shouldn't. I do pay the consequences: I crash for several days.

Ay, Ceci, who would have thought I'd be a middle-aged woman with the body of a senior citizen? That I'd be dependent on my pills? Remember how crazy my life was before? La comadre and I would pull all-nighters preparing papers and presentations, and make it through the next day without a problem. Now each aspect of my career requires careful oversight. I still love my work and my job, though. I'm off to teach a class. Thank goodness for the block system. We rotate intensive teaching and researching, so I have time to rest between teaching terms!

May 15, 2001

Hey Ceci,

I got a Fulbright Fellowship to conduct research in México, DF! I'm so excited! I can continue my work on Latina and Mexican women writers, plus gain some down time from my teaching obligations. I will be taking along students in our program abroad, however, so there will be some university work. I need to prepare myself for the trip, consult with doctors, have prescriptions filled. I'm on my way, México lindo y querido!

Baby Ceci will stay with the abuelitos in California until the second semester. In Mexico, I'll have her attend a bilingual Montessori. I also want to work with Claire Joysmith, who might collaborate with me in writing a border ethnography. Oh, I love to daydream about all the work I hope to do. But you know how things go, there will be some really good and productive days and others that will be a complete write-off. I am really going to have to maneuver the student program; it's pretty intense helping them to adjust to different instructors and a new environment. We need to make sure everything goes smoothly. I hope my energy level is up for this, I've been exhausted lately. We continue to adjust my medicines.

January 21, 2002
México, DF

Dear Ceci,

Wow! So many things have happened since our last communication. The 9/11 attack has inevitably and tragically been a transformative experience. Claire and I got together to talk about how Chicana/o Latinas/os were processing it and experiencing its aftermath. Guess what? We decided to do a book on the topic. We've got most of the testimonials together. I think this will turn out to be a great collection. Gloria Anzaldúa has sent an outstanding piece. In fact, we have titled the book from a phrase in her testimonio![14]

Ceci can't wait to go home; she misses her friends, but her Spanish is improving. She sounds like a Chilanga [a Mexico City native] now.

We are already starting to get ready for next year's calendar. I'll be back to a full-time load. In preparation, I'm experimenting with new treatments. You know I prefer the natural route. I'm also seeing a biomagnetist and an acupuncturist, and I'm going with Claire to the temezcales [herbal saunas]. I do get temporary jolts of energy once in a while. I have begun to notice that the fatigue has contributed to lack of focus and concentration, along with memory problems. No te digo, si no es una cosa es otra [Didn't I tell you, if it's not one thing, it's another]. But I am walking a lot here in Mexico City. And the food, well, rice and beans are great sources of energy.

July 1, 2002

Dear Ceci,

I had a great year in Mexico. Little Ceci is glad to be back home, though. Guess what? I think I forgot to mention that as a full professor, I'll have to assume the duty of chairing my department for the next three years. My colleagues want me to be department chair, and so does the administration. The payoff is that I'll have course release to be able to take on the extra responsibilities. I know it's crazy, but there I go. Onward into the pressure cooker.

Good and not-so-good news! Claire and I were awarded a fellowship from the Rockefeller Foundation to work for a month on the border ethnography project at their Bellagio, Italy, research center. (Hey, what do you think of the title "In What Language Do We Dream? Constructing a Transborder Autobiography/Testimonio"?) However, my doctors here recommended that I postpone the trip.

May 25, 2003

Querida Ceci,

You asked whether I'm jotting down my thoughts on the trying moments. Yes, at times I do feel compelled to write down what I'm experiencing . . . before I forget it? Before I forget how to explain it? I'm not sure why. It's telling that I even forget what I've written.

As I was looking for my medical history on my laptop today, I stumbled on two files I printed out for you. I wrote these brief fragments a couple of days apart last October, but they're the only writings I can find that capture those excruciating moments of great cognitive loss and agony for me. How can I—someone who makes a living in the halls of language— explain away the fact that I misplace critical words, even if momentarily? How can I justify my place in the academic world while losing the ability to retrieve those precious utterances that give fluidity to the most basic communication, that enable me to convey a grammatical construction, a theoretical concept, a personal issue, not only in teaching, but in everyday interaction? For now, I have to be patient with myself and beg patience of others around me. At what point does patience run thin? Let me tell you, sometimes I feel as if I'm trying to find true north without a compass. At other times, I feel I'm moving from theory to mimes, navigating through darkness while the storm subsides.[15]

Anyway, tell me what you think: Is this anything like what you experience?

The Rhythm of My Life
October, 10, 2002

The rhythm of my life, the slow movement in the dark recesses of my mind, gaps of memory, stolen words . . . what is happening? Is there a name for this? Where do I begin to make sense of it? Why is it so painful? Should I convert it into comedy? Admit a nameless handicap and find humor in the bits and pieces of rational thought processes still accessible to me? Something is slipping away much faster than normal aging would account for. The fluidity is abruptly interrupted. My mind stops for split seconds as the rest of the world continues on its course. Sometimes I'm in that flow, sometimes I'm not. My conscious mind struggles intensely to hang on to my last spoken word, to my last thought, not to let it slip away. Limbo for another split second. I return as quickly as possible to the puzzled faces of my interlocutors. Diligently I develop strategies to maintain continuity and fluidity in oral communication. I'm successful at times;

at others I face baffled gazes. If I have any energy left, I attempt to explain myself once more. If I don't, I let it go and hope I can lie down and rest for a few hours. I'm exhausted most of the time now. My mind feels thirty years older than my actual age.

Anxiety Dream
October 13, 2002

Last night, my anxiety over my incapacity to engage completely with the world around me manifested itself in a dream. I don't know whether this is the first time I have had such dreams, but this is certainly the first one I can remember.

I am in a room full of people to whom I need to communicate something important. Yet I am in a glass bubble, and no matter how much I struggle, I can't get through to them. As I exert tremendous efforts, trying to make them hear me, understand me, remain interested, I begin to feel extremely exhausted. My entire body and, more critically, my brain fall into an overwhelming numbness. The stupor draws me farther away into my bubble. From the echoes of my mind, I decipher an inquiring thought: Where am I going? Will I get enough rest there to be lucid when I return? How long will it take before I can return? Twenty minutes . . . two hours . . . five days? Will I be forgiven for my absence or forgotten in it? The uncertainty has no temporal frame. I cannot even recall how long this has been going on.

May 15, 2004

Ceci,

Qué te cuento, being chair is not so bad, barring personal issues, let alone legal ones. It's a lot of work, but I have a chance to turn things around with regard to our academic program. I do get tired, though. Now I have a pinched nerve to boot, so my arm is partially paralyzed. I keep wondering if my conditions are somehow related. My doctor has suggested that I get serious about therapy, meditation, and yoga to lower my stress level so that I can manage all of my duties with less impact on my body. I'm doing bikram yoga and pilates, but life itself is stressful. ¡Sí, ya lo sabes! Being department chair is a challenge, but it doesn't compare to my ongoing challenge with hyper/hypothyroidism. I have to say that I've learned a few important things along the way . . . especially with having an autoimmune disorder that is so difficult to diagnose in the first place. Pues, fíjate, in my case it took more than a decade. While it goes undetected and untreated, it insidiously affects and worsens other health issues.

Having this disease, though, has taught me that I always need a backup plan; I can't automatically count on my metabolism being stable enough for me to function normally. I'm still training myself to stop taking on projects that I cannot possibly do without burning out. Certain aspirations I realize, others I readjust, still others I completely transform. Enjoying each day and its accomplishments becomes more important with every new day.

5

Fat in America

A Latina's Personal Journey

"Christi"[1]

I just read an article, "Disparities in Health Indicators for Latinas in California," which reported that for Latinas "the prevalence of overweight is higher (42.7 [percent]) than for African Americans (40.2), non-Latino whites (24.2), and Asian/other women (16.3)" (Baezconde-Garbanati, Portillo, and Garbanati 2003, 49). Furthermore, the authors report that U.S. Department of Health and Human Services data "have also revealed an increase nationally in the prevalence of overweight among Latinas 20 years of age or older" (50).

In many ways, I feel like a living, breathing, corporal statistic, the incarnation of an ominous trend that is engulfing a vital segment of the female population that is already linked to alarming social risk factors. You see, I'm a woman, I'm a Latina, and I'm not only overweight, I am obese—meaning in technical terms that I am very overweight and have a body mass index (BMI) of 30 or higher (U.S. DHHS Minority Women's Health 2006b).[2] I can no longer shop in regular department stores but must go to specialty shops that cater to the larger-size (obese) woman. I am also a nonbeliever: I simply cannot believe that I actually got this big. I can't believe that all this happened in such a short time span (two years or so). And I just cannot believe that this happened to *me!* I have been a size 12 or 14 most of my adult life, and when I was a child, people would call me "skinny." (Back then, we had no car, so we walked everywhere, and we had meat only once a week—if we were lucky.)

When people who know me see me now, they do a double take: "Can that really be her?" They are also quietly noticing that I am physically changed; I am much bigger, and I occupy more space on the planet. Yes, my shoulders are wider, my thighs have doubled, my feet are big, and my waist has disappeared. In its place is an unsightly bulge under my belly button that forces me to buy a larger size of pants and look even bigger than I otherwise would. Then there's the double chin, the swollen fingers, and the heaviness in my breasts. There are other surprises: I have developed skin tags on my neck and upper legs that periodically need to be removed.

For some Latinas, being large is a badge of middle-aged wisdom and authority, but for me this state offers little consolation or power. My body feels very heavy, and I am tired all the time. I have less energy than before and find it hard to bend over to tie my shoes or pick up groceries. My blood pressure is on the rise, and I have developed gallstones. (Hypertension and gallbladder disease are among the health consequences of overweight and obesity, according to the Weight-Control Information Network.)[3]

My cardiologist indicates that I am also prediabetic, which means that my blood sugar levels are higher than normal but not yet in the diabetic range.[4] Let me elaborate a bit on this distinction. It is important because many Latinas and Latinos are prediabetic and don't even know it. A normal fasting blood glucose level is lower than 100 milligrams per deciliter (mg/dl). Yet someone like me with prediabetes has a fasting blood glucose level between 100 and 125 mg/dl. If my level goes up another 15 points, I will be diagnosed with full-blown diabetes and will follow the typical path of progression by developing it within three to eleven years after prediabetes. If this were not enough, as a person with prediabetes I also have a one and a half times higher risk of cardiovascular disease compared to those with normal blood glucose (American Diabetes Association n.d.b). I also have developed fatty liver disease, an abnormal buildup of fat in the liver due to excess caloric intake, another condition more common among people with prediabetes (American Liver Foundation n.d.).[5]

Not surprisingly, it is increasingly hard for me to celebrate the idea that real (Latina) women are big (anchas) and have (big) curves. Unlike the women in the movie *Real Women Have Curves* (2002), I do not dream of a boutique for large women; I want to get into the clothes I have stored in my closet. I do not celebrate my gordura (obesity), nor do I take kindly to terms of endearment that refer to weight, such as *gorda, gordita, ancha,* or *gruesa* (for more on these terms, see Delgado 2002, 293). Far from being a Latina icon, I feel I'm part of the American nightmare: the "mega-epidemic" described in a Director's Column from the National Center on Physical Activity and

Disability: "Obesity prevalence has more than doubled in children and tripled in adolescents since 1980, and diabetes has increased more than ten-fold at major children's hospitals throughout the United States. We're now beyond an 'epidemic' and into a full-blown 'mega-epidemic.' . . . Obesity is a major cause of disability, and people with disabilities have much higher rates of obesity and extreme obesity" ("Obesity Swells" 2006).

In "Latinas: A Call to Action," Dr. Adela González gives another perspective on the obesity health crisis among Latinas/os. She recalls being moved by the sight of throngs of Latinos (half a million) participating in the immigrant rights marches. She also recalls, "In the midst of this social movement, during all the speeches and rhetoric, my thoughts focused on other issues we face in this country, particularly that of health. . . . I paid particular attention to the number of overweight and obese children barely keeping pace with the elderly as they struggled to move their oversized bodies. . . . Watching the adult marchers reminded me of a . . . health issue among the Latino population: high rates of diabetes, obesity, and hypertension compared to the rest of the population" (2006). Dr. González ends her column in *Latina Style* with the hope that the next demonstration she witnesses will involve Latinas marching to reduce obesity.

I agree that obesity among Latinas/os requires a march for consciousness raising. In my own case, I was totally oblivious to the consequences and extent of this issue or to the severity of my own problem until family members commented on my escalating weight and the deterioration in my health became evident in blood tests and wellness checkups. I realized I must take action in my personal life if I want to be a part of a movement that puts health on the national agenda. And I must do it now!

You see, the future is here already, and it is daunting. I stand on the scale stark naked and am shocked to see the number: 235! ¡Dios mío! My God! I am supersized: I inhabit two bodies, one body at 117 pounds, the other at 118. There are also so many alarming psychosocial repercussions to my ailment I can't list them all. The other day at the post office I accidentally caught sight of my reflection in the mirror. Alarmingly, I could not see myself, only an obese body staring back. I had to do a double take. Was this really me? I asked. The answer, yes, provoked a sick, uneasy feeling in the pit of my stomach. Now I understand the reluctance some obese people feel about being photographed and their anger at television news clips that offer random snapshots of obese body parts when national ailments are discussed.

While reading Jane Delgado's essay "The Body We Have . . . The Body We Want," I became aware of a bodily contradiction that is true not only for me, but for much of America. In the United States, we get a mixed message: "At the same time that we get the 'thin,' 'thin,' 'thin' message, we also get the message 'to eat, eat, eat,' and to do so quickly" (Delgado 2002, 293). Delgado also offers some valuable insight into the meanings and practices associated with eating specifically within the Latina/o context: "Eating is what we do to celebrate. It is what we do when we gather together to talk with our comadres. And it is one of the major activities that brings [sic] families together. We grow up thinking of eating as one of the most important activities we share with those we love. And it is not just the eating that is important to us but every part of the sitting down to a meal" (2002, 294). I am not suggesting that Latina/o culture is responsible for my plight, although these positive associations with food likely contributed.

As I struggle to gain control of my weight, I think often about the societal stereotypes of people who are overweight or obese:

Fat people are lazy.
Fat people don't have much pride in themselves.
Fat people just don't try to lose weight.
Fat people enjoy being out of control.
If people are fat, it's their own fault.
Fat people are stupid. They don't understand that they are at risk
    for serious diseases and even death.

Personal experience and a visit to my doctor helped me to put things in perspective. One day he said, "It's a lot easier to gain weight than it is to lose weight." His words resonated with me, though they did not touch on the direct cause of my ailment. I'd need to look into the medicine cabinet for that. You see, my dramatic weight gain came as a result of a medication that I took for another ailment. In his article "Weight Gain in a Pill," Michael Woods, citing Dr. Lawrence J. Cheskin, states that "both doctors and patients overlook the possibility that weight gain can originate in the medicine chest, as well as [in] fast food restaurants and couch potato lifestyles" (2004). When I was prescribed this medication, I had no idea that it has been described as the "worst offender" for weight gain and as a "weight-gain drug" for some susceptible individuals. Although the weight started to pile on shortly after I started taking it, I was focused on the value of the medication for my ailment. I suppose I believed that a modest weight gain was an acceptable price for the vast improvement in my condition. Yet my weight gain continued unabated and eventually skyrocketed: I gained a whopping ninety pounds! I realized I now had two major problems—

the one I originally took the medication for and the obesity problem that ensued from taking a "fat pharm" drug.

I tried to curb my weight gain with exercise, but I could not exercise enough to counteract the weight gain, nor could I satiate my hunger. I was ravenous, out of control; I had lost the balance in my life. I even suspected that my excessive hunger meant that I was developing diabetes. Alarmed, I stopped taking the medication with my doctor's permission. Doing so stopped the weight gain but did not lead to weight loss. Almost two years later, I still find it hard to curb my appetite or alter the binging behaviors I developed while on the medication. Stopping the medicine did not change the negative effects of obesity on my health, either. I still crave food twenty-four hours a day, and I find it very hard to stop eating unless I'm in a space where food is strictly prohibited. Although I eat often and often overeat, I'm rarely hungry. That's the paradox—people in my condition aren't hungry even though they eat all the time. They actually have to reexperience what it means to be hungry in order to lose weight.

Because of the challenges associated with my ailment, I decided to seek help from family members. I explained that I could not tackle my problem alone: I needed active intervention, and I needed it *now*. With the help of a supportive doctor and my husband, I entered into a comprehensive program at my local hospital for people who are obese and suffer from heart disease, high cholesterol, or blood sugar problems. I had a great deal of anxiety about the program and how it would affect my strong attachment to food. I could not deny that I saw food as company, celebration, and entertainment. And—is it possible?—I saw food (and overeating) as healing. Incredibly, my world was getting smaller and smaller as I got bigger and bigger.

The medical intervention at this program is comprehensive: I keep a food diary; see a food psychologist; attend lectures by dieticians and cardiologists, a diet class, and a diabetes class; and follow an exercise regime. Keeping the food diary has been a major challenge because "everything that is eaten must be written." For some time, I've had an aversion to writing down what I eat, even though I like to write letters and reports and to write on the computer. In my youth, I was even the unofficial letter writer and secretary for my mother, who felt uncomfortable with written communication.

In previous attempts to lose weight, I had attended Weight Watchers. One of the reasons I had such a hard time sticking to that program was the requirement that I keep a food record. Writing down the food I ate somehow made my private drama public and real. I was not prepared to see in black and white on the page the amount I'd consumed; it meant—no bones about it—that I had to face my obesity and actually do something about it. Before that, my only food register was my little dog, who continually made the journey from the couch to the kitchen with me in hopes that she, too, could delight in another helping of food.

I don't want to underestimate the challenges associated with my struggle for health and wellness. Regaining my health is one of the hardest things I have ever had to do; it's even harder than when I quit smoking. Much harder. There's strong social sanction against smoking, which gives support to people trying to quit, but there's little social sanction against eating too much. When you are trying to lose weight, you realize that food is everywhere, a part of everything. And most of the readily available foods are not compatible with weight reduction. Instead, they have high amounts of saturated, trans-fatty, hydrogenated, or partially hydrogenated fats.[6] In my program, I have learned to read food labels to determine the fat content of various foods and to steer clear of these harmful fats (for more on food labels, see Delgado 2002, 285–86). I have also said adios to conventional salad dressings, sweets, mayonnaise, and my favorite—tortilla chips and potato chips. I have learned to welcome wheat bread, wheat tortillas, barley, brown rice, polenta, low-fat cereal, fat-free cottage cheese, yogurt, rice cakes, steamed tacos, and even Boca burgers.

I now adapt my native Mexican foods to avoid the artery-clogging cheese, fat-fried tortillas, and esophagus-wounding chili. Don't get me wrong: Mexican food is not all alike. For instance, my mother never cooked with all that grease, and as for lard, forget it! That just wasn't for her or us. I developed unhealthy habits after leaving home. At home, we ate in moderation, ate by five o'clock, and sat down together to eat. The chili was sparse, always of the mild variety, and the precious pinto bean was a staple and the crown jewel of our family palate.

If there is a silver lining to my obesity experience, it is that I am now experimenting with different kinds of foods and using a variety of cooking resources. I've been recently introduced to online recipe books such as *Platillos Latinos ¡Sabrosos y saludables! Delicious Heart-Healthy Latino Recipes* published by the National Institutes of Health (1996). As I assume the challenge to experiment with cooking traditional Mexican and Latino dishes in healthy ways, I find that my Crock-Pot is my best friend. In it I make frijoles (pinto beans), frijoles negros (black beans), lentejas (lentils), garbanzos, and pollo con vegetales (chicken with veggies). ¡Qué viva el Crock-Pot! More than any other means of cooking, the Crock-Pot helps me to prepare foods with loads of fiber that curbs my hunger. It also allows me to cook in bulk. I find that I must have healthy food available so that when I arrive home tired and hungry, I don't reach for the wrong things. So I have hearty prepared foods as well as lots of fruits and vegetables and salad at hand. And the brown lunch bag that I carry in my backpack is my salvation. When I need a snack, I grab my self-styled trail mix, composed of a mixture of low-calorie cereals, or I have fruit and cottage cheese.

As far as the diet segment of my program is concerned, the most challenging aspects are controlling portions, achieving a balanced diet, and monitoring my carbohydrate intake. My dieticians encourage me to measure the amount of food I eat (even when it's brown rice, cereal, or beans) and to follow a mostly vegetarian, low-fat diet. In my efforts to improve my diet, the American Institute for Cancer Research's "The New American Plate" has proven to be an invaluable Web resource because it provides visuals that encourage people to "start reshaping their diet by looking at their plate" (n.d.). The portion-control section asks questions to guide food choices: Is the greater proportion of your meal plant based? Are your portion sizes appropriate to your activity level?[7]

The other important part of my program is exercise. The positive feelings I get from exercise help me regain perspective and realize the truth in Delgado's statement that in order to lose weight, you must "be patient" (2002, 299). My motto is "Muévete: move it and lose it." A cherished friend gave me a pedometer, and I am surprised at how many steps I take each day. This little device hidden under my T-shirt has actually encouraged me to challenge myself by walking around the block, taking the stairs, and even making an impromptu journey when I am tired. (My pedometer has counted more than eight thousand steps in one day!) I need to mention two other important components of my exercise routine. One is informal: I put on my favorite music (Latina/o and oldies) and dance for about twenty minutes. This has the effect of connecting me to my culture and creative passions while lowering my stress level and blood pressure. The other is formal: a monitored exercise program in which my exercise and blood sugar levels are carefully tracked. This indispensable aspect of my program has provided me with much-needed data. Not only does my blood pressure go down with exercise, but my sugar levels also drop significantly. This is a good thing for me: people with prediabetes "can prevent or delay the development of diabetes by making changes in their diet and increasing their level of physical activity." The American Diabetes Association Web site also suggests that "just 30 minutes a day of moderate physical activity, coupled with a 5–10% reduction in body weight" can produce a reduction in diabetes ("How to Prevent or Delay Diabetes" n.d.d.).

For me, fighting obesity is a daily, moment-by-moment struggle that requires a great deal of energy, planning, and commitment on my own part as well as support from everyone around me. I have very good days and very bad days. Some days it's too easy to say, "I'll do my weight thing later on," but then I suffer the consequences of my inaction. Fighting obesity is also a process: my medical team and I predict that it will take two years to take off the weight—there will be no quick fix. I am not following a fad diet; I am learning how to alter my lifestyle. At times, I feel very impatient and frustrated at my slow progress (even though I have already lost twelve pounds—Yippee! ¡Arriba! ¡Arriba!). When I told my husband and mother recently that I was sick of it all, my family members were very kind. One by one they called me and told me to keep on going, that I was doing the right thing and doing very well. My husband got into action and into the kitchen to help get me organized for the day. My precious little dog rubbed against me and provided warmth. She even perked up her cute little ears when my husband said the magic word: *walk*. As a result, we took an unplanned stroll and had fun enjoying the beauty of nature and spicy conversation.

Another part of my process is a struggle for personal identity, to heal the profound disconnect between my personhood (who I am, how I see myself) and my actual (obese) body. Contrary to the notion of "my body, myself" popularized in mainstream feminist literature, my internal camera actually photographs my body as different from what others see. My body on the outside is often foreign; I do not feel like it belongs to me (or the image I claim that is stored in my memory). After doing the research for this essay, I have come to understand that this alienated body is a time bomb waiting to explode, that it is part of a Latina/o emergency and a Western/U.S. mega-epidemic. (Some say that obesity is a sign of a culture of consumption gone awry and of the First World's excess coming home to roost. This interpretation deeply troubles me, though, because the ones bearing the brunt of this epidemic are working-class Latinas.)

And yet I see that my body—this obese body—is more than illness and mega-epidemics and side effects; it is more than the ominous statistics and trend that I sometimes feel I am. This body is in dynamic transition, and it is starting to work with me instead of against me. And, lest I forget, this body also allows me to breathe, feel, love, work, teach, play, and experience the world and my place in it. Finally, this (obese) body is engaged in a struggle against obesity. This body does not want to be super skinny, adopt the "Twiggy look," or go the route of fashion models with anorexia and bulimia. What it desires is a healthy weight.

I have learned that, unlike other wars, fighting obesity is a battle *for* life.

I do not want to lose this battle, as many other precious friends and family members have. I realize that in many ways I am privileged: I have health insurance, a college education, and a wonderful, state-of-the-art health program at my disposal, along with a highly motivated interdisciplinary staff. I am also fortunate to have a supportive family, enough self-esteem, and a nonjudgmental environment to assist me in meeting the challenges posed by my weight. Finally, I have an active memory of a nonobese body. My goal is to let that vivid body, which lies buried in this obese body, see the light of day and materialize in the flesh. I want to reconcile myself with this memory. When I'm exercising along with other overweight (Latina) women, I feel the contours of this body—every step I take is a step in its design. When I dine with other obese people, every healthy meal we eat together is a step toward its reconstitution. When I commune with other people who are endeavoring to make positive lifestyle changes, I feel like I'm part of a movement that is remaking America itself, proving the pundits wrong, and challenging debilitating stereotypes that prevent others from seeing who we really are and how hard we're struggling for health and wellness. Most important, I am honoring the legacy of my mother, she who gave birth to me, raised me, clothed me, fed me, taught me, and continues to love me like no one else does. I simply cannot let her down. You see, she is the light of my life.

6

A Language for Healing

Finding Sacred Meaning in
Transcending Chronic Lupus

Concha Delgado Gaitan

Inward Mobility

We are healed
by a common language.
It's the belief in wholeness
a library of lessons
and the web of hands
that discipline our hearts
when fear shadows faith.
It's the flowering bond
in a universe of thoughts—
a peace that transcends
words
time
tears
like a cocoon unwrapping.
With mentors we join hands
listening to the poetry we make
the music we share
the laughter we hear
rekindling
the flickering candle

lighting the path
within.
Re-creating.

—*Concha Delgado Gaitan*

Standing at the stove, flipping her perfectly round flour tortillas on the black cast-iron griddle, my mother would say, "No hay mal por cual bien no venga" (There is nothing bad from which something good doesn't come). This statement impressed me deeply as a child, and whenever life has become overwhelming, I have always sought reassurance in Mom's belief that every black cloud has a silver lining.

I remember my mother's words regularly now that I am disabled with a debilitating illness, systemic lupus erythematosus (SLE). Lupus is an autoimmune disorder in which the immune system attacks the connective tissues surrounding different organs. It manifests differently in everyone, and flare-ups vary in frequency and intensity. Common symptoms include inflammation in tissues surrounding certain organs, severe fatigue, and pain in joints or a burning sensation in muscles. Weakness, especially in major muscles throughout the body, characterizes the illness. Women are more likely than men to develop lupus, and women of color are more likely to do so than are white women (Hugher 2000, 5).

For me, the onset manifested as severe joint and muscle pain, with distressing fatigue, respiratory impairment, and urological complications. It quickly spiraled my life out of control, leaving me dependent first on a cane, then on forearm crutches, and eventually on a power wheelchair. I reacted instinctively, seeking to fix my body, my work, and my relationships with the same commanding authority I always believed I had over my life. But with the onset of the illness, my body developed a mind of its own, disconnected from my will. Or so it seemed. My work, play, and daily activities became restricted, and I was stripped of my identity as a strong and self-reliant professional woman. Particularly problematic for me was the fact that my sense of self was intimately linked to working hard—something I gradually became unable to keep up.

Many of the messages I wrestled with when I became ill had their origins in my early life. Not long after my diagnosis, I hit bottom while reading dismal statistics and reports on what seemed a hopeless prognosis. Some sources indicated that only 4 percent of people with SLE healed. Most people who survived the major crisis would always have to deal with some symptoms (Dibner 1994, 7). Everywhere I looked, the word *disabled* marked my identity and my future. It defined how I felt and how I looked, but not how I thought. Confronting this bleak word enabled me to alter my focus. I realized I needed to reinterpret my condition in a way that did not pronounce me as a broken person. I clung to my faith practices in search of hope, joy, and new possibilities for healing. Instead of pursuing solutions to fix my body, I began a quest to find sacred meaning in my daily life. Through a supportive community, spiritual practices, and recreation, I learned to express gratitude, to trust the Spirit, and to forgive. This became my language of healing.

Thinking differently about my body, my work, and my relationships became possible within a supportive community. A heated pool, spiritual fellowships, inspiring Web sites, and loving family and friends formed a collective that cushioned my pain day in and day out. This community of loved ones supported the healing not only of my body but also of my life. I learned to trust abilities beyond my physical strength.

My healing journey has led me to question and embrace old and new faith traditions and to touch my inner peace. As I stretched my physical, emotional, and spiritual muscles, commitment to self-care became the core of my life. Before this point, attention to my general health had always come last on my priorities list, masked by chronic overwork.

As a child, I had learned new languages and cultures while keeping my own family's culture close to my heart. Speaking the same language, Spanish, and sharing cultural rituals formed strong family bonds, but it would take a crisis for me to understand the depth of those ties. Through crisis, we have an opportunity to discover our true power, to believe in something deeper than ourselves. Respect, faith, social justice, and hard work shape the language of my Mexican cultural tradition and my family life. These bricks and mortar built my foundation.

My daily journal provided continuity in what became a fragmented life. When I fell ill, I kept a written record of my feelings, observations, and changing identity as a woman, a professional, and both an able and a disabled person. I turned to my inner dialogue, tapping my inner spirit to advocate for myself when the medical system failed me, to change my work when it was time to grow, and to remember that *able* and *disabled* are cultural labels not to be confused with the person to whom they are attached.

A New Season

One early September fall breezes blew in a new school year as predictably as the leaves changed color. But this autumn I found myself in a different classroom. On sabbatical from the university for the fall quarter, I reveled in the easy pace of my days. One quiet Monday morning I was home alone, working at my computer, when suddenly I felt faint. I managed to call 9-1-1. A short ride later I was in the emergency room. I had become accustomed to periodic trips to the emergency room, but this visit would not be typical.

> From the gurney in the emergency room, I had one view: the dull blue curtain that closed around my cubicle, separating me from the neighboring bed. I could hear a soft woman's voice over the loudspeakers, paging doctors. Standing next to me, the nurse's hands moved quickly, stretching out my arm to inject a needle on the backside of my hand in order to insert the IV drip hanging on a pole next to me. The cold, sticky, round patches plastered on my chest were familiar: an electrocardiogram (EKG) was in progress. "Your heart looks fine," came the nurse's voice, which by now sounded as faint as my breath.
>
> "Your family doctor called and told us that you have a history of lupus," came a strong male doctor's voice.
>
> "Yes," I gasped.
>
> "Has this happened before?"
>
> "Yes," again I gasped.
>
> "Hang in there. We'll figure out where the problem is," the doctor said. "I suspect you might be having a lupus relapse."
>
> I closed my eyes, fantasizing that any minute the emergency-room doctor would come in and tell me about a new pill to eliminate all of my body's ailments. Little did I know that this hospital stay would turn into the longest I had ever had. I clung to a memory of being hospitalized as a child, when innocent prayer and my mother's words, "No hay mal por cual bien no venga," had erased my fear.

Surrounding our family's one-room house—literally a bathroom and a single large room that we divided up with curtains to separate the kitchen and bedroom—was a small yard where my sisters and I played. Calla lilies, geraniums, and short, thick, white daisy bushes encircled a patch of neatly mowed green lawn in front of the house. I was too young to remember what kind of spider bit me on that warm afternoon. For sure, it must have been one mean spider. My screams summoned my sisters, who were playing hide-and-seek with me. Mom ran out of the house to my aid. My foot instantly swelled up and turned bright red. Mom called our neighbor to take us to the hospital. I was scared, even though the doctor was very nice as he popped the large, pus-filled blister. I landed in the hospital until the infection broke. Mom gave me a small medallion of the Virgin Mary, saying it would protect me in the hospital. Clutching the medallion in my hand, I prayed the Our Father, which I knew from reciting the rosary. Then I fell asleep. After that episode, whenever I hurt myself or someone hurt my feelings, I prayed, confident that the words alone would lift the shroud of fear. Whatever ailed me God would rectify.

Prayers also kept me company in my preadolescent years when I was diagnosed with rheumatic fever. Children's Hospital was the largest building I had seen since we emigrated from Mexico. I spent years in and out of this towering white, sterile art deco building in Los Angeles. The most difficult part of being ill was the shame I felt—that there was something intrinsically wrong with me: Was I bad? Would my parents get mad at me for being ill? Would I lose my friends because I was sick? I felt miserable. I had failed at staying well. I lay in bed present in body, but absent in spirit, with no way of knowing where I would look for that spirit. My only resort was the litany of prayers I had memorized in church and at home.

Evenings at home brought a dreaded family ritual in our household: praying the rosary. Yet the silver lining of that black cloud was that it was the genesis of my meditation practices. I recall an intimidating male voice on a Spanish radio station who bellowed out Hail Marys and Our Fathers. For my parents, work alone could not have overcome the myriad of financial and social obstacles that poor immigrants face. Their prayers, I thought, created miracles. When our family's troubles seemed daunting, I saw Mom kneel to pray as if every problem had a solution. And sometimes that almost seemed true. The faith I learned in my early years kept me steady even when I consciously ignored it. And in my adult years, I frequently returned to this internal reservoir of faith.

> In the emergency room, my body was enveloped in what felt like a third-degree burn from shoulders to toes. My chest muscles struggled to pump enough oxygen. By now, I had abandoned my initial embarrassment that I was taking up hospital space for a silly fainting spell. I could barely muster enough breath for a whisper, and I knew that I had better use it to pray. Breathless, weak, and overwhelmed with pain, I stared at the dingy, pale blue curtain that surrounded me as I negotiated with God. I pleaded, "You've got to see me through this. Get me well. I've trusted you. I don't know what's going on or why this is happening, but if you get me through it, I'm yours. I promise to trust you, to live my life through you. You'll hear from me, not only in hard times, but every single day. I will accept your guidance day in and day out. I don't know what more to do." I surrendered.

I was a star student before we immigrated legally to Los Angeles from Chihuahua. Yet here, in my American school, despite my daily improving ability to read English, Mrs. Brown, my teacher, daily threatened to keep me in during recess until I learned to read English to her satisfaction, leaving me perpetually fearful and anxious. I missed my days in Mexico, where the language and books were familiar and where my friends understood me.

I hated school when I first arrived; my teacher's insensitivity was almost unbearable. On my first day, she immediately handed me a book and expected me to read the first page. I heard my voice, heavy with a Spanish accent, trying to sound out phonetically words I could not understand: "Di bois guent too deir jawus" (The boys went to their house), I stumbled painfully, trying to read aloud all the way to the end of the page.

Months passed, and my English conversations with classmates improved. I could say, "I like playing with my sisters" and "I like to eat in the cafeteria." But my teacher was still unimpressed by my progress in English. I was humiliated. I felt very alone.

School traumatized me. Most of the time I felt nervous just walking onto the grounds. This feeling worsened in the classroom. I wanted so much to show Mrs. Brown that I was trying the best I could. As she walked toward me, salt-and-pepper hair pulled tight in an intimidating bun, I fixed my eyes on hers. Her dull eyes showed no compassion. I felt like a captive, scared that my parents would find out I was not a good student.

One day the teacher instructed the class to fill in the answers to some questions in the reading workbook. I stared at the words on the page, but they meant nothing to me. Walking up to the teacher's desk, I told her that I didn't understand the questions. She looked at me and responded, "I've already explained it."

Embarrassed, I returned to my desk and looked around the room as if I expected to find the answers written on my classmates' foreheads. Instead, I saw a sea of blond heads tipped forward, reading their books. I was lost for answers, and my frustration got the better of me. I glanced across the row of single desks to my neighbor's paper, which was clearly exposed. But before I could copy anything, I felt the teacher's presence. She stood by my desk. "Let me have your paper," she demanded. I handed it to her. My eyes warmed with tears as I watched her tear up a sheet of paper that had nothing more than my name in the top right-hand corner. There it was. I had just learned what "Do your own work" meant. "You must work independently; it will not benefit you to get help from others" was the message—a message I carried with me into my illness. But that afternoon I felt my child's spirit fleeing the classroom, hiding in shame, leaving my empty body sitting alone at the rigid desk. Mrs. Brown never knew that years later, when I became a teacher, I would think about her and try to do everything the opposite of the way she had done it. The most important thing she taught me was what *not* to do. The loneliness and shame I felt for not knowing the answers left me devastated.

Fearing that I would be forever stuck in these feelings, I determined that I would not let Mrs. Brown get the better of me. I thought to myself, "I know how to read. I'll show you, lady." At that moment, I promised myself that I would successfully master this unfriendly place called school. I eventually did.

> In the hospital physical rehabilitation unit, sleep didn't turn on when the lights were turned off. How could I stop worrying about what would happen to me tomorrow? How long would I have to take chemo and steroids this time? My doctor explained that steroids reduced inflammation in the tissues, and when the inflammation did not abate rapidly enough, chemotherapy had to be administered to shut down the entire immune system in order, we hoped, to allow the system to heal itself. The dangerous part of this treatment was that the chemotherapy also diminished the system's response mechanism. In other words, it made my immune system even more vulnerable to infections and viruses. I wondered, When can I return to work? Supplications to God came from a place much more hopeful than my body's weakened vocal cords. Muscle weakness being a symptom of the syndrome that ravaged my body, I barely had enough strength to clutch my forearm crutches. I didn't know where my faith would come from. But a younger Concha knew. The chubby, eight-year-old, brown girl with austere eyes and short, wavy black hair was determined to get through these tough times. That little girl would help me find the faith I now needed.

After the initial diagnosis, visits to medical specialists became almost daily rituals for me. My rheumatologist and neurologist questioned me about how I managed in my daily life at home and at work. (Rheumatologists and neurologists play significant roles in many SLE cases.) That both specialists were women helped me to trust their understanding not only of my critical medical care, but also of my personal well-being. Every question reminded me of how disabled I felt and looked, relying on two Canadian crutches. And with every doctor's visit, my answers to those questions showed me how my life was becoming incrementally more restricted.

"Are you working? How much?"

"Are you driving your car? How far?"

"Do you do housework? What kind? Can you push a vacuum cleaner? How long?"

"What kind of help do you have at home?"

"Do you have a support system?"

Dr. Barrett wanted to know precisely what I meant when I spoke of "pain." In a flash, I was eight years old again, wearing uncomfortable, oversize, black-and-white oxfords that blistered my ankles, staring into the teacher's disapproving face. I tried to explain to her in a foreign language that I didn't know the word for the picture in the book. Many years later I ached for words to fill in the blanks of the doctor's quiz: a new language I resented having to learn, that of disabilities. I felt even more exhausted when I left Dr. Barrett's office. It was too much work to label the physical characteristics of pain. I searched for descriptors to capture the essence of the sensations that engulfed me: *PAIN! Burning. Stinging. Throbbing. Pinching. Aching. Stabbing. Shooting. Tremor. Pang. Spasm. Intense. Heavy. Tender. Thick. Severe. Unbearable.* Like HOT salsa running through my veins. *BURNING*— yes, that's it! But it's not that simple. "What degree? How much?" the doctor wanted to know. But it's impossible to quantify pain! I wondered, Is it pain if my arm feels thick but doesn't move or burn? I'm confused. I don't know what I think anymore! I can't feel my hips! They don't move when I walk. Why don't my legs bend? Is it pain if you don't feel a limb and can't use it?

How could I know if what I felt was not a first- or second-degree, but a third-degree burning pain? That was Dr. Barrett's question. A memory of a ten-year-old Concha flashed before me. It was a Saturday afternoon, and I was responsible for cooking the rice for the family's lunch. When the rice was boiling, I lifted the lid, and a burst of steam burned my thumb raw till the skin fell off. The doctors who bandaged it at the emergency hospital said I had a third-degree burn. And now with a body in perpetual pain, I found ways to simplify my routines at home. One night I was trying to bake red snapper in the oven, and as I reached in for the Pyrex dish, I felt a hot spot near my wrist. The sizzle I heard was not the snapper. It was my skin. The burn had created a hole about a quarter inch across and deep enough to show white tissue. I put ice, Polysporin ointment, and a bandage on it. A week later, I found myself in the emergency room with a respiratory complication. The attending doctor asked why I had a bandage on my wrist. I showed him the burn, and he asked me, "Does it hurt?"

"Not any more than the rest of my body."

"I'm concerned that it still looks raw."

"It's been that way for a while."

"That's a third-degree burn you've got there. It must hurt."

"Not any more than the rest of my body," I reiterated.

Without question, the pain in my body sometimes frightened me. But as severe as the pain was, I would soon deal with months of memory loss, which intensified my feelings of disability and shook my confidence and belief that I had anything left to offer the world. Losing track of time, destinations, concepts, and people's names made keeping a daily journal imperative. The memory loss was not in my imagination; my journal entries confirmed my suspicions that lapses were occurring, that pieces of time were vanishing from my life. My doctor helped me to understand that various types of memory loss were common in SLE and other immune system–related illnesses. She explained that the nervous system may not be as involved in SLE as in multiple sclerosis, but the severe pain and systemic fatigue may cause impairment in the patient's normal memory functioning. In my case, this impairment sneaked up on me insidiously. We all have selective memory at times, but forgetting chunks of one's life produces devastating confusion and fear. Facts, names, dates, ideas, and concepts leaked out of my memory bank until I felt blank. Teaching and research seemed overwhelming tasks. Thinking about what I had to do to conduct my community research projects, not to mention what I was supposed to write in the articles I was preparing for publication, became one strange odyssey. My connection with my childhood, family, and past experience was equally foreign. My relationship with much of my world was unraveling.

To help me deal with my growing fear and the fragmented parts of my life, I leaned on Luis. A wise Peruvian minister and psychologist, Luis has been my spiritual mentor for almost twenty years. He has taught me to live every day spiritually and joyfully, even through the worst adversity. Remaining peaceful through good and tough times is the foundation of the spiritual readings in which I immersed myself. One of those very influential readings was *A Course in Miracles* (1975). Advocating for myself was a new dimension in learning the language of healing. Luis's healing language and spiritual teachings called for three major practices: (1) observe, don't judge yourself or others; (2) know that you're not alone; and (3) always ask the Spirit for direction because it is our source and inner wisdom. I continued to care for my body in every way that complementary and allopathic medicine offered. Allopathic medicine—using remedies that produce effects different from those of the disease being treated—worked faster than complementary medicine. However, the limitations of drugs were clear: they did not heal. They masked the symptoms. In contrast, complementary medicine worked more on the premise that the body could heal itself with herbs and other such treatments, although it required a longer time to see results. The language of hope had now taught me that I had the choice to see any conflict from a place of oneness.

> Only a few days remained in the three-week-long hospital stay that evolved from the emergency room trip that had ruined my peaceful sabbatical. In preparation for discharge, physical and occupational therapists took turns teaching my body to sit up in a wheelchair and to do things I once took for granted. Julie, the occupational therapist, had her hands full helping me to strengthen my fingers and hands so that I could hold a fork and a pen, as I fantasized about being able to use my laptop again. For a moment, I felt desperately homesick and excited all at once. I missed relaxing on my own deck, gazing out at the bay. With a sudden realization of how much strength I had regained since entering the hospital, I smiled. I dreamed of being able to get out of my wheelchair—to make a cup of coffee in my own kitchen.

After my extended hospital stay, I returned home—not only to my comfortable house, but also to a place within me that I confidently called home. No, the road back to physical health was not bliss. My recovery was paved with both physical challenges and emotional losses that pushed me to embrace the dark just as tightly as I clung to the light. Yet I remained open to experiencing all that I am, pain and peace, thanks to Luis's constant spiritual mentoring. My situation no longer felt as if it were a problem, deficiency, or disability. Rather, I began thinking of my body as a reminder to choose a perception of wholeness and align with that inner power that houses wisdom, hope, and harmony—the language of healing that transcends my pain and transforms my life, keeping me focused on my inner strength in spite of my body's weakness.

Not long after I left the hospital, my rheumatologist closed her practice, sending me abruptly out into the cold in search of a new specialist. My experience through the ins and outs of traditional and alternative medicine led me to fantasize about having the services of a "health manager," someone who could assist me in deciding what type of healer or medical care would benefit me most at any given time. What I felt I needed then was a rigorous regimen of physical therapy and natural supplements. I did not reject Western traditions, but rather sought to use them along with holistic methods in order to speed up my healing. Maybe that wise health manager was within me, waiting for me to listen for the next step. But before I resumed my internal and external quest, I needed lots and lots of rest.

I spent more than half a year in a humiliating, frustrating, and physically strenuous search before I found a knowledgeable and caring professional willing to work with me. Dr. Berry, a cutting-edge nonsurgical orthopedist, has expertise in physical medicine, rehabilitation, and immunology, all focused on helping the body to heal itself. Her theory of healing is that the immune system can be supported in rebuilding itself through natural and holistic therapies. After completing countless tests, she comprehensively analyzed my case, concluding that she could help me. "But," she said, "you'll have to give me lots of time. After all, your problem has had years to get the way it is. It won't improve overnight."

She prescribed a daily, rigorous physical therapy routine at home for muscle strengthening and special physical therapy for the soft tissues twice a week at her office. The grueling, rolling motion of the therapy on my back was tantamount to torture. Frequent shots in the lower back, hips, and chest were uncomfortable, but they did ease my pain and improve my mobility. In addition, Dr. Berry prescribed a nutritional program that included potent supplements and herbal regimens. Between breakfast and bedtime, I took so many supplements that I dedicated one whole cabinet to them.

Along with Dr. Berry's therapies, I followed an intense Chinese medicine program of acupuncture, daily tai chi, and boiled herbs. And, of course, lots of rest. Herbs are considered food supplements in Chinese medicine. The tradition has a good attitude about food: that foods are healing if we eat what our bodies want. If I listened carefully, my body would tell me what to eat. If my body couldn't dictate what it wanted, I had a list of foods from my Chinese doctor. I could choose from stimulating, neutral, and calming foods, depending on how my body felt and what it craved. Warm summer days made my body crave cool, crisp carrots and ginger on a bed of lettuce. On the other extreme, when light fog and rain combined to chill my joints, I found myself in front of the stove, stirring up a pot of hearty vegetable soup with diced jalapeños.

This opportunity to practice the language of healing meant that my emotional work was cut out for me. When I returned home from the extended hospital stay, I had some difficult decisions to make. One was whether I would continue in my position as a professor at the University of California, Davis. The university's refusal to renegotiate my job description to allow me to work from home some days forced me to resign: there was no way I could commute to work daily in my current health situation. I let go, trusting that somehow I would be taken care of, regardless of what my next job would be or when I would be strong enough to work again.

Faith led the way. Letting go of feeling like a victim, I began healing this change of course in my career.

My mother used to say, "Cuando Dios cierra una puerta, abre otras" (When God closes one door, he opens others). Now I was in a position to strengthen my body and recommit to a new career, with my health as a top priority.

Although most of the time I had difficulty sitting up for long periods, a new career unfolded and a new season began for me with each strong step I took. From my newly organized home office, I found ways to hold a laptop computer and discovered new ways of writing—and a new industry. I learned new software such as Java and Unix, which years earlier I would have guessed were either gourmet coffees or endangered species. On the more creative end, I turned a new page into the world of writing classes, of writing coaches and video documentary workshops—of nonfiction writers' weeks, book agents, and book doctors. Imagine my surprise to learn that even books have doctors.

This new business of independent writing also meant a renewed commitment to forging a personal literacy that could read my body's rhythm and shape a career to match it. My health and my recent marriage to my loving husband, Dudley, were top priorities in this project. To my great surprise in 2000, the Council on Anthropology and Education of the American Anthropological Association honored me with the George and Louise Spindler Award. On my engraved plaque is written, "In recognition of your distinguished and inspirational lifetime contributions to Anthropology and Education." It was an unexpected, wonderful accolade for doing work with families and communities, which I love. Fundamentally, I like the person I have discovered while learning the language of healing—which is the best medicine not only for rebuilding my immune system, but also for sustaining a healthy marriage.

An important lesson I learned was that the body doesn't have a mind of its own, even though it might appear to. The primary source of my health is my inner power. I have come to learn that illness is a synchronicity of many parts of one's life. My life choices were couched in the contradictions of this historical time for women and minorities, when obligations and opportunities converged, leading to increased demands and making it impossible to maintain a balance between work and family. But recovering my health demanded that I take healing steps back to my childhood to retrieve the familial and cultural strengths of faith, which I needed to empower myself. I looked inward to craft a healing language founded on faith, gratitude, forgiveness, love, and harmony. Thereby, I came to believe that in the illness lies its own cure. In my case, getting healthy is my life's work, not only because of the chronic nature of my condition, but also because being healthy means discovering a day-to-day capacity to manage my vulnerabilities. Health is not an end, but a process. It is not a question of merely fixing my body, but of tuning my whole life through spirituality, community, and play. It's not even about relying on external remedies or even expecting my body to conform to my demands. It's about living life from that peaceful place in me that most contributes to keeping me strong. I'm particularly careful not to overwork. The language of healing requires that I learn good health habits and unlearn unhealthy ones. More and more I appreciate what I have always had, but at times forgotten—me.

With hindsight, I see that healing is a path of continuous opportunities to shift my perspective from separation to oneness. As my lupus health crisis unfolded, it became my teacher. Moreover, I became an advocate for the power of possibilities. My healing process has led me to embrace both the future and the past in the present.

Living with a chronic illness, I have learned that we need to speak about illness, about the potential for healing, and about building supportive communities around us to transform our lives. By giving voice, we move from a victim perspective to one of empowerment, gaining access to choices and possibilities for healing. When we can make decisions about our bodies and our lives, we are empowered. In putting a frame around this picture in my life, I seek to share with others how it is possible to use a crisis to liberate ourselves despite how our bodies look and feel. Healing essentially occurs as we are able to talk about it—and ultimately to connect with the healer within us and with those around us who support our healing process.

If my story resonates with you, perhaps I have successfully made my point. We all speak many languages, making every life a rich story. It's through language that we connect and share a common spirit. The challenge is to quiet down, look inward, and connect with our own inner healer, who knows best how to heal us. That's the lesson I have learned from this health crisis.

7

Debe ser la reuma /
It Must Be Rheumatism

Enriqueta Valdez-Curiel

"Debe ser la reuma," says my mother each time she has pain in her joints, "It must also be the years. At my age, it would be strange to have something that doesn't hurt. Ay, tu madre ya no sirve para nada, soy pura queja y queja" (Oh, your mother isn't good for anything anymore; I'm just complaint after complaint).

At sixty-five years old, my mom has suffered from osteoarthritis (which she calls *reuma*) for more than thirty years, but this is not the only ailment that has haunted her. She suffers from high blood pressure, high cholesterol levels, gastroesophageal reflux, recurrent depressive episodes, and too much pain of the kind that most doctors are not able to understand—the kind of pain that hurts your body and poisons your soul; the kind that takes away your sleep and tranquility; the kind that makes you feel like a rabid dog. Yes, that kind of pain cannot be eased with pills, and only time can cure it. She suffers from the pain of a soul outraged and trampled by the man she loved the most, my father.

Osteoarthritis is the most common form of arthritis. A chronic condition, it is characterized by the breakdown of cartilage in one or more joints. As a result, the bones rub against each other, causing stiffness, pain, and loss of movement in the affected joint. Osteoarthritis, also known as degenerative arthritis, affects the shape and makeup of the joint, causing bony spurs called osteophytes; unfortunately, it also affects the person's mental well-being because it can have profound social consequences in daily life. Based on U.S.

epidemiologic studies, the distribution of osteoarthritis in men and women is similar (Lawrence et al. 1998); however, the incidence of symptomatic hand, hip, and knee osteoarthritis increases with age, and women have higher rates than men, especially after age fifty (Dequeker and Dieppe 1998).

Osteoarthritis pain causes the person to cut back on social activities and activities of daily living, often leading to depression and isolation, further undermining the person's overall health and lifestyle (Bookwala, Harralson, and Parmelle 2003). In my mother's case, this dynamic played out in full force, exacerbated by my father's persistent misogyny and verbal abuse, which plunged her into severe and recurrent depression. In the patriarchy of traditional Mexicano culture, our family is hardly unique in suffering the consequences of domestic violence.[1] From my father's macho, Mexican male perspective, Mom was a mujer quejumbrosa, a whining, useless woman who did nothing but cost her husband money because she had to be taken to doctors and bought medicines—even though he never once did either, instead perpetually belittling her and her severe pain.[2]

> Rayando el sol, me despedí,
> bajo la brisa, ahí me acorde de ti,
> llegando al puente, del puente me devolví
> bañado en lagrimas, las que derramé por ti.[3]

These lyrics from an old Mexican song for years brought tears to my ojos de niña, my child's eyes, crying over my mother's absence. Year after year, as long as I can remember, my parents would one day wake me up at four in the morning, saying, "It is time. Wake up, m'ija, we have to go now." It was time to leave the family home, our home, and for us children to go to live with my father's family while my parents left our little town in Mexico to work in California. My heart, or the place in the chest where feelings are kept, would shrink, crumple up, and look for a place to hide in order to feel less pain. Some weeks ago, when planning a trip with my mother and discussing the best time to leave, I realized that the repressed memories of my sad childhood dawns made me detest leaving before dawn. Both my mother and I started crying over a past we could not change.

My mother was twenty-eight years old and I was four when we started our farewell vía crucis and our journeys between Jalisco and California. My father, after crossing the northern border many times with the Bracero Program, had been required by his boss to remain permanently in California, which gave him the opportunity to apply for U.S. residency for his whole family.

The United States represented for my mother an end to the poverty and misery in which my father had kept her. Now she could work and would never again lose a child because of poverty. During her seven years of marriage, she had had six pregnancies, but only two surviving children. Either her pregnancies had ended in miscarriages, or the children had died in infancy because of malnutrition, emotional violence, and the poor or nonexistent medical attention my mother and her children received because she was economically dependent on my father, who did not provide for his family. During that time, my father was already working in California under the Bracero Program, but he was spending most of his money on alcohol and mistresses, not sending it to us.

My brother, my mother, and I became the Mexican extension of a legal migrant to California. During the summer of 1967, the whole family set off for California. My brother stayed there for only two months, during his summer vacation, then went back to Mexico to continue his education. I started elementary school in Mexico some months later, when my parents lost their jobs in the fields due to the rains and returned to Mexico for the winter and part of the spring. My starting elementary school also began the cycle of mother-child separations that would submerge my mother into deep depression. When March arrived, my parents returned to California, and I remained in Mexico with my brother and paternal grandparents. I would have much preferred to go with my mom to the States, but there was no one to take care of me in El Norte while they were working; moreover, they rejected the idea of sending me and my brother to school in California, fearing that Mexicanos who attended gringo schools became hippies, drug addicts, and liberals. "Esos no muestran respeto por sus padres" (They show no respect for their parents), my father would say. "Acá la raza hace lo que le da la gana" (Kids do whatever they want there). Consequently, my mother and I suffered from repeated separations.

My mother started working in the strawberry fields in Salinas Valley, but, she told me, "my back did not allow me to do that job, m'ija. When I did that job, I felt like my waist was going to break. I actually finished my working days on my knees. That is hard work that I was not good enough for, and you know I am not lazy; in short, that is the only work I could not do because I have done all kinds of jobs." She also worked at weeding (in el desaije), but mostly she worked on the lettuce cuadrillas (harvesting teams), cutting lettuces. She did this work for more than fifteen years.

My brother and I used to visit our parents in the summer, remaining with them for two months. During this time, I viewed my mother's routine as normal and had no awareness of her great effort and sacrifice. She got up at four in the morning to make flour tortillas and to cook her and my father's lunch. She also left lunches for me and my brother. Sometimes she also had to cook for an uncle or my father's nephews, who used to stay with my parents for long periods. My mother did all this quietly, to avoid waking up her children and to allow her husband one more hour of sleep. My father never helped with or valued my mother's domestic chores, seeing them as every woman's obligation. Even though my mother worked more hours in the field or packing sheds than he did, and despite how tired she was, she always came home to cook our dinner and take off my father's work boots. By this point, she was already suffering intense waist, shoulder, and hand pain from arthritis. The physical labor and movements required to cut lettuces, working against the clock in damp fields, had caused severe deterioration in her joints. Cutting lettuce requires bending over, grabbing a head of lettuce with one hand, quickly and forcefully twisting the arm that holds the knife, and cutting the lettuce stalk. Injury to and overuse of joints are significant risk factors for arthritis, but my mother's life gave her few other options.

During this time, my mother never received any medical care because my father would always tell her that what she had was pura pinche güevonada (complete fucking stupidity). "¿Haber, por qué a mí no me duele nada?" he used to ask (Look, why don't I hurt at all?). Moreover, he was extremely jealous. He used to threaten that my mother could see the doctor only if he took her, but he never wanted to take time off from work to escort her. What a doctor could have offered her—for the arthritis, at least—would have been pain relievers such as anti-inflammatories and steroid injections to manage her physical pain. Although no treatment can cure osteoarthritis, early treatment can help reduce long-term damage to joints and bones.[4] Thus, year after year my mother eased her intense pain with Mamisan (an ointment veterinarians prescribe for inflammation in horses) and a concentrate of marijuana with alcohol. My brother and I sent or brought the Mamisan from Mexico for my mother, and she would get the marijuana from her partners on the lettuce cuadrillas, who used to smoke it to help them withstand the physical demands of their work.

My mother's physical pain was aggravated by the pain of not having her children with her and of our impending separation. She would cry at work and during her lunch hour from both types of pain: Would my grandparents and my father's other relatives treat us well? My father's parents did not like my mother, but they did like the money that she would send regularly and punctually every week for our maintenance. So fortunately my grandparents never mistreated us, and, in her own way, my grandma really tried, with affection, to substitute for my mother. But to me she represented my father, whom I already hated for his mistreatment of my mother.

My mother had to hide her tears from my father; she could not even look sad in front of him. When my mother could no longer repress her sadness and started crying during dinnertime, my father's words were: "Haz de andar de puta, hija de la chingada" (You must be whoring, you bitch), his universal explanation for any woman's sadness. "¿Ante esto crees que iba a llorar, hija?" my mother tells me now, "No, yo me aguantaba todo lo que podía y por eso llegué hasta la depresión. Además, cómo no deprimirse con un hombre como tu padre." (Facing that, do you think I would cry, Daughter? No, I tried as much as I could not to cry. That is why I became depressed. Plus, how could one not become depressed with a man like your father?)

My parents' routine in California was to work six days a week and on Sundays go to the laundry and grocery, then have lunch in a restaurant. The Sunday lunch was the only expense my father paid for. All other expenses of maintaining the household and us children my mother paid. My father ostensibly was saving his money to buy real estate in Mexico, but in reality he spent most of it on drinking and women. On Sunday afternoons, he would go visit his brother, then return home to sit on his sofa, drinking beer and watching television. Meanwhile, my mother ironed, cleaned the house, and wrote me sad and loving letters, always with a money order attached.

When they were in Mexico, my father would take my mother out only on Sunday and then only to the 6:00 A.M. mass to fulfill their obligation with God. My brother and I believed he took her to that service either to avoid being seen with her—which would have curtailed his love life—or to prevent other men from seeing her. She was a very beautiful woman, and my father was always jealous and afraid of losing her. My mother's version of these events, though, is that he was ashamed of her and did not want his mistresses to see him with her.

In Mexico, my father would prohibit my mother from leaving the house, even for a short shopping trip to buy some tomatoes at the corner store. As his infidelities became more and more evident, he increasingly threatened and intimidated my mother to prevent her from leaving him.[5] By that time, he was the only one among his brothers who was still living with his wife, a fact of which he was proud. He refused to become another "family statistic," no matter what he had to do to keep his wife from leaving him.

By the time my brother was in his fourth year of medical school and I was in my first year, the family violence at home had escalated to where my parents would fight almost every day. My brother, as a traditional man, would pretend not to notice what was going on and devote himself to living his life. I, however, fully understood that I was part of an extremely dysfunctional family and had already taken my mother's side.

I became my mother's protector; I started fighting with my father because of her or in her defense, and I took her, without his knowledge, to seek medical care for her arthritis. At some point in all their trips between Jalisco and California, my mother returned to Mexico with the news that she had two tumors in her breast. My brother and I, both medical students, were terrified that she had cancer, of which there is a history in our family. We said that we would take her to one of our gynecology professors. When my mother shared that news with my father, hoping, ingenuously, to find some compassion and support, he replied, "Ningún hijo de la chingada te va a agarrar las chichis" (No son of a bitch is going to touch your tits). My mother came to us sobbing, so my brother and I, pretending that we did not know what had occurred, told my father we were taking Mamá to the city to buy Christmas presents. Fortunately, her tumors were benign and disappeared after a short course of treatment. My mother denied that we had taken her to the doctor, and the subject was never broached again. Meanwhile, her episodes of sadness and weeping were becoming more frequent, but I did not understand then that she had depression; after all, I had seen her crying all my life.[6]

By 1987, my mother had developed obvious cervical spine deformities from the arthritis, causing severe backaches and headaches. Her eyes would appear swollen from inflammation in her neck muscles, and each day that my parents spent in Mexico, my mother would sleep more and more. I thought her lethargy was caused by the strong pain medication I was prescribing to relieve her head pain, but in reality it was due to a combination of the medicine and deep depression.

My father responded with anger and annoyed grimaces to the intensity of my mother's pains; he seemed to wish her dead. It was obvious how tired he was of my mother's situation, especially because by that time he was living with one of his longer-term mistresses—at least of those we knew about. Without a doubt, this infidelity was the one that hurt my mother the most. I think she felt she was competing for the love of a man whom, for reasons I will never understand, she loved more than her own life.

When they went back to the States, despite her pain, sadness, and drowsiness, my mother went back to picking lettuce in Salinas. The job she had been doing there for more than a decade consisted of filling a plastic bag with salad, pressing the bag firmly against her torso to expel all the air from it, and then hermetically sealing it. Years of doing this work in a cooled environment had deteriorated my mother's fragile joints, exacerbating the inflammatory and degenerative processes. In addition, the pressure she put on her abdomen to force the air from the salad bags caused a hiatal hernia that sent her to the emergency room twice because her coworkers thought she was having a heart attack.

By the time two more years had passed, my mother had to leave her job before the end of the day because she could no longer remain standing. Much later, I learned that Mamita would sleep in the car until her workmates finished their day and took her home. In this way, my father could ignore what was happening to my mother at work.

Finally, Mother could no longer hide her illness and somnolence from my father. She told him that she could not keep on working and that the best option would be for her to go back to Mexico and see the doctor there. His response was more violent than ever, and on two occasions, under the influence of alcohol, he threatened my mother with a gun, telling her that he was going to "mandarla a la chingada" (send her to the devil) because he was so tired of always seeing her moaning and full of pain. With her dead, he could live with his mistress. These episodes shattered what was left of my mother's nerves. Months later, my father finally called me to say that he was sending my mother on the next flight because she was in very bad shape. Of course, he never mentioned the death threats, and I found out about them from my mother only years later.

When I went to pick up my mother at the airport, her appearance and demeanor really affected me; the woman who stepped off the plane was far from the active and luchona (fighter) mother I knew. She was skinnier than ever, her face was tremendously swollen, she stammered, and she had the walk of someone totally defeated. For the five months that followed, she was in limbo, and I in hell. She ate little, slept most of the day, and woke up only to weep or engage in obsessive behaviors such as phoning my father's mistress at least fifteen times a day to tell her, "Eres una perra hija de tu chingada madre" (You're a dog born of your bitch mother). Her other obsession was to escape from home when I was out, to go to the drugstore to buy tissues to dry all her tears. I use the term *escape* because I did not allow her to go out alone; she was losing her grasp on reality. Not only would Mamita forget what day of the week it was or where she lived, but, while walking, she would list to the left and easily lose her balance. In addition, my mother, who had always been so meticulous about her appearance, now forgot to comb her hair and would button her blouse unevenly, giving her the appearance of a woman who was mentally disturbed. In fact, that's what she resembled. I was in my last year of medical school, and I had already cut contact with my father and my brother, so they did not talk to me, and I did not count on either of them for help.

A professor at the medical school I attended started a research project about the prevalence of depression in the city where we lived, and I decided to join the project and to write my thesis about the subject in order to understand it better. During much of the day, I had to leave my mother alone while I collected data for my thesis. I was in a rush to finish my thesis, get my degree, find a job as a physician, and become completely independent from my father. Yet leaving my mother alone at home became riskier each day because she was showing suicidal tendencies. I hid all the knives, scissors, and any medicines or objects she could use to hurt herself. I also asked my neighbor, Socorrito, to stop by the house as often as possible during my absence to check on her, but mostly I put my trust in God. Whenever I went out, I would ask God to protect my mother and please to keep her alive while I could not take care of her.

I spent the greater part of our savings taking my mother to different psychologists and trying various antidepressants, but neither the psychologists nor the drugs had any effect on her.[7] I finally heard about a very renowned psychiatrist and took Mamá to see him, although without much hope. The doctor prescribed a new antidepressant and gave me the usual warning, "We have to wait from fifteen to twenty days before we will see any effect." Meanwhile, I was in my own hell and had also started to lose my sense of time; I had lost all hope of seeing any improvement in my mother's state of mind. All I could think about was how I would start dying once she had been taken from me by her sadness. But this time the medication finally made a difference.

The best day of my life is also related to my mother's illness, but now to its absence. One morning, after almost two years of seeing her submerged in deep depression, I woke up to hear her singing. I immediately felt a chill that traveled throughout my body, paralyzing me: I thought she had finally lost her mind. I have never been more afraid in my life, not even years later when I got the news of my father's death. To see my mother go crazy—no, that I was not prepared for; besides, she did not deserve it. I got out of bed and saw through the patio window that she was hanging laundry out to dry. "¿Mamita, estás bien? ¿Por qué te levantaste tan temprano?" (Mamita, are you OK? Why are you up so early?) I asked her. "Me levanté a lavar; acuéstate, ya no voy a hacer ruido" (I got up to wash; go to bed, I won't make noise), she told me, smiling. I recovered my mother that day. Her sadness began slowly disappearing, and together we started rebuilding and strengthening her self-esteem. I asked her to leave my father, but she told me she was not ready for that yet. Given her fragile recovery, I realized that she could not be alone with my father again, so I left Mexico to live with my parents in California. I studied English and then applied for a master's degree program at the University of California, Davis. My mother's depression would recur each time my parents had an argument, but I was there to help her and reassure her that she would never be alone again.

Over the following years, my mom had two cervical spinal surgeries that helped relieve her backache and headaches. The arthritic cervical vertebrae that had been compressing her nerves were reconstructed, taking pressure off the nerves and relieving the terrible pain. She also had a third surgery to fix her hiatal hernia. In that process, we were forced to confront the impersonal and hierarchical health service in California. The worst was the cardiologist Mother saw for her high blood pressure, who treated her like an object. Because I had decided that no one was ever going to mistreat her again, I wrote the doctor a letter complaining about his behavior toward my mother, and from that point on an appointment at his medical office became almost like an inquisition. The doctor would request that a nurse be present at each of my mother's appointments as a witness that he was treating her well, and I would not allow my mother to go to see him without me. The cardiologist and I did not like each other, but at least we could talk knowledgeably about Mother's medical condition. My mother was eventually certified disabled because of her arthritis, and we returned to Mexico.

Once in Mexico, my mother distanced herself geographically from my father. She decided to live with me in Guadalajara, and my father, who did not enjoy living in the city, remained in our small hometown. Although my parents never divorced, their encounters became more and more sporadic, albeit no less aggressive; the difference now was that my mother had decided not to lose any more battles. My father was heavily invested in keeping up the appearance that we were a happy family and that his wife had not left him. Therefore, Mamá and I would visit him a few times a month, but we dictated the rules of engagement. He, in exchange, tried to be nice to my mother and helped her with the expenses of the house she was sharing with me. Why the change in my father? Simple. Mother was collecting disability payments. The money she collected would have been a pittance in the United States, but it was worth up to three times more given the standard of living in Mexico. My life was very stable, and I was able to support my mom both emotionally and economically. We did not need my father's money anymore, and we were less afraid of him. The abuser had lost his power.

In 2001, my father died as he had lived, violently. The former husband of one of his mistresses shot him three times at point-blank range, and he died instantly. My brother, mother, and I were in Guadalajara when we received the phone call with the news. I felt sadness but also relief. I thought that his death would close the long period of violence we all had suffered at his hands. My mother's pain was immense, but the worst pain came in attending her husband's funeral when the whole town knew the circumstances of his death. However, my mother endured it all with dignity. After all, this was the last hurt he could cause her, and it would be the last time she would be la pendeja del pueblo (the wronged wife in the town's eyes).

My mother still has episodes of depression, although less frequently, reminding us that that she will never be free of it—nor of the reuma. However, she has recovered her gusto por la vida, love of life, and there is no pain that can stop her. She goes out every day, shopping, traveling alone, visiting her friends, and seeing as many doctors as she wants. Mamita is healing the pain in her soul, and I am healing my pain as I see how she has been reborn.

8

My Spirit in Rebellion, My Body with Parkinson's Disease

Soy soldadera rebelde

Adaljiza Sosa-Riddell

My candle burns at both ends; it will not last the night;
But ah, my foes, and oh, my friends—
It gives a lovely light.
                    —Edna St. Vincent Millay, "Extravagance"

I discovered these lines of poetry when I was a sophomore in high school, fourteen or fifteen years old. They touched me so deeply and were so apropos to my plans for the future that I made them my personal canon, my rules for life. Yes, I have lived my life exactly in that frenetic manner. My parents came to the United States from León, Guanajuato, Mexico, in the early 1920s in the years following the Mexican Revolution. I am the eighth of ten children. Our family suffered extreme poverty as laborers in migrant agriculture, construction, and manufacturing. Despite my humble beginnings, I was always driven to achieve my dream of attending college at the University of California at Berkeley, following in my elder sister's footsteps. Despite working half-time throughout my college years, I studied hard, participated in campus activities, maintained close friendships, and stayed closely intertwined with my large Mexican family, who lived five hundred miles away.

Throughout my adult life I have suffered from many aches and pains, mostly minor, but always bothersome. The worst times came in the early 1990s, when my body began to feel completely frozen, gridlocked inside. I could barely move. I could not straighten my body. I felt all kinds of tensions inside, and the only way I could alleviate them was to cry or moan to no one in particular. These outward manifestations of the anguish within my brain and body had their own life and time frame. This was a new me who was much more emotional; my doctor told me "it was all in my head," and he was right, in a way. Yes, it was in my brain, but in the changes of the chemistry of my brain. I could do absolutely nothing about it. I was completely, totally helpless, at the mercy of these chemical changes. But I tried to fight back; I tried to swim back up to the surface of those emotions because I could not let myself drown in that way.

These feelings had been plaguing me for several years, but I had never given any thought to Parkinson's disease as a possible cause. I understood it as an "old man's" disease that more or less came with the normal aging process: "a disease, especially of the elderly, characterized by tremor (the person's head and limbs shake) and stiffness (muscular rigidity)" (New Good Housekeeping 1989, 253). Parkinson's seemed a relatively benign condition rather than a disease, except that I was always deeply disturbed by the illustration of a little old man, hunched over and walking with a shuffle, his hands curled up as if he were rolling something between his fingers. I always thought, "Oh, I hope I never have his disease." I never discussed my concerns with my doctor.

Finally, I made a list of my most frequent and bothersome symptoms, and from that list I composed a list of possible diseases. I presented my list to my physician, who consulted with a neurologist, and I received a letter officially confirming Parkinson's disease. I thought to myself: "What kind of disease is that to have? It's not even a glamorous disease." Upon receiving my diagnosis, I tentatively and skeptically grasped every lifeline my family, friends, and members of my various communities offered. I considered all cultural medical practices various people suggested and even medical practices I had previously scoffed at or dismissed. I had always considered each physical ailment I experienced as an isolated problem. Searching for answers, I went to my family physician, a physical therapist, an acupuncturist, a sobadora (massage therapist), and a women's healing project, but I received only superficial, temporary relief.

Many of the social norms I was taught in the first twenty years of my life

I had to reject in order to achieve my dreams. I refused to be restricted to traditional roles women played in Mexican American and Anglo-American society—specifically, the roles that a poor woman of color would end up playing. I rejected the notion that I would be a housewife or, at best, a secretary. It was unacceptable that I could not become an engineer and work in a man's world. The prevailing attitude among my teachers, my family, my peers, and most of my Mexican community that I could not attend the University of California at Berkeley because I was too poor was completely unacceptable to me.

A quintessential Chicana of the 1960s and 1970s, I have lived most of my life confronting and trying to change societal conditions I find unacceptable. I was at Berkeley in May 1960 when University of California students protested the hearings held by the House Un-American Activities Committee in San Francisco's City Hall. These hearings gained infamy because the police used fire hoses on peaceful demonstrators, a clear case of brutality. In this time period, when many anticolonial wars were beginning, more radical ideas were fermenting on college campuses. It was the time of the free speech movement at Berkeley. Ever since then I have refused to accept restrictive, oppressive, or unjust conditions. I have supported groups fighting to liberate colonized peoples from systems of world capitalism and have struggled against inequalities and injustices in my own nation.

Now I face a different adversary. I cannot just sit down and put the pieces together to solve this problem. My body is making me a prisoner. My spirit passed through walls and bars so all of my thoughts could soar, but now my body has become that stone wall, that prison of iron bars. How do I free myself? In short, I cannot; I must now learn to accept a condition that is clearly unacceptable, painful, debilitating. It is a condition beyond my control. Even if it does not immediately threaten my life, it does change it dramatically and irrevocably—the quality of my life and the quality of my body as it tries to live its life. I see myself now almost as two people, two separate personalities. Perhaps there will be even more personas in my future as I progress through the more advanced stages of Parkinson's disease.

The literature I initially read alluded vaguely to the pain, the contorted movements, and the bodily deformities that would come in the more advanced stages of Parkinson's disease. There were only oblique references to bouts of depression and agitation, writhing, and spasms. I did not understand, nor did the neurologist or even the literature explain, that these conditions would create a tremendous drain and strain on my spirit, my body, and my family. I asked myself, Must I resign myself to living with Parkinson's disease, or is suicide a brave way out? If I must accept this condition, how do I actually accomplish this acceptance? It took me more than ten years to admit that my minor problems were actually a cluster that formed one disease. Six more years passed before I realized that Parkinson's disease was a serious, intense condition that grew worse by the day. By this time, I was on small doses of dopamine supplementation, and the neurologist cautioned against increasing the dosage. Higher dosages usually result in intensified side effects; also, the effectiveness of the medication decreases over time as more brain cells are lost, so at that point high doses become necessary. I decided that, clearly, I needed more information, new approaches, and more aggressive treatment.

I still feel compelled to set myself free because there are many more things I want to accomplish. I want to see our daughter complete her doctorate because she wants to accomplish it. I need to be able to give her space and support. I tell her, "Citlali, m'ija, I made it through my doctorate, but I do not know if I can make it through yours." I want to see that happen while I can still understand what she has accomplished. Now that she has married a very wonderful young man, I want to see them start a family so that I can share her joy. My mother died seven years before my only child was born, something I regret very much. Mi amá was the long-suffering mother, la Santa Madre, of so many Mexican families. She would have quietly and fiercely loved my daughter. Their connection transcended the worlds of life and death. Her spirit looked over my shoulder, never letting me lose my temper with Citlali, strike her, or scream at her. I want to be able to weave that gossamer bonding with my grandchildren.

Many would-be articles, books, short stories, and poetry lurk nearly forgotten among my papers. I need to finish some of these projects, for I believe I have much of value to say about philosophy, society, and politics. I have much to write about the conditions and the future of the people with whom I identify: the Chicano and Latino people in the United States and Mexico. I expect to discover and learn of the importance of the ancient and contemporary indigenous world. I need to enhance my emotional connection with several people: my extensive extended family; my husband, Bill; my daughter, Citlali; her husband, Jorge; and my many, many friends.

The tremor on the left side of my body occurs almost nightly and always continues far longer than I can bear. I try to relax but cannot. I cannot even toss and turn. So I am more or less riveted to one spot unless I awaken my husband to help me turn. Then neither of us will sleep much. It is a very nice intimacy that at least we are still able to share a bed. Such an irony for my husband of fifty years (we were married on August 24, 1957), who was accustomed to the other spirit I used to be, the competent one. She ran a smooth household. He does not much like to run a household, although he is certainly capable of doing so. Now he finds himself having to take care of the new spirit, the new me, and almost all the household duties. Not only must he do all the chores I used to do, but he has to do personal things for me as well: help me dress, carry my food, put a bib on me, load my wheelchair into the car, help me in and out of bed. Because we both have always worked full-time, for years I hired a housekeeper so that we could spend time with our daughter. Now we hire a "personal assistant" for me, someone who can help me get dressed; keep my clothes clean, pressed, and organized; take me for walks; help with the housework; and keep me company.

I feel I do very little nowadays. I am wheelchair bound—the new me, the new spirit. I have to accept that and learn to deal with it gracefully, not angrily, because angry is no way to live. I have come to many crossroads in dealing with my infirmities and with Parkinson's disease. I am not an invalid, but I cannot walk. I cannot stand straight or walk even a few steps. I can do many intellectual things, but the simplest physical tasks—standing up, sitting down, going to the table, fixing my food, serving myself, and eating my food—are now exceedingly difficult. Yet I want to do them all because I love my independence.

Giving up my independence and privacy has been the most difficult adjustment. My physical limitations are now clearly evident to even the most casual observer. Every day people can see that I have problems with what researchers and psychologists call my emotions. But they are not emotions at all. They certainly are not *my* emotions. They are the outbursts of another person I do not even recognize. They are reactions to the chemicals—or lack of chemicals—in my brain. Although these "outbursts" do not seem to affect my cognitive reasoning directly, they do affect my ability to mold and shape my emotions in the direction that I want—to which I am accustomed and which used to be me.

I cannot remember exactly when these "outbursts" began because I had already had trouble falling asleep at night for several years. Strange thoughts crowded out rational thoughts inside my brain. I responded by thinking of my work or plans, anything rational to overcome the desire to jump out of my body, tear my hair out, bang my head against the wall, or do many other bizarre forms of self-mutilation to set myself free from my bodily prison. These disturbing thoughts I kept to myself. Soon after

I retired, I began to have these feelings during the day, and I began to notice a pattern. At first, these mental outbursts and the freezing of my body were not daily occurrences, but when they happened, it was always approximately one hour before I was due to take my next set of dopamine medications.

These conditions are not acceptable. Who wants to live like this? I do not. But then I read other people's comments. In "What Makes a Life Worth Living?" Lata Mani (2001), a woman of color who was a promising professor, writer, and star in the academic scene before she was injured and became disabled, asks, What is life? What kind of life is worth living? I try to think about that myself. Just because I cannot walk does not mean my life is not worth living.

Now I grudgingly accept the limitations of my body, but how to accept the unacceptable remains my challenge. To refuse to accept it is to live in the past. The present is here, and I might have a future. If I do not learn to accept these unacceptable limitations, then I cannot move forward. I know that my body is going to experience progressive deterioration. That is not so different from the normal aging process. For me, the process is accelerated and more extreme.

Searching recently through my old papers, trying to decide what to donate to the Special Collections Library of the University of California, Davis, I found a poem pinned to a drawing of a small rag doll. The poem has deeper meaning now than when I wrote it, and I thought I could use it for the ritual I was preparing to initiate my new stage in life, coming to terms with my own form of Parkinson's disease while continuing to live a useful life.

The Rag Doll

When I was a child I made her.
Pinned shoe-button eyes and my smile on her,
Covered her raggedy head with dark tresses,
Stuffed her soul full with cottony softness,
Lulled her with lullabies and gentle caresses;
Tossed her aside for provocative glances.
Dropping her lightly into this sleek marble tower,
Passing each hour interminably lonely,
Her cotton-soul stuffing screaming cushiony pain
For words left unspoken, her silence unbroken
Forgotten by me.

—*Adaljiza Sosa, 1972*

The idea of a grieving ritual came from a report titled *Living Well with Lupus* (Lupus Foundation of America 1995). The authors recommend a grieving period for anyone diagnosed with a chronic illness. I found, however, that grieving takes time, introspection, brutal honesty, and perhaps passage through specific crisis milestones. Nearly ten years after I knew my body was failing me, I finally acknowledged two crisis milestones: the day I received my wheelchair and the day I confessed to my neurologist I was experiencing depression, anxiety, agitation, and even thoughts of self-destruction. My decision was to put away my old body and spirit formally, quietly, and privately. I was once a spirit in tune with my body, and I decided to move on with my life as a person with Parkinson's and thus to become so again.

I began my grieving process with a ritual for my body and spirit, symbolized by the rag doll, the poem, and some words to remind her of all she had been and had accomplished before I placed her in her ivory tower. I gently lifted the doll from where I had hidden her long ago, in an imagined tower I had built when I was a child to protect myself from the pains of the outside world. This tower I thought could not crack, for it represented my cultural strengths: Mexicanas do not show pain; we do not flinch; no nos rajamos.

Curiously, I could not remember ever having named my doll. Recalling my past and considering my current passions, I named her Soldadera Rebelde de Aztlán, "Sol Rebel" for short. For several years I had wanted to develop an organization with this name, intended to defend nuestra raza Chicana/Latina/Mexicana and help us achieve some of our articulated goals. I held Sol Rebel tightly for a long time, stroked her hair, and told her the story of her life so that she would never forget her strong, daring rebellious spirit.

> Homenaje a mi espíritu y mi presencia,
> una soldadera rebelde de Aztlán
>
> You were always adventurous, una soldadera rebelde. You are the spirit who loved to walk along the top of track rails to learn how to keep your balance. You loved to run track, to run low hurdles, just to show that you could do what the boys could do and just as well. You loved to climb trees, play games, and study all the time. You are the spirit who wanted to be an aeronautical engineer and the first woman to land on the moon. You could still make it, Sol Rebel, for no woman has set foot on the moon yet.
>
> Remember, Sol Rebel, when you had to clean out the basement in our old house? You knew true fear then because you had to become

an expert on black widow spiders—their web styles, how to entice them out of their webs to kill them, their favorite hiding places, the different appearance of the male versus the female, their distinct eggs, and the beauty of their markings as the tiny brown spiders changed from black to brown to white decorative striping into that dreaded black arachnid with the bright red hourglass on its belly. Later, you and your sister hung old army blankets to divide that dark, cool basement into bedroom spaces, one for you and your sister, a room for each of your two brothers, and a space for your father. You were brave, but not brave enough to sleep in that dark basement alone.

Then there were the long, warm summers when you worked in the fields of Cupertino. A wisp of a teenaged girl, weighing a mere 110 pounds, you carried a sixteen-foot ladder and a bucket of fruit. You and your family worked from 7:00 A.M. to 8:00 P.M. six days a week, harvesting fruit or cutting apricots. The whole family lived in a packing shed without running water and used a creepy, dark, spider-laden outhouse.

The following summer you worked in a sewing factory and thought it quite an adventure because you made friends with Chicanas from San Fernando and Pacoima. It was a sweatshop of first-class proportions, 130 degrees Fahrenheit in a corrugated tin building without any air conditioning. You sweated like a pack animal as you steam ironed, running from station to station to earn seventy cents per hour in order to have money for your senior year in high school. The most difficult part for you, Apá, and your nineteen-year-old brother was commuting seventy-five miles from home to San Fernando every Monday morning, arriving at 7:00 A.M. and then living for the week in a friend's garage, without electricity, telephone, or other amenities most adolescents would not live without. On Friday you drove home, then did this all over again on Monday.

All the while you, Sol Rebel, harbored dreams of going to Cal. You dreamed that dream and made it come true. It was your spirit that wanted to build a house for your parents, and somehow you and your husband made that dream come true. You graduated from Cal and began teaching high school in your hometown, but you wanted much, much more. You spent your summers taking classes to obtain and upgrade your teaching credentials, completing your master's thesis in political science at the University of California, Berkeley, or enjoying the great outdoors. You and your husband took various members of your extended families hiking all over Yosemite National Park. You loved hiking and camping and taking the kids with you— your nephews and nieces, your daughter, and many friends. You had learned to swim at the age of twelve. "Mexicans do not swim," you were told. You loved to swim. You could do anything in the water.

When the Chicano movement began, you embraced it with all your being. It was you who marched in so many demonstrations that I lost count: the march on Gallo Wines in Modesto, the march in Watsonville, and so on. You were young, strong, daring, and fearless. Your spirit took you to Mexico City and to San Juan Teotihuacán to climb the pyramids of the Sun and Moon many times. You were the spirit who went to Cuba leaning on a cane; you made your way, mi soldadera rebelde.

Sol Rebel, I know how difficult it is for you to relinquish your mandamiento to struggle for the preservation of knowledge of your ancient ways, to spread our knowledge of the universal and our inter-twined presence with the land. It has been bequeathed to you from your indigenous ancestors in Mexico through my father, when at the moment of his death I saw and felt his rebel spirit come to rest on my shoulders. Smile, mi Sol Rebel; do not fret. That revolutionary spirit has already moved on to someone else or perhaps to many other people. Our spirit is free!

I then placed her gently in her ivory tower, my little doll, my spirit, where she is now to sit quietly, not frenetically as she had lived. Mi Soldad-era Rebelde de Aztlán is now limp, as if the spirit—and even the stuffing—has been taken out of her. I dare not turn my head to see her face, to look in her eyes, for if my spirit has been laid secretively to rest, then I should be resting there and mi soldadera rebelde should have her arm raised in our old Chicana power fist.

My ritual completed, I turned to other means of learning to live with my bodily limitations: I decided to go public; I applied the practical skills learned from my family members to my daily living; I continued to conduct extensive research on my condition; and, finally, I decided to keep working full time until June 30, 2000, utilizing my full rights under the Americans with Disabilities Act.

I went public by announcing my illness at the 1995 Conference of the National Association for Chicana and Chicano Studies, a professional academic organization of which I was a cofounder and very active member. I turned to my parents and what they had taught me about health. When any one of us was ill, my mother consulted her green book, *El libro médico del hogar* (The Book of Home Medicine) printed in 1936, a year before I was born. Of course, it was in Spanish, and it had color pictures of the human body, ghastly diseases, and treatments. Amá rarely used the old cures of her homeland, although she often told us stories about folk medicine. Both my parents had passed away by 1993, and I had only general memories of specific treatments they taught me. No one had ever mentioned Parkinson's disease.

Not surprisingly, three of my sisters had become registered nurses, and I often consulted them about any health problems. For my own interest, I studied medical encyclopedias, articles, and later, of course, the Internet. Article after article reiterated the lack of knowledge about the causes of Parkinson's disease and the very little knowledge about any treatments. The only thing the medical community seems to know is what does *not* cause Parkinson's. It does not seem to run in families or particular ethnic groups, and men and women are equally affected; it does not seem to have genetic links; it does not seem to be caused be any particular germ, a heart attack, or a stroke. The disease is caused by a loss of cells in the very central part of the brain, the substantia nigra. These cells produce a chemical neurotransmitter called dopamine that is important for coordinated muscle movement. Once the majority of these cells are destroyed, dopamine levels drop sufficiently to produce the symptoms recognized as Parkinson's disease. And it is a progressively degenerative disease. Still, there was very little information about it when I first started looking. I found the following entries:

1. "Parkinson's Disease: A slowly progressive disease usually occurring in later life, characterized pathologically by degeneration within the nuclear masses of the extrapyramidal system" (Miller and Keane 1983, 841).

2. "Parkinson's Disease: A common disorder of the brain. It develops because of damage to the extrapyramidal nervous system, the part which controls movement, posture, balance, and walking" (Lieberman et al. n.d., 1).

Finally, on the National Parkinson Foundation Web site I found: "Experts . . . believe that Parkinson's disease may be related to one or more of the following: chemicals called free radicals, [and] environmental toxins" (Lang 2005). Information available about Parkinson's disease prior to 1990 was limited, superficial, and not very helpful in diagnosis. And some of the new information has been speculative, highly controversial, and much debated. I recently found the book *The Family That Couldn't Sleep*, which argues that Parkinson's disease may be closely related to "mad cow" disease (Creutzfeldt-Jakob disease) and may be caused by misshapen proteins, or prions, inside genetic structures (Max 2006).

Throughout my life, I have tried to educate myself and discover solutions for my problems. I have always believed any problem can be solved. Are there any solutions to my current dilemma of living with a chronic disease? I can think of at least four. First, it would be wonderful to have a cure or even a way to control the disease. There are currently no treatments to slow the progression of the disease, only medical and surgical interventions that help make the symptoms more manageable. I have confidence that the scientific community is working on solutions despite the political entanglements. The much discussed stem cell research (whether using embryonic, amniotic, or adult stem cells) offers the most hope, but is stymied in the current political climate. The pills that I take, a carbidopa/levodopa combination, are already used extensively. They replace a small percentage of the missing neurotransmitter, helping to reduce symptoms. I expect researchers will come up with something more effective very soon.

There are other possibilities. I have already signed up to receive deep brain stimulation surgery (DBSS). It involves implanting in my brain a device that will send electrical impulses to parts of my brain in order to alleviate the tremor that courses through my body. It will help me somewhat, I hope. Just the possibility of DBSS offers me some hope for improvement. It is not a cure, but it may provide a great deal of relief.

Technological innovations can also help greatly, even without a cure. A power wheelchair, although extremely useful, is cumbersome, awkward, and limiting. I dream of getting around with a jet pack on my back in short hops, up stairs, and over curbs. It might also be interesting to live on the moon or a space station, where I would be weightless and more capable of keeping up with everyone else. At least we all would be equally awkward. Silly as these ideas may sound, they are the thoughts of a person who cannot move over the steps in our world that seem so small to everyone else. If I cannot have flat surfaces everywhere, I would love to have one of the robotic prototypes that are beginning to filter into the market and that would offer me the chance to walk as if in a robotic shell.

Finding the cause or causes of Parkinson's disease offers another approach. I have participated in a long-term study on possible causes, impacts, and prognosis for Parkinson's disease. I suspect either influenza or exposure to high levels of potent pesticides or herbicides caused my disease. Of course, all members of my family were exposed to large amounts of DDT when we worked in the fields from 1947 to 1954. Research in this area may yield valuable results, and I have made arrangements to donate my brain and body to science after my death.

I also recognize that my husband, daughter, and the rest of my family are also part of my illness experience and have to help me every day. I offer my husband's and daughter's words (written in June 2004) as a view into the impact of my disease on the people who care for me and love me.

William Riddell

My wife's Parkinson's disease is an annoyance with which we both have to live. Other people may express concern, but ultimately it is our problem as a couple. It is my commitment, my obligation to care for my wife, just as she has always cared for me. Sometimes I am afraid when I watch her slow movements, bodily contortions, and emotional outbursts. But mostly I feel helpless. I am also hopeful that a cure of some form will come very soon. I would see to it that Adaljiza would receive any helpful procedure. I also admire my wife very much because she has accomplished many good things, has a great attitude, and continues to work for good causes.

Citlali Lucia Sosa-Riddell

During my first year of college, I learned of my mother's condition. At the time I was just very relieved that she did not have cancer. . . . I really did not know what Parkinson's disease meant. I just knew that it was not exactly fatal, and that is what mattered most to me. I only found myself worried about my mother when she started having problems with her sense of balance. Oddly enough, she never seemed to hurt herself.

Over the years, she has slowly had more and more difficulty, mostly around her lack of balance and her inability to really walk. Her changes have happened so slowly that I have had time to gain acceptance. Most of the time I worry about her when she gets unhappy about her condition. I think it is especially difficult because she is one of the most tenacious people in existence today. It is at those times when her condition upsets me most. But I know that if our situation were reversed, she would never let me feel sorry for myself or be unhappy. She would force me to get up in the morning and help make the world a better place. So I know that I must do the same for her. I know that the best thing is to make her time with us as much fun as possible and try to keep doing some of the things that we have always enjoyed. Most of the time I am just happy to spend time with her and talk because that is when we have the most fun. In these times I am grateful rather than sad because my mother's mind is definitely as sharp as always, and while her body may fail I know her mind has not failed.

Message to Everyone

I also want to send some comments to all the people who have been by my side or are fighting the good fight in this world. I want you to heed my words and, I hope, learn from my experiences.

I am most pleased to have known you and to have been a part of a political movement that is only in its early stages. Chicana/o studies and Chicana/o politics are just beginning to change our world. It is my fervent hope that this movimiento we began a few decades ago will flourish and make the world a better place in which we all can live. You honor me by keeping these dreams alive. My burdens are more bearable and my world is much brighter knowing that I contributed to building something of value.

The next time you go to a demonstration, rally, or other political event, carry an extra sign, banner, or placard for me. Go forth fearlessly y con mucho corazón, with a strong heart. Speak all those beautiful words, mightier than any sword, louder than thunder, never again to be silenced. Honor me by writing, teaching, and pursuing community activity with passion and for the right reasons: to make the world a better place for Chicanas/os and thus a better place for everyone. Defend the defenseless. Siempre de la mano a los de abajo.

Even as I write these words, I know that a part of me will never resign itself to my limitations. The new me is just as radical as the old. I will find other means of contributing to a better world for my community and my family. Words are brimming over in my brain. I have little time and much work to do. Mi Sol Rebel is only resting. She will be back, stronger than ever. We remain soldaderas rebeldes de Aztlán.

9

"I Wake Up and Go to Bed with Pills"

An Anonymous Latina Speaks about the Not-So-Silent Killer (Hypertension)

Redacted by Angie Chabram-Dernersesian

In hypertension, or high blood pressure, the force of blood against the artery walls is elevated. Over time, it can lead to artery, heart, or kidney damage, as well as to atherosclerosis (hardening of the arteries), heart attack, and stroke. Although asymptomatic in most cases, severe hypertension may cause pounding headaches, visual disturbances, and nausea or vomiting.

Blood pressure is expressed as systolic pressure over diastolic pressure. Systolic pressure measures the blood pressure against the artery walls immediately after a heart contraction; diastolic pressure measures the pressure between heartbeats when the heart is relaxed. For adults eighteen and older, a reading at or lower than 119/79 is considered normal, whereas 140/90 or above defines hypertension. Recent, more stringent guidelines identify the range 120–139/80–89 as prehypertension, in recognition that even borderline high blood pressure can have significant health effects, is likely to progress to full-blown high blood pressure, and merits aggressive treatment (Yahoo Health 2004).

According to the most recent American Heart Association statistics, 18.2 percent of Hispanics have hypertension. The condition affects Mexican Americans in particular, among whom 27.8 percent of males and 28.7 percent of females have hypertension ("Hispanic Community" 2007).[1] In addition, according to a recent study, "Hispanic women's heart disease risk is comparable to the heart disease risk of Caucasian women who are about a decade older." Researchers found that although Hispanic and white women "scored similarly" in the areas of hypertension, diabetes, high cholesterol, and waist circumference (all of which are risk factors for cardiovascular disease), "Hispanic women's prehypertension rate (32 percent) was significantly higher than Caucasian women['s] (19 percent)" (American Heart Association 2007).

Hypertension is a significant contributing factor to heart disease and stroke, and heart disease is itself the number-one killer of Latinas, accounting for 29 percent of the 51,400 annual deaths (U.S. DHHS 2005; Georgiou 2006). My goal in this chapter is to increase public awareness and discussion about hypertension in this population. It consists of excerpts from my redaction of a conversation with a Latina hypertensive. Although she wishes not to be identified, she wants readers to know her story and understand her struggle with hypertension. For her, "information is power."

While reading, you should visualize the Latina subject of this story as a vivacious middle-aged woman who lives life to the fullest and loves to read, talk, work, and sing along with the radio, switching easily from Spanish to English. There are no chains on her tongue! Looking at her, no one would detect any symptoms of illness or a chronic condition. Nonetheless, she assures me, first in Spanish and then in English, that she's had high blood pressure for ten years and that despite its often being described as the "silent killer," it is not silent in her life. Not only does she recognize symptoms and risks associated with this chronic disease, but she has spent the past decade of her life speaking about it with family, friends, doctors, and relatives. In this sense, her level of awareness is far ahead of many of her compatriots'.[2]

Just as we are about to begin our conversation, my Latina interviewee asks, "Can we start in just a moment? It's late, and I haven't taken my pills. Ah, here they are. Just let me get a glass of water. . . .

"OK, now we can start. Do you know what, Angie? I talk to my friends and the women in my family about high blood pressure all the time. We talk about what makes our pressure go up, like bad people, injustices, work, family, and the sorrows of life. At times, we talk about how our lives have changed with high blood pressure. If you want, I can tell you about my life, my life before and after high blood pressure.

" . . . Like I said, my life was different before I got high blood pressure. No longer can I just get up, take a bath, eat, and go. I used to go, go, go, go. Sometimes I wouldn't eat all day long. I'd drink a lot of coffee too.[3] Like a cup of coffee here and another there. And more and more. Isn't coffee delicious? But it makes my pressure go up. Now I take it easy, I take care of myself. Only one cup a day, and one foot in front of the other. Bit by bit.

" . . . In the beginning, I hated taking the blood pressure pills, but now I know I need my pills.[4] I don't want to have a heart attack or stroke or suffer a serious illness. So I wake up and go to bed with high blood pressure pills.

"I know I have to be prepared. I know I need to organize the pills so I don't get confused and get sick.[5] And, of course, I always need to make sure I have enough pills! Once a month I have to buy them at the pharmacy. You know what, Angie? Before this I'd never taken medicine. I didn't know about medicines. Now I certainly know them. And at home we always talk about pills—the white pill, the pink pill, the yellow one, the round one, the big one, and the small one. We know the names of the pills as well: Atenolol, Benicar, and the water pill with the huge name [Hydrochlorothiaziade]!

"You know, these pills that I wake up with and go to sleep with every day are really expensive—really expensive! Now I know why the seniors are mad. I just don't see how they can afford them. Sometimes you have to pay forty dollars per prescription—and that's with insurance! They call that a co-pay? I'll tell you, I just don't know how poor and elderly people without insurance who have to take pills every day survive.[6]

" . . . I forgot to tell you something, Angie. You know, now that I think about it, I'm not the first one to get up and go to bed with pills in my family.[7] When I was growing up, my mom always used to talk about her blood pressure pills and her pressure going up. . . . When I was little, I didn't really know what this meant or how it felt, other than that she used to lie down when it happened. I do know that her pressure started going up when she went through the change [menopause] or felt bad from her nerves.[8] Now that I think of it, I remember that her pressure went up when her mother died. That was really hard. Her mom was a really strong woman, a seamstress who lost two kids in the span of a week. Imagine that! Her life was hard, you know. She crossed the border after the Mexican Revolution. She lived in an adobe house. She had to heat up the water and all of that. She burned tires for heat. She had to struggle to survive. There wasn't much food either.

"My grandmother had high blood pressure too. I don't think she took the pills, though, but I can't tell you for sure. The doctor would tell her to lay off the salt, but she didn't want to.[9] She liked her salt on her fideo [vermicelli] and her beans. She'd say that eating was one of the few pleasures in life. She loved to eat. Mi amá [grandmother] was a very loving person, you know. We loved visiting and talking to her. I think my grandmother gave my mom a lot of affection and support. Poor Amá, she was so good, and she spoiled all of us so badly. My mom is very strong, too. She kept it together when Amá died, but I think it really affected her—now a big part of her support, her apoyo, was gone.

" . . . I don't feel too good. Would you mind if we stopped for a little while? I have to take my blood pressure. I take it every day around the same time, around noon. It feels like it's high. You know how it feels? It's like you are driving up a hill or going up in an airplane. I also get a pain in the back of my head. Sometimes it feels like my head is blowing up like a balloon.

"Be right back, OK? I feel like it's high right now, I'll tell you in a minute. . . . My body speaks to me, it's not silent. My heart beats fast, and I start getting a little dizzy and hot. Then I feel tired. Sometimes I get a pain in my back. My eyes get a little blurry. And if I'm outside, I want to get out of the sun. Where's the machine? Oh, it's in the living room. I forgot to put it away yesterday.

"Look at it, it's really old, you know. I use it so much. I take it every-where. OK, my girl, Angie, let me show you how I do it [take my pressure]. First I put on the cuff, right above my elbow. Then I adjust the little hose thing right here in the middle of my arm. Then I press here, start.[10] You have to stay really still. Oh good, 138 over 84! Thank God! Well, not great. You know what the doctor says, Angie? The doctor says its supposed to be 120 over 80, but it's never like that, not even with three pills. Sometimes it's 165 over 95. It can even go higher. It can go to 170 over 115. That's when I get real dizzy and my heart starts beating even faster. When it gets that high, I either call the doctor or head to the emergency room.

" . . . Once I went to a talk about high blood pressure, and they said that it's better to take a few pills at a lower dose instead of one strong pill. That worked for me. Before then, it was horrible. You don't know how I suffered. They prescribed a pill that gave me a horrible headache. I also got depressed. I began to forget things. I couldn't sleep. My eyes got really dry. It was awful! At the doctor's office, he'd look at me, like asking, 'Why can't you adjust to the medicine?' As if my body was weird or something like that.

"When I'd try to talk about side effects, he'd tell me I'd only get ner-vous if I kept reading the paper that comes with the pills. One doctor even told me I had a 'thing' about pills. Like a phobia or something. And he was younger than I am. I was furious. I flat out told him, 'You are a doctor of the body, not the mind!' He didn't expect me to come back for a month, so that he wouldn't have to see my face for a long time. No way, José! I went back and back and back. He got tired of me. But in the end I had to go to another doctor to find a solution. The new doctor was nice, he listened, he understood me, and he tried what the lady at the conference said: more than one pill at lower doses.[11]

" . . . I'm glad I didn't give up. It took so long to adjust the medicine, I can see where people would say, 'The heck with it, this is making me feel worse than the high blood pressure.' Many times it did make me feel worse, I couldn't do things, I had to lay down all day. It was really depressing to suffer the side effects of some medications.

"But you have to be patient, you know. You have to work with a good doctor, little by little, and you have to keep going while they adjust the pills. You know what? I think *you* [the patient] are the one that really does most of the work. You have to pay attention to your body, your head, your heart. You have to take your pressure reading, you have to go to the doctor. You have to tell him how you're feeling. You have to write down your pressure measurements every day. It's all about you and you and you. Good health takes work. That's life.

"Sometimes people tell me to calm down, even when others are angry at me and they blow a fuse. But you can't suck the life and feeling out of yourself; you have to feel things. You have to respond. Sometimes I think they want us Mexicanas and Latinas to be bland, without life. I'll tell you something, Angie, I won't lose my spark. I have to take care of it. I'll give my spark a comfortable place to live.

"They also tell me 'no stress.' It's not easy when you're working and working, and there's a lot of pressure to work harder. More and more work. I've always worked very hard, you know, and I love to work. But I take care of myself now. I don't go beyond my limits.[12] I'm not a crazy workaholic anymore. Sometimes people get annoyed with me. Sometimes people want to guilt-trip you when you say 'no' or try to help them in another way that doesn't hurt you. I love helping people, but I am old enough to make my own decisions. Yes, I've reached the age where I give myself the right to say 'no.'

"Bit by bit I want to change things, not just take pills. I want to lose weight so I can bring my pressure down. At one point, one of my doctors referred me to the physical therapy office, where they taught me how to breathe. Diaphragmatic breathing, I think it's called.[13] I also like to work in the garden like Amá used to. You know, she and Apá [Grandpa] lived a lot outside. As soon as he'd get home from working in the sun all day, they'd sit there until late and watch the stars and talk and talk. He loved doing this, even though he was a gardener who worked in other people's yards all day long, and his skin was red from the hot sun. People talk so much about relaxation therapy. But, you know, I think my grandparents had it right. They ate a lot of corn tortillas, beans, and chicken, and they talked to each other every day. They didn't just sit in front of the TV. They didn't think that life was work.

"I'm tired. Let me rest for a minute, Angie. They say that if you talk too much, your pressure goes up.[14] Let's see if the pill worked. Let me breathe a little bit. Do you want to learn how, Angie? OK, Angie, I'll teach you. Breathe from your stomach, like babies do. In and out. Forget about the flat belly. Breathe in and out. No, Angie, don't hold in your tummy like they tell you to in the magazines. Do you know what they'd tell me? 'Breathe in the relaxation, breathe out the high blood pressure.' Now I'm going to take my pressure on both arms. Sometimes the pressure isn't the same in both, you know.

"The numbers are still a little high. But of course, I forgot to take the water pill that makes you go to the bathroom all the time. You see, you need to have your stuff together, be organized. I usually keep everything in this little bag, so it's all together. That way, I don't have to see the pill bottles all day, and I get on with my life. I have to live my life.

"Many people have helped me, and I hope that I have helped others, too, you know, especially the ones who have high blood pressure like me. I think I've also helped people in my family who were later diagnosed with high blood pressure. First I took the pill, then my sister took it, then other people in my family took it. I hope my experience was good for them. Ah, I'm sure it was. The other day I went to visit my sister, and we were just about to have breakfast. She's a great cook. Before we started to eat our enchiladas and beans, someone said, 'I forgot to take my pills.' It was so funny—we all got up and got our purses and our pills right away. We've always done so much together, and now we are doing this together. First the food, then the pills, then the wonderful plática [chat]. Later on, my mom and I take our pressure. We pass the machine and say, 'How was yours?' Then we say, 'It's good' or 'Don't worry, it will go down soon.' We are all doing the same thing, healing and supporting each other. Curing ourselves. Curándonos. And that's how I like it. Yeah, I like it like that."

10

A Tapestry of Illness

A Latina Physician's Family Gives Voice to Diabetes and Illness

Jessica Núñez de Ybarra

As the youngest of eight children, my twin sister and I had many influences. The strongest in my life was always our mother, Carmen. As long as I have known Mother, she has been a defender of justice—not only in my immediate family, but, even more important, in our community. With her language and cultural skills, she became an intermediary for those who could not defend themselves. She did this without question and never expecting compensation.

When I think of my mother, her mystical ways and connection to Mexican American traditions always come to mind. When I am fearful, I just have to look at my own hands, which remind me of hers, and I feel suddenly strong and calm. I remember her hands healing by virtue of their gentle touch—whether they were rubbing our sore legs or preparing dinner, paying bills, answering the phone, reading her Bible, or tending to her garden. My mother's wisdom has guided my life. Her deep sense of spirituality and Catholic faith embody core Mexican American values. She has always lived a very selfless life, with a strong sense of purpose. I have always admired her no-nonsense approach, maybe too much sometimes, and yet she has also taught me about compassion.

In her lifetime, my mother has been exposed to many types of pain: the pains of poverty, separation, childhood illness, sexism, prejudice, sorrow and loss, violence, alienation, childbirth, motherhood, arthritis, osteoporosis, heart disease, cancer, and diabetes. My mother's pain history and life story are a vibrant cascade of triumph and miracles, despite horrible twists and challenging odds. Her stories run through my mind like a beautiful tapestry, like my own special road map for life. I feel privileged to have had such deep dialogue with my mom for so many years.

This road map has been especially valuable in my work as a physician. I do not know how my childhood experiences led me to pursue a medical career—it just has always been my calling (since third grade). My mother used to say, "You want to be a doctor? Strange, I love you so much, but I really hate doctors." My career choice never really sat well with her, but she always supported me wholeheartedly.

My mother's life narrative revolves around an illness that has plagued my family for twenty years: diabetes mellitus, a chronic condition that should duly be respected and dreaded. Diabetes mellitus is a condition that is not discussed enough. People with diabetes find it difficult to accept the necessary lifestyle changes, health risks, complications, and emotional toll. Denial is often their most powerful coping mechanism. However, in order to understand our battle with diabetes, one first needs to understand the disease.

As of 2002, an estimated 18.2 million people in the United States (6.3 percent of the population) are living with diabetes. Of those, some 13 million people have been diagnosed, and the other 5.2 million do not yet know they have it. According to the Centers for Disease Control and Prevention, "Mexican Americans are over twice as likely to have diabetes as non-Hispanic whites of similar age," and diabetes affects an estimated 8.2 percent of all U.S. Latinos (CDC 2004b). The reason for the higher rate of diabetes among Latinos is unknown but may involve genetic factors or environmental assaults.

If untreated, diabetes results in excessive blood sugar (glucose) levels due either to the body's failure to produce insulin (type 1 diabetes mellitus) or to a combination of insufficient insulin and a resistance to its effects (type 2, or adult-onset diabetes mellitus) (American Diabetes Association n.d.a). To paraphrase my mentor, Dr. Lois Jovanovic, people with type 2 diabetes mellitus have outgrown their pancreas by becoming overweight.

The hormone insulin enables blood glucose to enter all the cells in the body except those in the brain. Without glucose, the cells in the body "starve." Moreover, when glucose cannot enter the cells of the body, it accumulates in the blood until it is cleared out by the kidneys and voided in urine. Although much is still unknown about the disease, persons with diabetes can reduce complications by controlling their levels of blood glucose and by maintaining as normal as possible blood pressure and blood lipid levels. Plenty of exercise, weight management, and a healthy diet are vital in accomplishing these goals.

My family has always been very close, yet each of us has our own idiosyncrasies. I sometimes think the only thing we have in common is our love for God and each other and our fear of diabetes. Everyone we know on Mom's side of the family has eventually developed diabetes (mostly type 2). Diabetes and its complications have already either severely debilitated or prematurely taken many of my mother's brothers and sisters. She often feels pangs of remorse and guilt for surviving so many of them.

My knowledge of diabetes was enhanced through my medical education; plus, as a family, we were able to learn together from my mother's personal struggle with medications and diets. One reason my mother has managed her disease so successfully is that she has always had a very large and supportive network, including her husband, children (one of them a physician), grandchildren, prayer group, church, friends, and siblings. My mother is still here with us, but it has taken a village to keep her.

The most interesting aspect of Mom's condition, from my perspective as her physician daughter, has been to hear her complain about how strict her doctor is: "Why do I have to take insulin?" Other people she knows manage their condition with diet and medications alone, so why can't she do the same? Managing insulin therapy requires great skill because once the insulin is administered, blood glucose levels drop rapidly as the glucose enters the cells of the body. If the levels drop too much, the brain is affected immediately because brain cells receive glucose directly from the bloodstream without the mediation of insulin (American Diabetes Association n.d.a).

Insulin therapy has several unpleasant side effects: it creates unnaturally strong sugar cravings, induces fat storage (causing weight gain), and must be administered by injection, usually multiple times per day. Over time, the skin gets sore, and "knots" of scar tissue develop at the injection site, creating additional discomfort. An individual on insulin therapy cannot leave home without it or skip meals, must store it in a cool environment, and must carry glucose testing and injection supplies. And receiving the therapy requires money or a good insurance plan.

In my mother's case, she also has to take pills, vitamins, and supplements around the clock and to monitor her diet in order to manage her diabetes, diabetic neuropathy (functional or structural nerve degeneration or damage), rheumatoid arthritis, hyperlipidemia, hypothyroidism, cardiac arrhythmia, thrush, gastroesophageal reflux disease, and osteoporosis. The diabetes has caused retinal detachment in both eyes, so my seventy-nine-year-old father must administer her insulin injections for her. She has also had great difficulty managing her condition even when she follows all the doctor's instructions perfectly. She gets faint and perspires profusely if she does not eat on time (a result of low blood sugar from long-acting insulin), and her blood sugar levels are difficult to control no matter what she and her doctor do. Her tongue is especially sensitive because of a combination of factors (neuropathy, medications, thrush, and possibly vitamin deficiencies due to the poor functioning of her digestive system). Except when the neuropathies in both feet cause occasional severe pain like burning pins and needles, her feet are numb, and she cannot feel anything that she steps on, placing her at risk of injuring herself without realizing it. She is very sensitive to any kind of infection, and her skin is slow to heal. Now just add to this mix a history of heart (coronary artery) disease, breast cancer, and rheumatoid arthritis, and you will understand the pain reference.

The one thing that seems clear from my family's experience with diabetes is that people tend to become remorseful only after symptoms have already developed, and at that point they are mostly irreversible. Furthermore, if you throw up your hands and say, "Ah, heck, forget about it!!!" the situation just goes from bad to worse.

My mother's narrative paints one distinct portrait of our family's experience with diabetes. Perhaps an equally compelling narrative is that of my first cousin Robert (my mother's nephew). For years, Robert and I commiserated about his childhood struggle with diabetes and about his loss of sight, kidney function, and toes after he became an adult. Whereas my mother was diagnosed with diabetes as an adult, my cousin's experience is particularly poignant because he was diagnosed at age eight—with a rare combination of both type 1 and type 2 diabetes. Robert has always provided me with the best insights into the complexities of life with diabetes:

> For me, living with diabetes is much more than dealing with just one disease. It is living with the inevitable threat of kidney failure, neuropathy, blindness, and heart disease, to name a few. It is living with the constant struggle of balancing the food I eat with how much insulin I take.
>
> My journey [of self-management] began one week into my seventh-grade summer vacation in 1981. I was thirteen. While my friends were out riding their bikes or playing ball in the park, I was learning how to measure two types of insulin and the difference between them. I was being taught how to give myself shots in my arms, thighs,

and stomach. I took two shots daily. In a time before fancy glucose meters, I learned how to draw blood, place it on a strip, time it, wipe it, time it again, then figure out the result by matching the color of the test strip to a color or number chart. I had to do this four times a day. I also had to test the sugar level in my urine—every time I used the bathroom.

All my doctors said that being healthy and staying healthy were up to me, that the choice was mine. Then I was told of all the horrible complications that could develop. That is a lot of pressure to put on anybody, let alone a thirteen-year-old. At the time, I was not told that there are many factors that may cause my blood sugar to fluctuate. Stress, mood, and infection are just a few of these kinds of factors. Back then, I felt like it was my fault if my sugar was high and that I would be "in trouble." It caused me sometimes to lie to my doctor when my levels were not normal. I would try so hard, and still my levels would be up; I felt like a failure. Many times when I'd give myself more insulin in hopes of getting my sugar under control, [my sugar level] would go too low, and then I would have an insulin reaction. My head would hurt, I would start to sweat, I would get shaky and confused, and all within just a few minutes. In response, I would usually drink some juice to bring my sugar back up. To this day the feeling of an insulin reaction is so scary to me. I have over-compensated many times, then my sugar goes too high. It was and is a constant struggle.

Only my immediate family knew that I had diabetes. I kept it a secret. I remember finding out that a person I knew had diabetes. We talked about it, but I still did not say anything. I was ashamed of it. It took me years to tell my friends.

When I was about eighteen years old, after months of countless tests and trips to different doctors, I was diagnosed with peripheral neuropathy. The pain in my legs was so bad that I was unable to walk for about three months. I remember needing a wheelchair during a family vacation. After a year or so, my symptoms subsided. During that year, I kept asking, "Why me?" I felt like I was a good person, but still I was hit with illness. On a more practical level, I tried so hard to take good care of myself. I did what the doctors told me. I checked my blood sugar often, I exercised, and I watched my diet. I just could not understand. I was so frustrated that I just gave up for close to two years. I stopped checking my blood sugar and took insulin only about once a week. The only thing I did right was stay away from sweets. I realize now that even though I felt good during this time, damage was being done, but I felt fine. Even now I often feel better when my sugar runs high than when it's at perfect levels.

Finally, I decided to start taking better care of myself, so I made an appointment to see my doctor. He referred me to a diabetes workshop. There I learned about the insulin pump. With the pump, I do not have to keep such a tight schedule. It gives me the freedom to eat when I want. My blood sugar levels were down to normal after just a few weeks of wearing it. By this time, I had had diabetes for a little more than a decade. I had not had any serious problems with my eyesight. That was about to change.

One morning while lying in bed, I noticed that when I closed one eye, some things disappeared. It turns out that I was developing a retinopathy from diabetes.[1] I underwent several laser treatments, but my vision still got worse. I had to stop driving, which took my independence from me. I then had to rely on others to get me places. I fell into a deep depression that lasted for years. I kept thinking that I had done something wrong, that it had to be the time that I stopped taking good care of myself. I kept telling myself that it was my fault. If only I had listened to the warnings. My vision was getting worse. I had more involved surgery to try to save my vision. After three vitrectomies, two surgeries to reattach my retina, surgery to implant a valve to drain excess fluid from my eye, and countless laser treatments, I have about 40 percent vision in one eye. My eyesight is such that if something is in my line of vision, I can see it. But if something is in one of my many blind spots, I don't. Only recently have I begun using my cane, but I'd much rather fake being able to see. I'm sure there are many people that I come in contact with who have no idea that I have any issues with my sight. The same way I kept my diabetes a secret, I try to keep my poor eyesight secret, but I've tripped and fallen too many times.

By then, I was starting to feel better emotionally and was even going to take some classes at the Braille Institute. At a routine doctor's appointment, I was referred to a nephrologist to check my kidney function. At that appointment, I got awful news. I was told that I would be on dialysis within five years. I didn't know how to deal with that information. I had seen my dad on dialysis, and I knew that I wouldn't be able to handle it. Well, four months later I was on dialysis.

Maybe I should have kept a better schedule. Maybe I shouldn't have drunk alcohol or smoked. Maybe experimenting with drugs wasn't a good idea. But even had I done everything "by the book," who knows if I'd still have the same complications. I know some people who did everything perfectly, and they're going blind. On the other hand, I know some people with diabetes who drink, smoke, and do drugs, and they're fine.

For the next two years, every Monday, Wednesday, and Friday I sat in a chair for three and a half hours, hooked up to an artificial kidney. I chose to take the first available time slot, 4:45 A.M. I figured that I'd just sleep through it. I was wrong. Many times I couldn't fall asleep, and if I did, I'd often be woken up by the beeps and alarms of the more than twenty stations. Or I'd get excruciating cramps in my hands, legs, or feet. I had three operations to give me an access for dialysis. In the meantime, I had tubes hanging from my chest. When those became infected, one was inserted in my neck.

Dialysis is horrible. For something that was keeping me alive, it sure did suck the life out of me. When I'd get home, I'd sleep for at least four hours. Then the rest of the day I'd feel drained and lethargic. Only on the days when I didn't have dialysis did I feel somewhat OK.

The only way I would not need dialysis would be to get a new kidney. After many blood tests, tissue typing, and meetings with surgeons, I was put on the transplant list. Several family members went through the screening process to give me a kidney. One by one, each was disqualified, mainly because diabetes runs in our family. Each time I got the news, it felt like a door slamming in my face. The news was especially bad when I considered that the average wait for a kidney is at least four years.

After hearing that my family could not give me a kidney, Lisa, a very close friend (to whom I am now engaged), offered to be a donor. She knew how much dialysis was wearing me down, both physically and emotionally. She was the one I would confide in when I had no one else to talk to. After thinking long and hard about it, I accepted her offer, but we still needed to find out if she was a match. As it turns out, she was. She completed the full workup, and we were going to set a date for surgery. Finally, an end to dialysis was near.

The day before we were going to set the date for surgery, I got the call. Miraculously, after being on the waiting list for about only eighteen months, a match had been found. I was so happy that only I would need to have surgery; Lisa would not have to go through the painful recovery of giving up a kidney. But at the same time I felt sadness for the family and loved ones of the person who had died. While my family and I were excited and cheerful, someplace else there was a family grieving. It's a strange, almost eerie feeling.

After twenty-three days in the hospital, I was allowed to go home. I had about fifteen new medications, and I had to take about twenty pills twice a day. I had to record my blood pressure and temperature three times a day, as well as how much I was urinating. Three times a week I had to be at the hospital by 6:00 A.M. to have blood drawn, then see the doctor at 8:00 A.M. to discuss the results. Because of the high doses of immunosuppressive drugs I was taking, I wasn't allowed to be in crowded places for three months. As time went by, everything decreased. Now, three years later, I have to see my transplant doctors only every three months and take only about nine pills twice a day.

No one ever thinks of pain as a gift, but pain is what lets our bodies know when something is wrong. Because of my neuropathy, I have little or no feeling in my lower legs and feet. When something is wrong or I am being hurt, I feel no pain. There have been times when I've cut my foot and not known until I notice a trail of blood.

I learned the hard way to keep shoes on my feet and never to go outside barefoot. About two years ago, I got a message from an elderly woman saying that she was in trouble. I thought that the call was from someone who lives on the opposite side of my apartment complex. I went to check on her, and, thankfully, she was OK. On my way back to my apartment, I realized how hot it was and that I was not wearing shoes. It was at that moment I knew something was wrong. Sure enough, in the short time it took me to walk about twenty yards, I had burned the bottoms of both feet, and they were already blistering. I saw my podiatrist that same day and was given an ointment and bandages to apply twice a day. Because my antirejection drugs keep my immune system low, I am prone to infection. Over the next year and a half, I battled an infection that settled in my foot. I was admitted to the hospital four times and had three surgeries. Ultimately, a toe was amputated. By the way, the call I got that day was a wrong number.

Right now I'm on the waiting list for a pancreas transplant. If all goes well, I will be insulin-free for the first time in twenty-two years. I will still have the health problems I do now, but they will not worsen and, if I'm lucky, may even improve. I will not have to worry about whether I give myself enough insulin when I eat or, worse, too much. There are a lot of risks involved with the operation and no guarantees, but there never are.

I think that if I had the chance to do it all again, I wouldn't change but one thing. I would have kept better blood sugar logs and would have always taken my insulin. (I don't drink often, but if I know that I'm going to be drinking, I check my blood before I leave, then check it again when I get home. This way I know for next time how my sugar will be affected.)

In 2005, while this book was in preparation, my cousin Robert died from complications of diabetes. I am still inspired by his courage, generosity, and compassion. Much has changed in the treatment of diabetes since 1981. Diabetes often attacks cells before the person even senses or feels any physical pain. That constitutes our biggest challenge in the battle to control diabetes. Most symptoms of diabetes manifest at the end stages of the disease and are signs of permanent disability (American Diabetes Association n.d.a). Prevention and early detection are therefore of paramount importance in order to begin managing the disease in time to ward off permanent disability or premature death. Both my mother and Robert learned how to maneuver through the challenges in life gracefully despite their battle with diabetes. As for my brothers, sisters, and me, the miracle in our lives is that we all have had each other to lean on—thanks to our parents' devotion and love.

The Caregiver's Role

My father, Thomas, has known my mother, Carmen, since she was fifteen years old. He knew he loved her and proposed marriage when she was nineteen years old. After proposing, he asked his godmother to ask Carmen's mother for Carmen's hand in marriage because both his parents and her father had died. That was the Mexican tradition. They were married on November 17, 1956.

When I asked my father to describe his caregiver role, he thoughtfully wrote the following:

> My responsibilities caring for my ailing wife for more than twenty years have been very informative. I am very thankful to the Almighty for giving me the opportunity to do my part, as my wife's husband, to help her. I try to do whatever I can to lessen her workload. Taking care of a loved one with diabetes is very complicated.
>
> I have assumed many responsibilities that I took for granted when I was working to support my family. But now that I am retired, I realize the work that my wife had been doing daily to raise our eight children for so many years. For example, I now do the grocery shopping and pay the bills. I help her with bathing and dressing. I also assist with the laundry and kitchen duties, including cooking preparations and so forth. I even bring her Holy Communion on Sundays when she can't join me at mass, which is very gratifying. . . .
>
> She hasn't driven a car for some time now—so I do the driving. We usually don't travel out of town much because it is very tiring for her. I take her to her doctor's appointments. I help her with her medication by opening the pill containers and setting out her weekly doses in a special container; this makes it easier for her to remember which medications she has already taken.

My father has certainly been very strong, quiet, and valiant during these difficult years. I felt so touched when I talked to him about his relationship with my mother. Yet he has given as much love and devotion to his children as he has to his wife. This, in turn, has grounded me in my own life and my life choices. My parents raised me to be an independent woman and clearly supported the work and career choice I have made as a preventive medicine physician—even if Mother didn't completely like it initially.

Unlike most of my siblings, who live close to my mother in southern California, I see her only two or three times a year now that I have married and moved to northern California. Yet I am still present in Mother's life. Each phone call lasts at least an hour, and, as my mother says, "It feels as if we are never apart." I love our phone conversations, but early in my career it was sometimes difficult when she asked me questions about her condition or newest treatment. She would get angry because she wanted me to be both her doctor and her daughter. But over time she has come to terms with the fact that I am her devoted daughter first, and it would be unethical for me to treat her. I do not think anything has been lost—we talk about everything, the way only mothers and daughters can.

My mother has always offered me such practical advice and amazing insight. She certainly has become an expert on many challenging issues, including the ethics of caring for patients, death and dying, and the essential elements of comforting the sick. If I have learned anything from her over these years, it has been to listen to the patient.

My mother describes diabetes as a never-ending struggle. Sometimes she gets upset because just as she gets over one thing, something else develops. She gets depressed sometimes and wishes it all would come to an end. But then she finds herself surrounded by her loving husband, children, and grandchildren, who say, "What would we do without you?" Those words renew her energy and faith and give her the strength to keep living. The most powerful form of love for her is the continual and dependable visits from family and friends—one of the benefits of all her toil and labor with eight kids. The children and grandchildren continue to come and go; every day it is a different family with a different array of needs, concerns, and stories.

As a physician, I have come to respect the gift of life and relationships and have learned to put my faith in a higher power when treatment fails because disease or disability is severe or death is imminent. My family narrative of diabetes puts a human face on a disease that is increasingly endangering the health of the Latino community. Managing the disease is a daily struggle that requires patience, vigilance, support, and courage from the person with diabetes as well as from those who support him or her. May our tapestry provide for others some insight into those challenges and encourage in them a renewed respect and sensitivity to the issues.

11

"Working toward Wholeness"

Gloria Anzaldúa's Struggles to Live with Diabetes and Chronic Illness

AnaLouise Keating

When first diagnosed with diabetes, your response was denial. This couldn't be happening, hadn't your body paid its dues? Why now, when you had the time and means to do good work? Digging in your heels you refused the reality—always your first line of defense to emotional pain. But the reality intruded: your body had betrayed you. . . .

Gradually the pain and grief force you to face your situation, the daily issues of living laid bare by the event that has split your world apart. You can't change the reality, but you can change your attitude toward it, your interpretation of it. If you can't get rid of your disease, you must learn to live with it. As your perception shifts, your emotions shift—you gain a new understanding of your negative feelings. By seeing your symptoms not as signs of sickness and disintegration but as signals of growth, you're able to rise from depression's slow suicide. By using these feelings as tools or grist for the mill, you move through fear, anxiety, anger, and blast into another reality.

—Gloria E. Anzaldúa, "now let us shift"

Born in 1942 in the Rio Grande Valley of south Texas to sixth-generation Mexican Americans, Gloria Anzaldúa was a leading cultural theorist and a highly innovative poet and fiction writer. As one of the first openly queer Chicana authors, Anzaldúa played a major role in redefining lesbian and Chicana/o identities. And as editor or coeditor of three groundbreaking multicultural-feminist anthologies—*This Bridge Called My Back: Writings by Radical Women of Color* (first published in 1981), *Making Face, Making Soul / Haciendo Caras: Creative and Critical Perspectives by Feminists of Color* (1990), and *this bridge we call home: radical visions for transformation* (2002)—she has played an equally vital role in redefining feminist theory and developing inclusionary multicultural movements. *Borderlands / La frontera: The New Mestiza*, Anzaldúa's most widely acclaimed book, first published in 1987, has become a classic of sorts—frequently anthologized and often cited by scholars in a wide range of academic disciplines, including (but not limited to) American, Chicana/o, composition, cultural, ethnic, literary, and queer studies.[1]

In all of her writings, Anzaldúa draws on her personal experiences to create what she calls "autohistoria-teoría," a type of reflective self-awareness employed in the service of social justice.[2] She uses her personal experiences—revised and in other ways redrawn—to develop a theoretical lens with which to reread and rewrite the cultural stories into which we are born. Through this lens, Anzaldúa exposes the limitations in existing paradigms and creates new stories of healing, self-growth, cultural critique, and individual/collective transformation.

Anzaldúa approached her health in a similar fashion, viewing her physical difficulties and chronic illness as containing messages, lessons to be learned and then shared with others. Thus, in this chapter's epigraph, taken from one of the final essays published during her lifetime, she depicts her struggle to accept the diagnosis, her attempts to live with diabetes by reframing its role in her life, and her efforts to learn from and survive her condition. Diabetes mystified her, and Anzaldúa tried to make sense of it in both her writing and her life. As she explains in an unpublished manuscript, "I am undergoing what feels like a tenderizing of soul, un amasamiento. But I don't have the language nor the set of images to describe this inner experience. How to talk about this sentiency?" (Anzaldúa 1999).

Anzaldúa was diagnosed with type 1 diabetes in 1992, at what she considered to be the height of her career. Type 1 diabetes is an autoimmune disease that accounts for only 5 to 10 percent of all diabetes cases. Unlike type 2 diabetes, which disproportionately affects people of color, type 1 affects Caucasians more often than other racial or ethnic groups (National Institute of Diabetes 2006). As Anzaldúa explains, "The body's immune system attacks and destroys the insulin-producing cells of the pancreas. Not able to enter the cells of the pancreas and not able to enter the cells, glucose builds up in the blood and the body's cells literally starve to death. To stay alive I have to inject insulin three times a day which means I have to prick my fingers to test my blood. Every day I make at least six holes in my body" (1999). Type 2 diabetes is generally preventable through attention to exercise and diet and can often be treated with oral medications and lifestyle changes. In contrast, type 1 diabetes is caused by a combination of genetic and environmental factors and requires more intensive management, including taking insulin by either injection or pump. There are to date no known cures.

The onset of diabetes drastically altered Anzaldúa's life on every level, from her self-image, daily activities, and relationships with family and friends to her writing projects and speaking engagements. The diabetes forced her to reexamine her sense of self-identity, her relationship to her body, her eating habits, her social life, and her worldview. Like many people diagnosed with a chronic illness, she initially reacted to her diagnosis with denial, disbelief, and anger. Yet even in these early stages, she began researching diabetes and altering her life to accommodate and treat this disease. She applied her extensive research skills to learning as much as possible about its causes, its effects on the body, treatment plans, and recent medical breakthroughs. She attributed the onset of diabetes to a combination of factors, including genetics, the pesticides in her childhood environment, a 1980 viral infection, and the stress she experienced as a self-employed, politically engaged writer attempting to support herself financially while producing provocative work that challenged existing belief systems.

Anzaldúa was extremely conscientious and diligent in managing the diabetes. She ate healthful foods, exercised regularly, and monitored and recorded her blood glucose levels several times a day; she carefully coordinated her exercise and her food intake with her blood levels and insulin injections, making adjustments as necessary. In addition to following a conventional treatment plan, which encompassed insulin injections and regular medical visits, she explored a variety of alternative healing techniques, including meditation, herbs, affirmations, subliminal tapes, and visualizations. Monitoring her health consumed her life and greatly interfered with her writing projects and her relationships with family and friends; however, despite these strenuous efforts, her blood sugar levels often careened out of control. This difficulty in stabilizing her blood sugar levels increased the severity of her condition and led to many health-related complications.

Diabetes might almost be considered a cluster of diseases because it affects so many organs of the body, including (but not limited to) the skin, mouth, eyes, feet, kidneys, heart, nerves, and stomach. Common diabetes-related complications include gastroparesis (the slowing or stoppage in the movement of food through the stomach), heart disease, stroke, high blood pressure, kidney disease, blindness (due to diabetic retinopathy, or damaged blood vessels in the retina), periodontal (gum) disease, and numbness of the feet or other extremities (sometimes leading to amputation). Anzaldúa experienced many complications, including severe gastrointestinal reflux, Charcot foot (softening of the foot bones), neuropathy (nerve degeneration), vision problems (blurred vision and burst capillaries requiring laser surgery), thyroid malfunction, and depression.

Anzaldúa's attempts to address her health needs proactively were complicated by her difficulty in retaining the insurance necessary for quality medical care. An independent scholar, she could not secure affordable health insurance, and for much of the year before her death she was without insurance and did not schedule adequate appointments with the various specialists treating her. In mid-May 2004, she passed away from diabetes-related complications.

Diabetes was only the most recent in a string of physical challenges that shaped Anzaldúa's entire life. At age three months, she began menstruating due to a "very rare hormonal disturbance or dysfunction" (Anzaldúa 2000, 19) that led to extremely painful menstruation throughout her childhood, the onset of puberty at age seven, and a complete hysterectomy thirty years later in March 1980. This extraordinarily early menstruation marked her as different, "abnormal," and "unnatural" very early in her life. As Anzaldúa explains in the following conversations, which took place in 1998 and 1999, she resisted the feelings of shame triggered by this sense of difference. Instead of trying to fit into some type of externally dictated physical normalcy—whether by denying, hiding, or attempting to alter her body—she accepted her physical differences and used them to forge an identity and a pathway outside the norm.[3] She developed a variety of strategies and created a spiritual worldview that enabled her to make sense of her life and to build inclusionary communities that profoundly challenged conventional identity categories.

A Conversation on Identity, Spirituality, Chronic Illness, and the Body

ALK: In earlier conversations, we've talked about recognizing that our flesh is spiritualized, and I'm interested in hearing you talk a little about how this idea goes with your health. For instance, diabetes has had a huge impact on your life, and before the diabetes, there were other things. . . . If the flesh is spiritualized, can you use the spirit to heal the flesh?

GEA: Yes, but you have to have a tremendous discipline. In a PBS show, I heard Carolyn Myss talk about her book *Why People Don't Heal and How They Can* [1997]. I was struck by her statement that in order to will your spirit to heal your body, you have to have great belief and great discipline. Our mind, our flesh, our energy system are all connected. What people think affects the body, and the body's physiology depends on how people think. If someone believes that modern medicine is the only answer to healing certain diseases, the diseased person is virtually helpless and depends on the doctor as an all-knowing God. She can't participate in her own healing; it all has to be done with injections and drugs and vitamin supplements. That belief system has to change. You have to start believing that "I *can* effect healing in my body. I'm not going to give in to external authoritative figures." But it's very hard to change a person's belief system.

ALK: Because everything outside us is saying the opposite—that *doctors* heal us.

GEA: Yes. You have to bypass the surface mind and maybe the middle mind, go into the deeper mind, and reprogram it. I really believe in subliminal tapes. We have these belief systems because someone told us over and over and over and over, "You're a bad boy, you're no good, you'll end up in jail, you always mess up." These repeated statements become a belief. We can change these beliefs by telling ourselves the opposite: "You're a worthy human being: you're loving, you're worthwhile." You can reprogram your belief system, but it takes a lot of energy, and sometimes it takes a lot of trauma—like the trauma I'm now going through with the diabetes. I have to open myself up to the belief system that I *can* heal myself, that my body can heal itself with the help of the spirit. That's one of the things I'm doing, and I don't know how long it's going to take. Maybe with some people it can take place instantaneously. With me, I spent the first year or so denying, resisting the fact that I had diabetes and another year being angry: "Did I deserve this? Where did I fuck up?" Now I've gotten to the point where I'm able to detach myself and say, "Gloria has drama, this chronic illness, because she gets out of balance." I don't have that detachment yet, but I'm working on it, and I'm waiting to see if there's a meaning to this disease, to this struggle: What is it teaching me? What am I learning?

What's the pattern I'm repeating, the belief system that I'm hooked into? Besides the genetic element, there's a component of the environment, of everything I've learned and of my belief systems. I can't blame it all on the physical body. I can explain the genetic part of it: it started when the Europeans came to this country and introduced things that the native peoples' immune systems couldn't handle. The more the mixture of Indian and whatever, the higher the rate of diabetes. Mexican Americans have diabetes, often more than Mexicans, whites, blacks, or Latinos. So there's a genetic, historical explanation for it. Then there's the environment: I breathed in a lot of chemicals when I was growing up—the pesticides and other poisons—but that still didn't do it, because when I moved to California, I started eating healthier and exercising. And there was one other, the third switch: I had developed a viral infection that provoked my immune system. Those three components—your genes, the environment, and an infection—guarantee that you'll get diabetes. So I fucked up with two of them. Environmentally, I could have started taking myself away from the poisons a little earlier, and I could have taken care of myself physically (the condition that led to the operation in 1980 was emotional and whatever). If I had prevented one component, I could probably have been borderline genetically, but never gone into type 1 diabetes. My responsibility is not with the genes, or maybe it is, maybe I chose to have these genes. But I am not at the point where I can detach completely and see myself struggling with this disease—say, if I activate the spirit, discipline the spirit, and ask it to heal the body, I believe that it will heal the body, it will heal. There are people who can do this, people who have remission, who are supposed to die from cancer, leukemia—sometimes it [the healing] will last for a long time, and sometimes they lose it and go back to the cancer. I think that self-knowledge as well as the information about the external world will give us the means to be able to heal our bodies.

ALK: I want to ask you a related question, about the various things that have impacted your identity. How would you say your experiences with physical illness/disease, like the very early and painful menstruation and diabetes, . . . have impacted the ways you define and think about *other* aspects of your identity, such as being Chicana, being queer, being female, and being spiritual?

GEA: They have impacted me totally. My body has played a large role in shaping my identity. To move from the physical illness and pain to the spiritual, I had to have that concrete, physiological experience. It set me apart from the herd. I had to figure out, "Why was I so different? Do I want to go with the herd, or should I resist and rebel?" My resistance to gender and race injustice stemmed from my physical differences, from the early bleeding and my early growth spurt (I reached my adult height when I was twelve, but I weighed only eighty pounds). I was extremely shy and vulnerable, and it all stemmed from the fact that people saw me as "flawed."

Part of my resistance was escape from the physical world that was so harsh, but the other part was a survival mechanism, a capacity I had to use to survive the physical world; I had to be able to go to the fantasy, the imaginal, and the spiritual. I was a dreamer, but I was the firstborn, and my mom discouraged everything impractical because she wanted me to help her with the household chores and with the other kids. She tried to force me—like the culture forces all women—to be a practical person connected with concrete reality when much of my life was really in the imaginal world. This is where I got the idea that spirituality is the ultimate resort of people who are extremely oppressed.

I developed this way of "being" in my mind, my imagination, and my spirit. It was a result of having a particular body and of my interactions with other Chicanos—especially my family. I found that whenever I got "normalized," when I began to fit in, something would slap me down again. I'd have another near-death experience or I'd have horrendous pain with my menstrual periods, pain so horrendous that I'd fall on the floor and go into convulsions. These experiences kept me from being a "normal" person. The way I identify myself subjectively as well as the way I act out there in the world were shaped by my response to physical and emotional pain.

The diabetes also has had a large impact on me. Here I was: I bought this house, I was finishing up my second attempt at a PhD, I was traveling all over the world, I was gone six months out of the year, I had all this energy, my writing was going great, and then POW! Diabetes. I had to stop everything. For a year, I could hardly function other than to take care of myself. I was doing some reading and writing, but I had to withdraw from people. At the beginning, my friends got pissed because I wasn't interacting with them. I was so busy just surviving from day to day. I realized that I was going too fast and overextending. I love to be involved with everything, but when I'm doing too many things, I don't do anything justice. I might have been getting too ambitious, I might have been thinking myself a "big shot" as a writer on the fringes of the academy. I never got into the "star" mentality, but there were certain temptations. The diabetes just knocked all that out. I had to go back to basics: "What do I want from life? What do I really want to do?" I wanted to stay home, write more, and not travel as much. Now I can't travel as much because my neuropathy causes my feet to swell. I get dizzy and mentally foggy when I'm having a hypo [hypoglycemic attack, or very low blood glucose level]. I lose my equilibrium and fall. Gastrointestinal reflex has me throwing up and having diarrhea—sometimes simultaneously. At one point, I thought I was going to have to start wearing diapers. I tell you, things like these change your image of yourself, your identity.

Some greater self or total self is guiding me to be a certain way; it has instructions for how I should live my life, instructions that the "little me" subselves don't know. Now I'm trying to get information on which way to go; I'm trying to listen more to my inner voice because before diabetes I was too much out in the world. But it's also not good when I hide in my castle. I have to find balance, so I go back and forth. Evidently, I haven't balanced my body because my blood sugar keeps changing. No matter how well you're taking care of yourself, no matter how controlled your diabetes is, there's always that percent[age] that's failing. The whole thing with diabetes is having a balance in your blood sugar; if you don't have a balance, it affects your eyes. I had blood clots; I had hemorrhaging in my eyes almost two years ago and had to have laser surgery, or I'd have gone blind. The immune system killed the thyroid hormone–producing cells. I gained thirty pounds, which I haven't been able to lose. I have to be on a supplement. I walk around like a duck, my metabolism is so low. How do I balance all this? I have to have some exercise, the food has to be nutritious, the amount of insulin has to be in conjunction with how much I eat and exercise. Sometimes I have to take more insulin and eat less; other times I have to eat more and exercise less or exercise when my blood sugar is higher. It's very dangerous when the insulin is high because it strains your kidneys, your heart, your blood vessels in your eyes, *everything*. But for me it's scarier when it gets low because I could go into a coma. Before, I could tell when I was going into a hypo because I'd start sweating; I'd be hot and itchy; plus, I couldn't think or hold a thought. With no food going into the brain, the thinking function gets disrupted. Now I don't work up a sweat. I could be having a conversation with somebody, and all of a sudden it hits me, and I barely have enough time to take some glucose tablets. So, it's all about balancing, but it takes so much energy, energy that I resent having to give to diabetes when I could be using it for my reading and writing—that's where the anger came from. My body has played a large role in shaping my identity. . . .

ALK: Que feo. I had not realized the hypos were so severe. But that's what I thought and what I tell my students: since first reading your work, I've believed that your body played an enormous role in shaping other aspects of your identity.

GEA: The importance I place on the body may also be a reaction against the New Agers, who want to transcend the body. You have to work everything from the body. They're trying to do the opposite: they ignore the body.

ALK: Sometimes New Age people believe that they can immediately materialize whatever they want just by visualizing it.

GEA: Some have no idea of the full script they've programmed for themselves or have been programmed with. You have to work through all the layers.[4]

Conclusion

As this brief conversation indicates, Anzaldúa's efforts to make sense of and live with the diabetes were both complicated *and* enhanced by her holistic worldview. Throughout her career, she posited a radical interconnectedness among body, mind, spirit, and soul. As she asserts in *Borderlands / La frontera*, "every cell in our bodies, every bone and bird and worm has spirit in it" (1987, 36).[5] This meaning-filled, holistic belief system compelled Anzaldúa to view her physical health within a larger framework. She read her body as a text with messages about her life, with instructions for living. In this holistic framework, her body served as a bridge of sorts between her inner self, or what she describes in the preceding dialogue as an "inner voice" or "total self," and her conscious mind, or what she refers to as "the 'little me' subselves."

Yet Anzaldúa had great difficulty in interpreting her own embodied text; the diagnosis of diabetes was difficult for her to accept, and she repeatedly questioned its meaning in her life. She depicts some of these difficulties in the following passage from "now let us shift." Using a second-person voice, she narrates her reactions to the doctor's diagnosis:

> Three weeks after the doctor confirms your own diagnosis [. . .] the reality of having a disease that could cost you your feet . . . your eyes . . . your creativity . . . the life of the writer you've worked so hard to build . . . life itself . . . finally penetrates[. . . .] You're furious with your body for limiting your artistic activities, for its slow crawl toward the grave. You're infuriated with yourself for not living up to your expectations, not living your life fully. You realize that you use the whip of your ideals to flagellate yourself and the masochist in you gets pleasure from your suffering. Tormented by self-contempt you reproach yourself constantly and despair. Guilt and bitterness gnaw your insides and, blocked by your own grand expectations, you're unable to function. (2002, 550, unbracketed ellipses in the original)

Anzaldúa went through a number of stages as she grappled with this chronic illness, beginning with denial and moving through anger, depression, and despair. By the late 1990s, she had shifted into a stage of self-reflection, in which she attempted to fit the diabetes' meaning within larger life patterns. Thus, for example, she read the diabetes as a "wound" and speculated that it contained a message (a warning of sorts) about imbalances in her life: "The spirit eating me from the inside was telling me I was being eaten alive by my responsibilities to others. The academy was not giving back to my spirit what I in my teaching images and words was giving it" (1999).

Anzaldúa continued to reflect on the diabetes' meaning in her life—not just for herself, but for others as well. Two years later, she had extended her insights even further and tried to redefine "health" in more holistic terms. As she explained in a 2001 interview Irene Lara had with her,

> I don't define health as the absence of disease, but as learning to live with disease, with dysfunction, with wounds, and working toward wholeness. If you're human you don't have a whole integrated body, being, soul, whatever, because of the traumas and difficult lessons we've gone through. Health also has to do with holism. You can't just heal your appendix; you have to look at your whole body, your mind, and your soul. They're all one. Since Descartes we've split them and view them as separate compartments, but they're interwoven. I believe in holistic alliances, holistic health where you consider the whole, not just the part. In that respect, taking it into spiritual activism, you don't only consider the best interest of your group, your organization, your race. You consider the best interest of the whole, which means white people, black people, *everybody*. This perspective makes me a "race traitor." . . . When you start thinking about holistic alliances you're stepping across barriers, gatekeepers to cultures that want to keep you out, and your own culture that wants to keep you out. You're given only two choices: assimilate completely or separate out completely. (Lara 2005, 51, emphasis in original)

I have quoted this passage at length because it beautifully illustrates how, after living with diabetes for almost ten years, Anzaldúa had developed ways to acknowledge her personal concerns, yet also to move outward, connecting her physical body to the body politic and using her personal struggles with her health to refine her theory of spiritual activism. Anzaldúa's assertions here are especially remarkable given the diabetes' increasingly severe effects on her body and life. By 2001, diabetes-related complications had drastically altered her life: she was far less mobile; she could no longer go on hikes or take long walks; she did not feel confident driving long distances because of her vision problems. Her health needs had also greatly increased, making it difficult to complete her writing projects on time, to keep up with her research and the large amount of correspondence she received, or to go on the speaking engagements that she required to support herself financially.[6]

At the time of her passing, Anzaldúa was still working through these issues and attempting to gain an even greater understanding of diabetes' meaning in relation to her holistic worldview. Despite her inability to make full sense of the diabetes, she refused to reject her holistic beliefs. In conversations with friends, unpublished essays such as "S.I.C.: Spiritual Identity Crisis" (Anzaldúa 1999), and e-mail exchanges with disability scholars, she continued to reflect on these issues as well as on many others. Her self-reflective analyses and provocative insights offer vital building blocks for those of us struggling to understand chronic illness and the complex interrelationship among body, spirit, and soul.

12

When the Joys of Pregnancy Bring a Shocking Discovery

A Latina Epidemiologist Confronts Gestational Diabetes

Lorena García

Going in for my oral glucose-tolerance test was just another routine in my prenatal care. Testing for gestational diabetes mellitus (GDM) occurs between the twenty-fourth and twenty-eighth week (the seventh month) of pregnancy in order to safeguard the health and well-being of both the pregnant woman and the developing fetus. This is the time when the fetus accomplishes most of its body growth and when intervention can prevent complications if GDM is present.

Being diagnosed with GDM came as a shock. I was immediately alarmed because I knew from my training as an epidemiologist and public-health researcher that GDM might have life-threatening consequences for me and my baby during and after pregnancy (which I discuss later). But then I thought that the result must be a mistake, a false positive. I was not at high risk; in fact, I had almost *none* of the risk factors.

There was no history of diabetes on either side of my family. My mother had not experienced GDM during any of her three pregnancies and had maintained a very healthy lifestyle, with a good diet, appropriate weight, exercise, and medical care. I had always followed her example, being conscientious about my health and lifestyle. Growing up, I recall always having fruits and vegetables at home, with soft drinks and candy only for very special occasions. My grandmother taught me that having a good diet would lead to a healthy body. She told me that she used to scold my mother if she bought candy with her allowance and instead encouraged her to eat fruit. My mother actively encouraged my participation in sports; she enrolled me in swimming lessons and supported me when I joined the track and softball teams at school. She recalled her own fond memories of participating in sports in her youth and wanted me to have the same experiences. She told me that my grandmother would jump rope with her when she was a little girl, saying that exercise would give her a good physique. Good hygiene was another aspect of health that was important to my mother and grandmother, and they taught me to be diligent with my personal hygiene at all times.

I did, however, possess two unmodifiable risk factors for gestational diabetes: I was older than age twenty-five and a Latina. Becoming pregnant in my late thirties was a conscious choice that I made early in my career. I wanted to finish my doctoral degree and begin a career in academia in order to offer a better life for my spouse, children, and myself. I was raised to believe that both educational attainment and family were extremely important. But I remember an incident during graduate school that brought home for me the knowledge that this dual focus was not the norm for everyone. After the sudden death of an administrator at the university, my classmates and I were discussing what we wanted others to remember us for after we died. Many said that they wanted to be remembered for their work; one in particular stated that she wanted to be remembered as a great employee, one that always got the job done. Their responses puzzled me, but this last one shocked me: Why would anyone want to be remembered as a great employee? Was this how they viewed their existence? I felt sorry for this classmate and thought that surely she must have other goals in life. When it was my turn, I responded, "I want to be remembered as having been a great friend, a wonderful wife, a good daughter and sister, someone who made a difference in others' lives, and a great epidemiologist and researcher." My classmates looked at me in puzzled silence, as if I had said the wrong thing.

During my pregnancy, most of the health-care personnel who treated me behaved as if, because I was a Latina, having diabetes was somehow normal. But for me it was not normal. I questioned myself: How could I have prevented this? How could I, a well-educated Latina who had planned her pregnancy for so long and gone to such lengths to ensure her own health and her baby's health, be a diabetic? It just couldn't be possible. I come from a long line of strong-willed and intelligent Mexican women who had had healthy pregnancies. I had followed the advice of my mother, my grandmother, and my aunts.

I remember my mother emphasizing that when she got pregnant with me, she immediately went to consult a specialist (i.e., an obstetrician-gynecologist) who came highly recommended by friends and family. She encouraged me to do the same because I would need to trust this individual with my and my baby's health. She also warned me to eat well during my pregnancy, expressing concern that I often would forget to eat when I became consumed with work: "Necesitas una buena nutrición, tu cuerpo necesita muchas vitaminas por el desgaste normal durante el embarazo, así tendrás un bebe sano y fuerte" (You need good nutrition, your body needs many vitamins for normal gestation; that's how you'll have a healthy, strong baby).

My grandmother also emphasized taking good care of myself: "Cuídate mucho, debes de acudir a un ginecólogo para tu embarazo. Cuida mucho tu aseo personal, para evitar una enfermedad. Y no te creas en los mitos de que debes comer por dos, es mal para ti y el bebe" (Take good care of yourself; you must seek a gynecologist for your pregnancy. Take care with your personal hygiene to avoid illness. Also, don't believe those myths that tell you to eat for two; it is not good for you and the baby).

So where had I gone wrong? I had chosen a profession that was stressful, and there had been plenty of times when I did not take as good care of myself as I would have liked. Nevertheless, my female relatives also had had stressful lives, yet they did not have gestational diabetes.

Prior to becoming pregnant, I had sought preconceptional care. I consulted with physicians and had my overall health evaluated. My husband had been just as involved and had been conscientious about his medical care. I began taking prenatal vitamins, continued my healthy lifestyle, and avoided any harmful exposures. I tried to read as much health literature as possible so that I could be better prepared for my pregnancy. Because my family had a history of good health, I assumed I would have an uncomplicated pregnancy. My parents had always had health care while I was growing up; whether we lived in the United States or Mexico, preventive health care was something I had come to expect. A high-risk pregnancy was the furthest thing from my mind; the prenatal screenings were just supposed to be routine.

As I lectured in my courses about GDM and the risk factors involved, I had difficulty seeing myself as someone with this health condition. It was as if I were speaking about someone else. It took quite a while for me to come to terms with the diagnosis. I also had irrational feelings of guilt—I had somehow done something to put my baby at risk—even though my mother repeatedly reassured me that it was not my fault.

I was deeply concerned about my baby's health. I was mortified at the thought that I could be harming my unborn baby. I prayed and asked God to give me strength. I contacted friends, family, and colleagues, anyone I could think of who might have some insight or information. The literature I found did not provide me with all of the answers I now needed.

I finally decided to participate in a GDM study, hoping I could find some answers to my questions. A part of me also hoped that the results might help other pregnant women. Maybe GDM will be a thing of the past someday! As part of the study, I was given the usual care for gestational diabetes: a consultation with a registered dietician and a nurse educator. My husband accompanied me to these appointments, offering me emotional support. The dietician went through my diet and made some changes: I was to reduce the number of fruits and breads or cereals I consumed and replace them with more protein and fats. For me, this was quite a change because I had always eaten a low-fat, high-fiber diet. The diet outline she gave me reminded me of the Atkins diet (which eliminates almost all carbohydrates), to which I was strongly opposed because of the high fat and cholesterol content. No wonder some diabetics go on to develop heart disease! I was not very good at diets, but I knew I was going to have to be good at this one for my baby's well-being.

Meeting with the nurse educator was easier; she taught me how to check my blood glucose with an electronic glucose monitor four times a day, every day: once in the morning while I was fasting and again two hours after breakfast, lunch, and dinner. Even though the lancets that drew blood from the tips of my fingers were small, they still hurt. I was then taught how to handle safely the test strips and lancets, which were later to be returned to the hospital in a sealed biohazard container. I couldn't imagine having to perform this routine four times a day for the next three months. It was going to be a big change in my lifestyle; I had never monitored my diet so closely and received instant feedback on my food choices (via the glucose monitor).

This experience gave me a new respect for diabetics. I realized that, unlike the situation for most diabetics, my condition would last only during my pregnancy. I realized how fortunate I was that I would not have to go through this routine for the rest of my life. It gave me an insight that I could not have obtained through reading books or journals or attending conferences. At home, both my husband and I changed our eating habits; when we went out, we had to select places that had the types of food I could eat. When I visited my family, meals had to be modified for my needs, and we made special trips to the grocery store so I could adhere to my new diabetic diet. Everyone dear to me changed their lives to accommodate me, the effects rippling out beyond my baby and me to encompass family and friends. I no longer ate when I was hungry but followed a schedule of meals equally spaced out throughout the day. I quickly discovered which of my favorite foods were off-limits: high glucose readings kept me away from bagels, fruits, tortillas, and pasta. I ate foods that I would not normally choose, such as peanut butter and cottage cheese. The glucose monitor became like an appendage; it went everywhere with me. I discovered how difficult it could be to check my blood glucose levels wherever I happened to be at the time. I personally did not feel comfortable testing my blood in public; I preferred doing it in my office or home, but this was not always possible. I had to overcome being self-conscious about testing myself in public places such as restrooms.

My parents and, indeed, my entire family were fascinated as they watched me test my blood sugar—after all, I was the only one in the family who had ever had to do so. All the attention was rather amusing: my mother, father, sister, and niece intently observing me as I went through the process of testing my blood glucose. They were quiet at first, then everyone spoke at the same time: my father, "¡Ay, mi niña, como te ha de doler! ¿Cuantas veces al día lo haces?" (Oh, my dear, how it must hurt! How many times a day do you have to do this?); my mother, "Hija, no te preocupes, todo saldrá bien" (Daughter, don't worry, everything will turn out fine); and then my sister and niece, "Can I check my blood glucose?" Out of concern and curiosity, my parents told their physician that their daughter had been diagnosed with gestational diabetes and asked him to test them as well. It did not surprise me when their blood glucose test results came back normal.

At first, I didn't want my relatives to find out about my condition. I wasn't sure yet how I felt about it myself yet, especially considering that none of them had diabetes. In my tight-knit family, "family" meant both immediate and extended relatives: aunts, uncles, cousins, grandparents, and godparents. But when my mother contacted my relatives in Mexico about my situation, everyone was supportive. My mother kept them up-to-date on my health status. I discovered that it helped me to communicate with my loved ones; they were reassuring and told me that I was a smart woman, "una mujer con educación" (an educated woman), and that, as an epidemiologist, I would know how to take good care of myself. They had faith that I would have a healthy pregnancy and promised to pray for both my baby and me. I felt better, much better. My husband got used to our receiving phone calls from Mexico regularly on Saturday afternoons.

As hard as it was for me to change my lifestyle, I focused on doing it for my baby's health. I walked, I exercised. Throughout my last trimester, I followed my new diet religiously. Despite these efforts, I gained forty pounds! I was horrified! My doctors were not concerned, though, because they said that I had been a bit thin and had had a low level of body fat when I got pregnant. Despite my weight gain, I was still within my appropriate body mass index (a weight-for-height measure that indicates whether one's weight is within the normal range). Go figure, no one was more surprised than I was.

Looking back, I wish some of my physicians had better informed me about GDM or spent more time discussing my health. At the health-care facility where I sought prenatal care, the ob-gyns worked as a team so that all patients and physicians would become acquainted. I was not enthusiastic about this approach at first, but I quickly changed my mind. My regular ob-gyn was always in a hurry to get out of the room; she would sometimes listen to my concerns, but her answers sounded like a scripted monologue. On more than one occasion as I left the facility, I would see her at her computer, on the phone, or in conversation with her assistants. I thought to myself, This is what she was rushing to? I felt that I did not matter as a patient and that my health was not important to her. So I decided to find a new doctor. My new ob-gyn immediately stood out: she spent more time with me, listening and answering my questions. I felt that I was important to her as a patient. I also liked the fact that she, like me, had had her pregnancies after age thirty-five and had been diagnosed with gestational diabetes. She was sympathetic, and I felt safe with her.

On the day I went into labor, I was both excited and nervous. My husband and parents were with me during the labor and delivery, and I was very glad to have them with me during this special time. I began labor around 5:00 A.M.; at first, I wasn't sure I was in labor, but the increasing pain and intensity of the contractions soon dispelled any doubts. I was quite calm, considering this baby was my first, and waited until 10:00 A.M. to tell everyone. My husband was nervous, but not my mother; she had been through this process. She asked me to describe my symptoms and calmly told me it was too soon to go to the hospital. She monitored my progress and let me know what to expect at each stage of labor. She kept reassuring me that everything would be all right and that we didn't need to hurry. It would be better to labor at home during the initial stages because once I was in the hospital, I would not be allowed to move around, which would substantially slow down the labor. She then told me to take a hot shower because it would help the labor progress.

At around 11:00 A.M., I began to get ready because I had a prenatal care visit scheduled for that afternoon at 1:00. At my appointment, I discovered that I was five centimeters dilated. My ob-gyn was amazed at how well I had been managing my contractions; she squeezed my hand and told me I was ready to check into the hospital.

My son was born on his due date, June 18, 2004, at 1:59 A.M. He was healthy, weighing 7 pounds, 15.5 ounces and measuring 20.5 inches. I felt so fortunate that a loving family surrounded me and my son during labor and delivery. Even though my regular ob-gyn was not supposed to be on call that day, she went out of her way to make sure that she was present to deliver my son. The next morning she returned to see how we were doing. I was touched because I knew that she had two small children of her own and probably had not had enough sleep.

During labor and delivery, both my blood glucose levels and my son's were constantly monitored. They were normal. Finally, I was able to bring closure to my experience and take my son home.

Gestational Diabetes Mellitus

In the United States, 4 percent (135,000) of pregnant women annually experience GDM, and it is estimated that many more women are unaware that they are at risk for it. Research indicates that the prevalence of GDM is increasing (Ferrara et al. 2002; Ferrara et al. 2004; Dabelea et al. 2005). The condition cannot be prevented, but with proper medical attention it can be treated and maintained under control. It is of major public-health importance because if untreated, it can lead to life-threatening consequences and chronic health conditions for both the mother and the unborn child (Casey et al. 1997; Joffe et al. 1998; Hedderson, Ferrara, and Sacks 2003).

The Expert Committee on the Diagnosis and Classification of Diabetes Mellitus defines GDM as "any degree of glucose intolerance with onset or first recognition during pregnancy" (2003, S10). Hormones released during pregnancy play a key role in glucose intolerance. This type of diabetes occurs only during pregnancy and usually disappears soon after delivery. Women who have had GDM are at higher risk for developing type 2 diabetes and GDM in the future. For many women, GDM is the first time they have had exposure to any type of diabetes.

Risk factors for GDM include a family history of diabetes and obesity as well as a personal history of GDM and glucose intolerance, or glycosuria. If a woman has any of these risk factors, she is considered at high risk. She is considered to be at low risk if she fits the following profile: "less than 25 years, normal prepregnancy weight, not a member of an ethnic/racial group with a high prevalence of diabetes (i.e., Hispanic American, Native American, Asian American, African American, or Pacific Islander), no known diabetes in first-degree relatives, no history of abnormal glucose tolerance, and no history of a poor obstetric outcome" (Setji, Brown, and Feinglos 2005, 18; also see American College of Obstetricians and Gynecologists 2001). Prevalence estimates of GDM vary according to the diagnostic criteria used (Coustan 1995; Turok, Ratcliffe, and Baxley 2003; Setji, Brown, and Feinglos 2005). Mexican American women have a higher prevalence than white women: 4.5 to 5.1 percent for Mexican American women versus 1.5 to 3.4 percent for white women. In one study, the prevalence of GDM increased over a three-year period: from 2.8 percent to 5.1 percent for Mexican American women and from 1.9 percent to 3.4 percent for white women.

The American College of Obstetricians and Gynecologists recommends that all women be screened for GDM during their second trimester, between the twenty-fourth and twenty-eighth week of pregnancy. However, a woman who has had a previous pregnancy with GDM is screened earlier, in the first trimester of pregnancy.

A woman with any one of the risk factors for GDM is scheduled for an oral glucose-tolerance test. The woman's blood is drawn to determine a baseline fasting glucose level. She is then given 50 grams of oral glucose and within one hour has her blood drawn again. If the plasma glucose level is higher than 140 milligrams per deciliter she is further tested at a later time. This later test is more extensive and time consuming; women should be prepared to spend an entire morning and should either bring someone with them or be dropped off and picked up. Again, the woman's blood is drawn while she is fasting. Afterwards she is given 100 grams of oral glucose, and her blood is drawn three times at one-hour intervals. GDM is diagnosed if two or more of the plasma glucose levels exceed established thresholds. (There are two competing sets of guidelines, both endorsed by the American Diabetes Association and the American College of Obstetricians and Gynecologists.)

A woman who is diagnosed with GDM is monitored more closely throughout her pregnancy and delivery. If the woman's blood glucose is not kept at a healthy and constant level, then the blood that reaches the fetus through the placenta contains too much glucose. The fetus's system will work hard to counteract the high blood glucose level by producing additional insulin, but it is not sufficient. The excess blood glucose is converted into fat. Thus, the fetus gains too much weight and is very large for its gestational age, a condition known as macrosomia. Macrosomia can create complications during delivery such as shoulder dystocia (an injury that occurs during the time the fetus travels through the birth canal) and fetal distress, which may necessitate a cesarean section. The newborn infant may then be at higher risk for respiratory distress syndrome and later in life is at higher risk for obesity and type 2 diabetes. For pregnant women, complications due to uncontrolled GDM can include preeclampsia, a serious condition that includes all of the following: hypertension (high blood pressure), proteinuria (abnormal levels of protein in the urine), edema (swelling of the face and hands), urinary tract infections, and cesarean section. Most important, though, these complications can be prevented if pregnant women with GDM receive proper medical care and nutritional counseling and engage in physical activity.

The treatment for GDM depends on the woman's individual situation. For some women, a diet and exercise plan is sufficient. Others require insulin as well. It is important that women meet with a registered dietician and nurse educator as soon as they are diagnosed with GDM to formulate an appropriate diet plan and learn how to test their blood sugar four times a day. They will also be asked to keep a journal of their blood glucose readings and review them with their health-care practitioner during their regular prenatal checkups in order to ensure that the current approach is effective. During the course of the pregnancy, these women may receive additional ultrasounds to monitor the fetus's health and development. During labor and after delivery, the women's blood glucose levels are monitored closely, and insulin may be given if the levels are high. In addition, the health-care providers watch closely for potential complications due to GDM.

One Year Later

My experience with GDM seems as if it happened long ago, and yet it has been only one year. Would I have done anything differently? No. I look at my son, and I thank God that he is here with us.

I am proactive about my health and my family's health. I have made sure to take my son to every scheduled visit with his pediatrician and give him the best preventive health care available. It is rewarding to have the pediatrician say that my son is healthy, happy, and thriving; it is exactly what I want to hear. To lower his risk for diabetes or other health problems later in life, I provide him with varied and nutritious foods and activities that allow him to have fun and be physically active at the same time. But they would have been priorities for me anyway, even if I had not had gestational diabetes. I have come to realize that my healthy lifestyle, family values, and profession as an epidemiologist were the determining factors in my healthy decisions.

Various health specialists have offered different perspectives as to why I was diagnosed with GDM: some have said it is probable that I carry the diabetes gene, whereas others believe it is because of my advanced age at first pregnancy, and still others believe that it is an interaction between the diabetes gene and advanced age at first pregnancy. For now, because I have no family history of diabetes, I believe it was most likely a combination of my advanced age and the recent stricter diagnostic criteria for the oral glucose-tolerance test. More than one health-care professional has told me that my blood glucose readings were borderline, and had I been pregnant a few years ago, I would not have been considered diabetic. In fact, a prominent diabetes expert (who also has diabetes) commented that some of my blood glucose readings were too low and argued that I should have increased my food intake.

Communicating my experience in the classroom has also helped me to become a better professor. When I lecture about GDM, I share my experience with students so that they can gain a more personal perspective. I hope that sharing my experience will help them become better health-care providers. Having GDM has also made me aware of all of the positive and negative realities of the health-care system. Although I lecture on and promote preconceptional care, I realize that not all health-care facilities are prepared for or want to provide this service. It was not easy for me to schedule a preconceptional visit. I was questioned often and made to feel that preconceptional care was not important enough to justify a separate appointment. Some health-insurance plans do not cover preconceptional care, and others will cover it only if the woman is considered high risk (i.e., during pregnancy) or if the primary care physician makes a referral.

So what now? When and if I decide to get pregnant again, I will go through preconceptional care as before. I will eat well, exercise, and make sure that I take care of my health. I will try to prepare myself mentally for pregnancy. I realize that I will probably have to go through the GDM testing and counseling much earlier on, probably around the second or third month of pregnancy. So, in the meantime, I guess I had better enjoy eating lots of fruits and pasta, and, yes, once in a while treating myself to strawberry Häagen-Dazs ice cream and Godiva chocolate truffles.

13

A Retrospective on the Narratives of Latina Health

What We Can Learn

Angie Chabram-Dernersesian
and Adela de la Torre

The narratives gathered in this book illustrate firsthand what it is like for a selected group of Latinas to experience and combat serious, chronic, and debilitating illnesses within various representational, social, cultural, ideological, and intersubjective contexts. Yet the value of these narratives is not just testimonial. They also provide important information regarding the naming, construction, and translation of illness and healing experiences by Latinas from different generations, social and geographical contexts, and worldviews. In addition, these Latinas articulate the significance of naming their ailments, using mixed treatment modalities and therapeutic speech, exploring identity formation, and being supported by family and community in caregiving and healing.

Metaphors of Illness and Naming Practices

In *The Wounded Storyteller*, Arthur W. Frank suggests that "seriously ill people are wounded not just in body but in voice" and that they "need to become storytellers in order to recover the voices that illness and its treatment often take away" (1995, xii). He urges his readers to "hear" the body in the ill person's speech. Our Latina narratives provide numerous opportunities for hearing this type of embodied speech, including instances where speech draws on bilingual and figural expressive language or on metaphors of illness that attach specific meanings to the illness experience.[1] For example, Adaljiza Sosa-Riddell provides a complex description of Parkinson's disease that brings together mind, body, and spirit in these striking metaphors: "My spirit passed through walls and bars so all of my thoughts could soar, but now my body has become a stone wall, that *prison* of iron bars" (emphasis added). Her descriptions of her immobility repeatedly conjure up the idea of being buried alive: her body feels "completely frozen, gridlocked inside." In this way, she articulates how Parkinson's targets her body, mind, and spirit differentially: whereas she does not feel any loss of intellectual powers, she has to live and work with severe physical limits to her mobility that make doing the simplest of daily tasks very difficult. Yet she struggles unceasingly to maintain her independence, a legacy of her working-class childhood, which forced her to assume responsibility and self-sufficiency beyond her years, as when she overcame her fear of black widow spiders to kill them in a dark basement she had been told to clean. As a child, Sosa-Riddell was exposed to pesticides in the fields of California, which she feels is a possible cause of her current condition, as Gloria Anzaldúa also believes of her diabetes and Clara Lomas of her thyroid condition. Although no one can say whether environmental toxins caused these illnesses, the exposure to them is another manifestation of how these women's working-class Chicana childhoods position them to speak about and interpret their illnesses.

Lomas's description of living and working with Graves' disease also emphasizes the importance of independence in the face of a chronic, life-long illness, but her letters evoke a contrasting set of metaphors about health. She presents the image of a body in constant movement—in a *revolution* against her—with frightening heart palpitations, inordinate perspiration, racing thoughts, double vision, and weight loss. Her illness is synonymous with speed, "unfathomable speed," "warp speed," yet even at this pace Lomas realizes that "there aren't enough hours in the day." In addition, living with an unstable metabolism often means managing a metabolic *roller coaster*, which can plummet her from the highest to the lowest energy levels and requires careful balancing of lifelong medications as well as the demands of career and work. Because Graves' disease is an autoimmune illness, her constant battle is to regulate her own body not to revolt against itself. This disease is almost unknown within the literature on Latina health, so Lomas provides a unique perspective, and we hope

Latinas and their doctors will see through her eyes the consequences of failing to diagnose it.

Like Lomas, Concha Delgado Gaitan also speaks of feeling that her body has a mind of its own, but her illness leads her on a quest for balance between life and work, body and spirit. She ultimately realizes that the body and spirit are not in opposition, but that she can harness both of them for healing. Similarly, Anzaldúa's discovery that her body had "betrayed her" initiates an intensely spiritual quest in which her illness becomes a metaphor for everything that separates her from the mainstream and gives her the courage to define a self-identity as a queer feminist.

Angie Chabram-Dernersesian's redacted narrative of a Latina living with hypertension—rising and going to bed in time with her medications— also renders an account of a life regulated by medications whose dosage must constantly be adjusted. For this Latina, the effects of hypertension are expressed in metaphors of driving up a hill, ascending in an airplane, and feeling as if her head is an inflated balloon. This markedly visual language emphasizes elements of height or inflation. However, the Latina's health challenge does not end here: lowering her blood pressure has meant enduring serious side effects of medications that can make her feel even worse than when she started taking them, persevering with her treatment, and working patiently with the doctor little by little until together they find the right combination of pills.

Hypertension and heart disease are in combination the biggest single threat to Latina/o lives, and this Latina's narrative gives an important human voice to how Latinas feel as we treat this deadly disease. The feeling of inflation is not only a sensation, but also a metaphor for how perceptions of the disease may impact compliance with treatment regimens. As with other chronic health conditions, daily vigilance and knowledge of how to manage this disease are necessary to prevent a false sense of security that tells us las pastillas are unnecessary or, worse, are always causing our symptoms. Thus, as we compare these descriptors of symptoms, it behooves us to note how they may be important in developing a new vocabulary for explaining treatment.

Delgado Gaitan's lupus narrative also provides striking illustrations of the importance of unbridled expressive speech and creative metaphors. The process of translation and comparison are essential to the work of Latina health, as when she tries to quantify her pain: "I ached for words to fill in the blanks of the doctor's quiz: a new language I resented learning, that of disabilities. . . . It was too much work to label the physical characteristics of pain. I searched for descriptors to capture the essence of the sensations that engulfed me. *PAIN! Burning. Stinging. Throbbing. Pinching. Aching. Stabbing. Shooting. Tremor. Pang. Spasm. Intense. Heavy. Tender. Thick. Severe. Unbearable.* Like HOT salsa running through my veins. *BURNING*—yes that's it!"

If Delgado Gaitan's "thick" description of lupus pain as "hot salsa" reveals the importance of culturally grounded reference points and multiple discursive fields for communicating states of Latina health, Jessica Núñez de Ybarra's account of her mother's lifelong experience with pain (and chronic conditions) unconventionally redefines this ailment across a large spectrum of Latina experiences: the experience involves "the pains of poverty, separation, childhood illness, sexism, prejudice, sorrow and loss, violence, alienation, labor, motherhood, arthritis, osteoporosis, heart disease, cancer, and diabetes."

To this list we can add the pains of nonsupport, infidelity, and domestic abuse from the multiple scenarios that arise within Enriqueta Valdez-Curiel's narrative, factoring in the "wounding" language (verbal abuse) that permeates it and exacerbates the depressed condition of a mother who shoulders multiple burdens across national and gender borders. For this woman, all the pains of life are subsumed under "la reuma." Similarly, Yvette Flores's account of her mother's struggle with dementia incorporates a wide definition of pain that includes "the pain of her marriages" and her husband's infidelity. For her family, the thought of dementia is too painful to accept, so they make an unspoken decision to interpret Aura's illness as madness. Their refusal to name her illness accurately constrains how they respond to it.

In turn, Adela de la Torre links chronic pain to empacho (pain of the heart from "loving too much"), the emotional pain of women who must work rather than fill traditional roles and who do not receive recognition for their life choices. Yet, in this narrative, pain is also a monster that invades the body, a torturer that "commands respect and compliance as it eats away at [one's] mobility, vitality, and optimism by relentlessly piercing and destroying the cartilage."

In Gabriela Arredondo's breast cancer narrative, pain is metaphorically linked to female "silence" and lack of empowerment: "Part of the pain that follows me about my 'uelita's short, fierce struggle with breast cancer is my own guilt. After all, I knew older women could get breast cancer. . . . Somehow, though, I never talked with her about breast cancer."

In many respects, the issue of pain intersects an array of domains for Latina women. The pain from emotional abuse from both family members and social institutions, the pain from physical ailments such as arthritis and medical treatments such as radiation for cancer, and the pain of not knowing the medical outcome of a disease because of its chronic and unyielding nature. Understanding the complexity of pain in neurological, emotional, and physical terms is indeed a new, uncharted research domain. It is as much a focus of the illness narrative as the definition of the illness itself. The importance of pain in the expression of disease suggests a need to know more about it so that we may improve the treatment of the chronic conditions that plague our families and threaten our mortality.

Metaphors of food and its preparation, important aspects of Latina culture, also abound. For Arredondo, food and cooking contextualize the illness experience. It is in the kitchen where her grandmother displays the radiation that had "cooked the skin where her breast was removed" and likens her scar to a popular Mexican food: pork rinds. Granddaughter and grandmother are ultimately linked by the absence of a breast, a scar resembling a chicharrón (pork rind), and a desire to reveal to the world the effects of medical interventions on the body. The grandmother's phrase "mira lo que me hicieron" (look at what they did to me) becomes an intergenerational cry of a Latina body that has endured the scars of a dreadful disease and a medical establishment that cannot heal without further wounding. Here the body is without doubt the silent witness.

In "Fat in America," the obesity of the (individual) body is a metaphor for another obesity: that of the national body and the larger Chicana/o and Latina/o community. Obesity is a metaphor for America itself and its capitalist consumer economy that leads Americans to believe that "the bigger the better" is true of everything "from churches, cities, malls, and companies to campaign budgets" (Lévy 2006, 241). U.S. culture encourages unbridled consumption while promoting standards of beauty that border on the anorexic, creating an untenable situation for the obese person who already bears the consequences and risks of overconsumption, cannot adhere to mainstream norms of beauty, and is already marked with serious disease. In contradistinction to the idea that "bigger is better," Christi testifies that as her body gets bigger and bigger, her world gets smaller and smaller, and she strives to reconcile her body as it is now with the memory of the body that once was hers.

Within the context of current medical narratives, obesity is defined as the result of behavioral problems that can be "fixed" with more exercise, less food, and a healthier environment. This obesity epidemic discourse, however, ignores the emotional reality of most Latina women. Many of us view our bodies and ourselves within a norm different from the mainstream American cultural norm of beauty, and we experience stressors that place us at greater psychological and physical risks than the average American woman. Moreover, food has social meaning with the context of an increasingly dynamic and heterogeneous community. Preparing, sharing, and eating food with friends, partners, and family members are social rituals with multiple meanings. Aside from allowing for intense negotiations around reproduction of labor, community, and identity, these rituals can create bonds within and across generations of family and community members as well as opportunities for cultural expressions of affection, pride, and remembrance. In the best of instances, these rituals can provide regenerating moments when the daily stressors of life are shifted aside as we prepare our special meals. Whether it is tamales during the Christmas season or menudo for a family brunch, the consumption and overconsumption of food subsume both cultural meaning and resistance for most Latinas. As Lorena García points out, her diabetes changed the dynamics of family gatherings because she had to bring her own food. Thus, dietary modification strategies within the Latina population must consider how we interpret the meaning of food and its place in relation to health, cultural norms, and traditions.

Serial Illnesses and the Social Contexts of Latina Health

Adela de la Torre, Adaljiza Sosa-Riddell, Enriqueta Valdez-Curiel, Gloria Anzaldúa, and Concha Delgado Gaitan's narratives also outline "relational" illnesses, or cluster(ed) health discourses, that must be spoken about and considered together if Latinas are to be successfully treated: arthritis, depression, and empacho; emotional upset and Parkinson's disease; lupus and the pathology of fear. In their individual ways, all these speakers also express the need to heal the body, mind, and soul holistically. The experience of Jessica Núñez de Ybarra's diabetic mother, Carmen, demonstrates the importance of factoring "serial conditions" into the narratives of Latina health. As Núñez de Ybarra explains, "Sometimes [my mother] gets so upset because just as she gets over one thing, something else develops." Without an understanding of the magnitude of the serial health conditions that some Latinas experience, it is impossible to treat them comprehensively or to provide the emotional support these women need when, as a consequence of so many illnesses, they wish "it were all over."

The narratives of Latina health reveal other connections important for understanding the health outcomes of Latinas who live and work with chronic illnesses. For instance, there is a strong relationship among occupation, work, and illness: years of filling salad bags in a chilled environment not only exacerbates Valdez-Curiel's mother's arthritis, but compounds it with a hiatal hernia severe enough to mimic the symptoms of a heart attack.

Finally, Concha Delgado Gaitan emphasizes that other relational factors—life history, personal options, and a lack of synchronicity among the many parts of life—may play an important role in the emergence of a chronic illness. Her choices "were couched in the contradictions of historical times for women and minorities." In this context, "obligation and opportunities converged," leading to overwhelming demands and making it impossible to maintain the balance between career and family necessary to maintain good health. Gloria Anzaldúa echoes similar sentiments, talking about how a combination of genetics, environmental exposure, a viral infection, and overwork set her up for her diagnosis of diabetes.

Familial and Generational Affiliations and Disaffiliations

Family and generational histories are another important factor in Latina health, and several family profiles appear in these collected narratives. One is Adela de la Torre's telling family portrait: "As I child, I witnessed my grandmother's struggle with the disease. Her gnarled, arthritic hands would daily brush my long black hair and gently fold the locks into two neat trenzas (braids). In the innocence of youth, I would rub her bumpy knuckles, transfixed with the idea that her worn hands would comfort me as she rubbed my head to help me sleep." This passage begins a relational family history of arthritis: we learn that not only the child's grandmother, but also her mother, the mother's cousins, and she herself will live with arthritis, although all have different manifestations of this complex illness. In this way, her narrative not only confirms a family predisposition toward the ailment but also a generational profile that probably encompasses at least two sets of mothers and daughters, including a daughter who now understands that her own hands may soon resemble her grandmother's.

One of the most powerful generational links to be found in the narratives is Jessica Núñez de Ybarra's narrative of her mother's arduous struggle with diabetes, which dates back more than twenty years and is framed within a tragic relational history of meaningful affiliations: "Everyone we know on [my mother's] side of the family has eventually developed diabetes (mostly type 2). Diabetes and its complications have already either severely debilitated or prematurely taken many of my mother's brothers and sisters. . . . For years, [my cousin] Robert and I commiserated about his childhood struggle with diabetes and about his loss of sight, kidney function, and toes after he became an adult."

In turn, the story of a Latina with hypertension points to a family predisposition toward this chronic condition that extends to mother, grandmother, and some siblings who share not only rituals, but also these vivid memories of hypertension: "When I was growing up, my mom always used to talk about her blood pressure going up. When I was little, I didn't really know what this meant or how it felt, other than she used to lie down when it happened. . . . My grandmother had high blood pressure too."

Family links also surface in Clara Lomas's letters, when all her siblings discover they have thyroid problems. However, their condition is not intergenerational because, interestingly, their parents and grandparents don't demonstrate any of the typical symptoms.

Yvette Flores's testimony locates a different family affiliation. Her uncle's experience with dementia is crucial to the family's response to her mother's illness: "We were not unfamiliar with Alzheimer's in the family. Mom's only (legitimate) brother had spent years under its hold. It had started like Mom's, with memory difficulties, repetitive questions, preoccupations about money and the children, an exacerbation of all the things that as a good husband, father, and provider he had worried about all of his adult life."

In contrast, other Latina stories dispute the idea of a larger family profile or predisposition toward a particular ailment. Lorena García's gestational diabetes narrative, for instance, strongly denies any evidence of diabetes in her family. Ada Sosa-Riddell also refutes the idea that Parkinson's is a family disease.

There is a tremendous need for research into the intergenerational genetic links across the spectrum of diseases affecting Latina women. The fact that most studies on Latinas are population based and look at a moment of time makes family narratives such as those in this collection critical for understanding and interpreting intergenerational illnesses. Thus, these narratives pose important research questions and challenges for the medical and scientific community. To what extent are our illnesses part of our genetic code? And if we are able to untangle this code, can we begin to treat our illnesses more effectively and minimize the fear and speculation in our communities?

Mixed Resources and Treatment Options

Concha Delgado Gaitan establishes a generational link at the beginning of her lupus narrative: "'No hay mal por cual bien no venga' (There is nothing bad from which something good doesn't come). . . . I remember my mother's words regularly now that I am disabled with a debilitating illness. . . . I clung to a memory of being hospitalized as a child, when innocent prayer and my mother's words, 'No hay mal cual bien no venga,' had erased my fear." In this excerpt, the importance of a female cultural legacy and memory of therapeutic modalities emerges as surely as it does in Jessica Núñez de Ybarra's depiction of her own mother's hands—a memory that brings strength and calm in the face of adversity. Yvette Flores records the psychological healing that emanates from a mother's "untamed tongue" freed by dementia: "Dementia freed [my mother] to speak her truth. When she accused my father of having an affair with 'the Mexican woman,' she was disclosing the details of his long-term affair with a family maid in Costa Rica, an affair that produced two daughters. . . . I finally understood why we had left Costa Rica and come to the United States."

In addition to memory, the Latinas in this collection draw from a wide spectrum of resources as they face health challenges and endeavor to process, learn about, and explore their health conditions and treatment options. Even while fighting her own anger and denial, Gloria Anzaldúa began applying her "extensive research skills to learning as much as possible" about diabetes, "its causes, its effects on the body, treatment plans, and recent medical breakthroughs." Gabriella Arredondo and her husband educate not only themselves but also the doctors on new treatment research in breast cancer; Clara Lomas conducts lengthy Internet searches on Graves' disease, which she later shares with her family members; Ada Sosa-Riddell reads widely about Parkinson's disease and consults the Internet; Lorena García participates in a study on gestational diabetes that she hopes will shed light on this ailment even as she carefully monitors her glucose levels and diet. Concha Delgado Gaitan, Clara Lomas, and Ada Sosa-Riddell write in journals in order to get through different phases of their respective ailments, whereas Christi initially resists the requirement that she record "in black and white" every piece of food she eats. The anonymous Latina in the hypertension narrative devises a series of rituals to help her reduce her pressure. Yvette Flores relies on her professional training, her children's words, and a colleague's opinion as she pushes for accurate diagnosis of her mother's dementia. Enriqueta Valdez-Curiel literally becomes her mother's protector, defending her first from her husband, then from herself. Adela de la Torre's mother, Mimi, relies on "an ointment made of chili powder called Capsaicin, . . . her favorite 'old lady's perfume,' Ben Gay, and a good dose of Tylenol." Jessica Núñez de Ybarra's mother, Carmen, follows a complex regimen that involves taking pills around the clock, monitoring her diet, and receiving insulin by injection several times a day.

Remedios are the remedies used by our mothers and grandmothers, yet they intersect all our lives even within the context of twenty-first-century pharmaceutical drugs and technologies. Medical practitioners may dismiss our alternative healing practices as quackery, yet we know that for thousands of years our indigenous ancestors survived with their knowledge of herbs, use of potent animal and insect venoms, and rituals that deeply touched their souls and their bodies.

As we reflect back to our past behaviors and practices to cure ourselves, we learn the importance of the power of our intuition, cultural legacies, political affiliations, spirituality, and knowledge in selecting our preferred treatment modalities, or combinations thereof, for disease and illness. Although the Latinas in this collection make use of conventional medicine, they also draw on alternative therapies, including folk medicine, herbs, wisdom, prayer, conversations, relaxation techniques, political memories, and spirituality. As Gloria Anzaldúa points out, a sole reliance on conventional Western medicine disempowers Latinas, leaving us at the mercy of the omnipotent doctor: "Our mind, our flesh, our energy system are all connected. What people think affects the body, and the body's physiology depends on how people think. If someone believes that modern medicine is the only answer to healing certain diseases, the diseased person is virtually helpless and depends on the doctor as an all-knowing God. She can't participate in her own healing." Anzaldúa herself meticulously monitored her blood sugar and followed a regimen of insulin injections. Yet she balanced this medical intervention with acupuncture, herbs, affirmations, the native feminisms of women of color, and spiritual growth. Most important, perhaps, she, like all the contributors to this book, drew on the therapeutic value of self-expression.

The Therapeutic Value of Speech

Concha Delgado Gaitan explains that an "inner dialogue" allows her to tap into her spirit to advocate for herself "when the medical system fail[s] her" or when it is necessary to grow or "to remember that *able* and *disabled* are cultural labels not to be confused with the person to whom they are attached." Therapeutic speech is also crucial for the Latina with hypertension who participates in a conversation that helps her to understand that her chronic condition is part of life, not life itself. Clara Lomas writes letters to her sister that include lengthy dialogues recounting different aspects of her struggles for health and helping her to make sense of the confusing state of her health. Telephone calls from relatives in Mexico on Saturday afternoons reassure Lorena García. Ada Sosa-Riddell's grieving ritual centers around a lengthy monologue to a doll who represents the woman she used to be and the spirit that still lives within her, helping her to come to terms with her frozen body.

Shared life experiences and pláticas (heartfelt talks) are also essential for two cousins/soul sisters, Lupe and Mimi, who support each other through the debilitating effects of arthritis over a lifetime: "For as long as I can remember, whenever I heard a hushed voice in my mother's bedroom, I knew my mother was talking to Lupe; sometimes I would hear a quick chuckle, but when she hung up the phone, I could tell from the look in her eyes that she had cleansed her mind through deep conversation." Given the value of these pláticas, it is not surprising that Lupe's death prompts a worsening in Mimi's arthritis. Significantly, Mimi can manage her pain only by seeking counseling, another form of therapeutic speech: "I would marvel at how in order to meet with her therapist, my mother would struggle up three flights of stairs with a walker—something that was beyond her normal daily living activities."

When we speak and are listened to, we are able to begin healing the wounds created by our past and present lives. Pláticas open the door to healing in ways that a simple medical encounter cannot. The doctor's diagnosis and recommended treatment of the disease is just the beginning of our healing process. Nervios, susto, coraje (anxiety, fear that shakes the soul from the body, and anger) emerge and cannot be treated without a limpia (cleansing) of some sort; pláticas are an important part of this cleansing process for Latinas who treat disease holistically by reconnecting the mind and the body with the soul.

It Takes (Comm)Unity:
The Role of Family, Friends, and Caregivers

Together, these Latina dialogues confirm that the issue of Latina health extends beyond individual Latinas, their bodies, treatments, and particular healing practices. Entire extended families (parents, siblings, aunts and uncles, cousins, children) as well as community members are enlisted into the orbit, work, and discourse of Latina health. Several narratives in this collection emphasize the importance of family; in some, family members actively participate in the narration to describe their involvement as caregivers or the effect of their loved one's condition on them, such as Citlali and William Riddell (Adaljiza Sosa-Riddell's daughter and father), and Tomás Núñez and Robert (Jessica Núñez de Ybarra's father and cousin).

Support from an extended family is particularly striking in Yvette Flores's narrative, where her parents' apartment is filled with women who have left their own homes (some in another country), spouses, and children to come and support the ailing parents and the caregiver daughter, yet without ever acknowledging the mother's health condition or that their "visits" are motivated by her need for help. Christi initiates her weight-loss journey by seeking her family's help, and her husband takes a walk with her when the food cravings hit. Lorena García's entire family is affected by her gestational diabetes, changing their eating habits to accommodate her dietary requirements. Jessica Núñez de Ybarra's "whole family has come a long way in taking care of her mother"; and in another family, the Latinas routinely monitor their blood pressure, take their hypertension pills together, and support one another. In Adela de la Torre's arthritis narrative, family members struggle to provide a safe haven for an ailing parent; Clara Lomas's extended family offers much-needed child care and support; and Enriqueta Valdez-Curiel organizes her entire life around caring for her mother, even choosing to immigrate to the United States for a period in order to protect her.

In many respects, our narratives reinforce and confirm the health literature that identifies a strong, supportive family structure as a protective factor against adverse health outcomes, yet this structure is itself flexible and includes multiple manifestations and expressions, shifting gender and sexual roles, and female-centered households and communities. Moreover, anthropologist Carlos Velez-Ibáñez (1996) has suggested that the resiliency of Mexican families, even despite intermarriage, is evidence of his "black hole theory," wherein Mexican families, particularly in the border region, expansively draw in new family members. Thus, even despite the intergenerational class mobility also evident in these narratives—many written by women who grew up in working-class circumstances and through education, protest, and determination achieved economic stability and positions of respect—Latinas' diverse cultural identities, reciprocal familial obligations, and social networks continue to play a key role in their health narratives, suggesting that even beyond our geographic borders, ever-dynamic family cultural ties are key to how we treat illness.

The Challenge of Shifting Identity Formations

As we have seen, extended family networks are crucial for Latinas who must deal with a variety of symptoms and ailments, challenges, and complications from both short-term and chronic diseases. These networks are also crucial for Latinas with illnesses as they navigate the challenges of shifting identity formations and actively confront the "I of yesterday" (the Latina before the illness) and the "I of today" (the Latina that has emerged from the disease process). Christi probably expresses most clearly the feeling of being one person on the inside and not recognizing the person she sees in the mirror, which is the person to whom others react: "I simply cannot believe that I actually got this big. . . . And I just cannot believe that this happened to *me!* . . . When people who know me see me now, they do a double take: 'Can that really be her?'" Her fight is about more than losing weight; it is about regaining her former identity and congruency in her personhood.

Likewise, Gabriela Arredondo is estranged from her previous self by the transformations in her body. The loss of a breast and of her hair propel a shift in identity from academic, mother, and wife to cancer survivor: "There's something very anonymous about being bald—not just bald, but having no body hair at all. I look in the mirror—before the makeup—and I don't see myself at all. I look like all those classic cancer patients I see on posters for fund-raisers: smiling faces with no hair, no eyebrows, no eyelashes. Perhaps it is this look that friends and family expect to see? Who knew that hair could be such an integral part of personalizing oneself?" She also discovers that this identity as a cancer patient is incompatible with her Latinidad when she is unable to find a wig that doesn't either stereotype her or Anglicize her. Yet her role as a wife and mother transcends her physical identity, and she expresses gratitude that she can still don a bathing suit and play in the pool with her husband and son—bald head, "Latina" hips, missing breast, and all.

Adela de La Torre's family narrative is another that illustrates a sharp contrast between the past and present identities of someone whose life is altered by arthritis: "As young women, [Lupe] and [Mimi] would play tennis on weekends on the Oakdale High courts, exchanging quick volleys and smashing backhands. . . . Yet all too soon [Lupe] was forced to trade her stilettos for orthopedic flat shoes and throw her prized wooden racket in the trash."

Mimi, who once joined her vivacious cousin on the tennis court, also suffers from debilitating pain and disability. As she struggles to rebuild her life through her healing process, she "clings fiercely to her independent status," even when her condition makes this option difficult and her children disagree with her decisions. A significant component of her healing is reconciling the identity she had as a master teacher in the public elementary system for forty years with the identity she had wanted, that of devoted Mexican mother.

None of the Latinas in this book let the image of suffering define her identity or social condition, and all fight for full and meaningful lives in the face of disability and illness. Yet Ada Sosa-Riddell also acknowledges that Parkinson's has shaped her identity in ways that she must openly acknowledge and that go beyond the merely physical and visible. In contrast to Lupe and Mimi, Sosa-Riddell insists on what appears to be a necessary rupture with a previous self (Sol Rebel) and sees herself as almost two different people. The "almost" is important here, for if this narrative can be read as a memorial to Sol Rebel, who helps Ada to grieve and lay to rest the healthy, able-bodied, self-directed child and activist she was, as well as the assumptions about health that supported this image, it also registers significant traces of that rebel spirit, whose profile emerges in the affirmations of self-determination and the desire for wellness, the remembrances of the past and lifetime achievements, the dreams of fulfilling many projects, and the possibility that there will be other serial personas in her future who can transcend a self that appears to be indelibly split.

Lorena García's reflections on gestational diabetes also focus on the relationship between identity formation and health status. She recounts how the diagnosis of gestational diabetes came as a surprise to her and produced a form of alienation: "As I lectured in my courses about [gestational diabetes] and the risk factors involved, I had difficulty seeing myself as someone who had this health condition. It was as if I were speaking about someone else." García bears witness to the splitting of identity that can occur when one is diagnosed with an unexpected illness or is forced to come to terms with a chronic health condition. For her, coming to terms with gestational diabetes means leaving behind a series of health assumptions, recognizing her membership in another identity formation (that of people with gestational diabetes), and reconciling her identities as a professor and researcher of Latina health who lectures to others on the dangers of gestational diabetes *and* as a person with that very condition. She also speaks tellingly to the fact that people, particularly women, are complex amalgamations of multiple, sometimes conflicting identities when she responds to fellow students who define themselves as their profession by saying instead, "I want to be remembered as having been a great friend, a wonderful wife, a good daughter and sister, someone who made a difference in others' lives, and a great epidemiologist and researcher."

The contradictions that blur the boundaries between health-care provider and patient or family caregiver in one's own home space are also evident in Jessica Núñez de Ybarra's moving story of her mother's struggles with diabetes. Suggesting that family caregivers, too, must make important adjustments to their professional identity and career vision, she speaks of needing to separate her identity as a doctor from that of caregiver and caring daughter. She needs to be the loving support her mother is looking for in a daughter, not one more health-care professional monitoring her mother's physical condition.

Yvette Flores's testimony of her mother's dementia retraces both the progressive loss of identity associated with this ailment and how these signposts are "missed" by everyone but her from her unique perspective of professional psychologist and daughter intimately attuned to the changes in her mother's personality. Because of the nature of dementia, it is not surprising that a strong contrast emerges between the Latina of yesterday and the Latina of today—or that these shifts in identity are spoken of from a daughter's creative imagination. In addition, Flores creates a bridge from past to present that links the mother who once was with the mother who now is. As disorientation and loss of memory, purpose, and identity rob her mother of her self and life history, the daughter creates a lasting memorial to that person as she speaks for her mother and gives her a voice, a history, a memory, and a sense of personhood. In the process, the daughter offers a symbolic re-creation of her mother's newfound identity, which incorporates traces of the past, in this moving poetic tribute:

> You are no longer who you were
> But your maternal instinct
> Cannot be extinguished
> You still perceive
> What I do not tell you
> You still foresee
> The dangers blind to me
> You still read the desires
> Invisible even to me

Both chronic pain and memory loss affect Concha Delgado Gaitan's personhood and prompt a number of shifts in identity that require her sustained attention. She explains how at one point lupus shook her confidence and threatened to "unravel" her connections with the world, her work, her family, and herself (the Latina of yesterday). Reclaiming a Latina identity and a sense of personhood in the present means not only engaging in memory-affirming, culture-affirming, and spirit-affirming practices that can connect her to herself, the universe, and others, but also confronting and rethinking her professional identity (as a professor), crafting a new career that complements her healing process, building a personal life with a new spouse and a new identity, and cultivating an altered philosophy of life founded on the idea that getting healthy is her life's work. At the same time, she affirms herself as whole and complete in her present as a person with lupus—"I realized I needed to reinterpret my condition in a way that did not pronounce me as a broken person"—rejecting the messages of health-care providers who defined her as a lifelong sufferer of disease who would never be whole again.

Shifts in identity formation in relation to professional identity and work practices also appear in the narrative of hypertension. The Latina speaking subject draws a strong contrast between a present life of measured engagement where she puts "one foot in front of the other" and wakes up and goes to bed with pills, on the one hand, and an earlier personal history of workaholism where she risks the serious and debilitating effects of the not-so-silent killer, high blood pressure (an ailment that is often linked to stressful situations and type A, or reactive, personalities), on the other. In contrast to the Latina of yesterday, the Latina of today takes care of herself, doesn't go beyond her limits, thinks carefully about what she volunteers for, and says "no" when necessary, even if others resent her proactive health stance.

Similarly, Clara Lomas's letters draw a sharp contrast between the youthful Latina superwoman academic-mother of yesterday and the middle-aged Latina of today who occupies what feels like the body of a senior citizen. She, too, needs to adjust her life and professional identity in light of the fact that every work commitment demands careful scrutiny for its possible health consequences and effect on her quality of life. She has learned that she will have to give up some dreams and always have a backup plan because she can't automatically count on a stable metabolism. Yet her narrative confirms that she remains successful, productive, and fully engaged in life, even if "there will be some really good and productive days and other days that could be better."

This need to scrutinize every aspect of one's life leads to reprioritizing and reforming one's identity around its core elements. Gloria Anzaldúa had lived with a series of debilitating illnesses from childhood, so her physical body and its illnesses were at the core of her identity formation, including even her willingness to declare her lesbian identity openly. As she explains, the physical differences between her body and other children's "set me apart from the herd. I had to figure out, 'Why was I so different? Do I want to go with the herd, or should I resist and rebel?'" Then the onset of a new chronic illness in adulthood—diabetes—required her to reexamine her identity and worldview, to shift her time and energy away from her career to take care of herself:

> I was finishing up my second attempt at a PhD, I was traveling all over the world, I was gone six months out of the year, I had all this energy, my writing was going great, and then POW! Diabetes. I had to stop everything. For a year I could hardly function other than to take care of myself. . . . I realized I was going too fast and overextending. . . . I had to go back to basics: "What do I want from life? What do I really want to do?" I wanted to stay home, write more, and not travel as much. . . . So, it's all about balancing, but it takes so much energy, energy that I resent having to give to diabetes when I could be using it for my reading and writing.

Enriqueta Valdez-Curiel's account is arguably the most tragic and jarring of the Latina narratives in this collection, with its mixed profile of Latina ailments, domestic abuse, verbal abuse, transnational migration, and poverty. If the title "Debe ser la reuma" announces the confusion of a mother who does not recognize her multiple ailments, the narrative itself incorporates shifts in identity that take us from a beautiful, youthful mother (captured in photographs) to an elderly and downtrodden woman who is unrecognizable to her own daughter: painfully thin, with a swollen face, unstable gait, and disheveled appearance that make her look as if she were mentally ill. Yet with a number of combined treatments and her daughter's unwavering support, this Latina recovers her love of life and embraces a new identity: someone who does what she wants, when she wants, and with whom she wants.

Rafael Campo has suggested that the surefooted movement of writing may help to re-create an integrated sense of self and that literary forms such as poetry can empower through the construction of "transformed identity, as the patient, after her illness finally identifies with the illness" and initiates another type of healing (2003, 96, 97). Most of the narratives in this collection bear him out. Similarly, they constitute an important type of outreach, from the authors to comadres who live with serious ailments and can find a forum of sorts in this collection—a story similar to theirs where empathy prevails.

Learning to Listen / Listening to Learn:
The Lessons of Latina Health

Concha Delgado Gaitan refers to her lengthy hospital stay as a kind of classroom experience and to lupus as her teacher. With this characterization, she recognizes the important link between healing and learning, a connection echoed by Gloria Anzaldúa, who interpreted her diabetes as presenting lessons to be learned and then shared with others. Thus, much of her writing reflects her struggle to accept the diagnosis, her attempts to live with diabetes by reframing its role in her life, and her efforts to learn from and survive her condition.

Yet, as the chapters in this collection attest, not all health-care practitioners are ready to learn this lesson. Some refuse to take calls from patients, listen only superficially, and speak from scripted dialogues. Others minimize patients' concern over the side effects of medications, treat them disrespectfully, or draw stereotyped conclusions about Latina psychology. Yet these practitioners do not represent the whole health-care community. The best health-care practitioners do listen—not only to the patient but also to family members and caregivers. They see the whole person, not just the disease. They educate others about the importance of learning and social communication for healing. They, like Concha, recognize that healing is a "life's work" and that "health is not an end, but a process." They acknowledge that health takes work and are careful not to overwork their patients. They pay close attention to the situational aspects of Latina health (to family, work, and social and historical environments) and to the stories of Latina health that extend beyond this book and exist in everyday life, everywhere, for those who are willing to listen, write, translate, and record them.

As we move into an increasingly technology-driven society, we must continue to reinsert our personal (Latina) narratives into health professionals' medical script. As a data-driven society, we benefit from research and the best medical technology, but at the same time we increasingly risk losing our own human face and agency as patients. Physicians often excel in reading the lab results from outsourced private labs, yet never question the underlying significance of their placing greater value on the report of an anonymous technician than on the patient's own intuitions and interpretations of the illness. By recentering clinical discourse on the patient, we can recover an important balance in treating illnesses and diseases. We need to understand and treat illness with the wealth of current medical knowledge, but also within the interpreted context of what it means to the patient. Despite the fact that indigenous healers around the globe have taught us the value of listening to the patient's words before diagnosing and treating a disease, this important aspect of care has been lost in how we train our contemporary medical providers. Thus, an important art in the healing process has been lost in our drive for technological superiority in medicine. In an era when medical care is driven by "cost containment" and doctors are pressured to give each patient no more than a fifteen-minute appointment, the idea of pausing to reflect and listen to a patient in a medical encounter may appear frivolous, yet the voices in this text attest that in the long run it is the only way to improve health for everyone.

14

Latina Health

Empirical Realities, Alternative Interpretations, and Policy Recommendations

Adela de la Torre

Dolor de oídos

Cuando se trata de dolor de oídos se aplica a las mismas una cucharita de almendras o de oliva, lo cual se introduce a gotas a una temperatura elevada pero que no queme. (Wagner 1952, 56)

Earaches

With regard to earaches, you apply to them a small spoonful of almond or olive oil, which you introduce drop by drop at a high temperature, but not so high that it burns.[1]

As a child, I remember my abuelita keeping her yierbas conveniently tucked away in a kitchen drawer. Whenever my sister or I was ill, out came her myriad of pomadas, laced with an assortment of prayers and holy cards. For our chapped lips, she would rub on honey and then whisper a brief "Santa María"; for a fever, she would wipe us with rubbing alcohol and rub our panzas, muttering "sana, sana, colita de rana"; and for our scraped knees, she would pull out sulfur, purchased from her comadre Mechita at the Mexican pharmacy, and pray to Santa Teresa. She seemed able to cure any illness without antibiotics or visits to a physician. Her faith and healing powers made us feel safe, both physically and mentally.

For many Latinas, staying healthy requires looking at how we feel both physically and spiritually. Advances in medical science over the past twenty to thirty years have made it difficult for us to hold on to our traditional cultural beliefs about health and health care. Nevertheless, the personal narratives in this book reveal that many Latinas still maintain important links to their cultural expressions and unique spiritualities, which frame how we cope with and interpret our illnesses. These narratives ground Latinas in the material realities we live with each day.

Here, I juxtapose these health narratives with what is known empirically about Latinas from U.S. census and health data. These data are important in informing us of the value and use of our traditional healing processes. They also allow us to describe our social and relative health position in the United States. I place this summary of who we are and what our illnesses are within the context of examples of traditional remedios (remedies) rooted in our deep indigenous heritage. My source for these vignettes is my grandmother Adela's sourcebook in caring for her family: *Plantas medicinales y remedios caseros* (Medicinal Plants and Home Remedies, 1952, originally published in 1936), by Federico Wagner. This wonderful book blends indigenous, Mexican, and European home remedies to treat the illnesses most common in Mexico. Those I selected mirror to the extent possible the disease categories we focus on in this book as well as "los remedios populares"—that is, the remedies common, affordable, and accessible within the context of traditional healing practices.

These extracts remind us of the importance for Latinas of traditional healing practices rooted in the espíritu of our indigenous past. Knowledge of traditional healing practices empowers Latinas to inform health providers of how health care should be delivered to us and our families. Our contribution in this book is thus to offer knowledge about how the practice of medicine can respond to Latinas' multifaceted cultural needs and practices.

The following background information is an important beginning that shows where we fit within the broader parameters of risk and health in the United States. It informs us of our material conditions and grounds our health narratives in data, albeit at times limited, to guide our future directions and strategies for our own and our families' health.

Latinas in the United States: Who Are We?

Latinas are a significant and growing population in the United States. As members of the largest national minority group, they comprise slightly more than half of the overall Latino population and represent more than eighteen million U.S. residents (U.S. Census Bureau, Population Division 2002, table 1). Latinas share with their male counterparts the distinctions of being on average younger than the general U.S. population and of falling disproportionately within the ranks of the working poor (U.S. Census Bureau, Population Division 2002, table 14.1).

Nearly two-thirds of all Latinas self-identify as Mexican origin. Yet these forced census classifications hide the rich tapestry of Latina hybrid identity formations. Thus, I do not want to project a unified or rigid Latina identity on the basis of government statistics. Rather, I suggest using such statistics as one tool in an array of tools that can capture a glimpse of who we are today, while acknowledging that the term *Latina* alone may gloss over important differences.

One important variable to consider in examining the overall Latina population is age. Latinas are an extremely youthful population, with more than one-third being under eighteen years old (U.S. Census Bureau, Population Division 2002, table 1.1). In addition, more than 40 percent of Latinas fall within the prime childbearing years of twenty to forty-four (U.S. Census Bureau, Population Division 2002, tables 1.1, 1.2). This demographic profile places a significant number of Latinas in the portion of their life cycle when childrearing and family obviously play central roles. Indeed, Latinas have the highest fertility rate of any group in the United States (U.S. DHHS HRSA 2004, appendix table 1) and have become a primary force in propelling the native birth rates in the United States, making this country one of the few global industrial countries not facing zero or negative population growth.

Latinas' increasing demographic presence is clearly visible in the rapidly growing ethnic enclaves throughout the United States. However, their social position is largely constrained by their economic and political placement within these communities. In 2001, the median income of U.S. Latinas was $12,583, approximately three-quarters of the median income of all U.S. women (U.S. Census Bureau, Population Division 2002, table 1). This wage gap between Latina and non-Latina U.S. women exists across all income categories and is attributed to how much Latinas work and where they are employed. Overall, Latinas have increased their labor-force participation but still fall behind the overall U.S. female participation rates. As of 2002, 58 percent of all Latinas older than sixteen were employed in the civilian labor force, compared to 60 percent of U.S. women as a whole (U.S. Census Bureau, Population Division 2002, table 9.1). Yet many Latinas work as mothers and family caregivers, providing the social network and family support that sustain Latino communities. Thus, this labor participation rate indicates only paid employment, not the significant contribution that Latinas make to their families and social networks through unpaid labor.

The most striking feature for Latinas who have paid employment is that many work in those sectors of the economy with the lowest wages and fringe benefits, particularly in terms of health-insurance coverage. The two major employment sectors for Latinas are service occupations (28 percent) and technical, sales, and administrative support occupations (37 percent). Compared to non-Latino white women, Latinas also have higher numbers of women in one of the lowest-tier job categories: operators, fabricators, and laborers.

As these statistics demonstrate, many Latinas work in physically difficult and demanding jobs, with little if any job flexibility and very low pay, which disproportionately situates them within the working poor. Latina poverty rates are nearly double those for all U.S. women: 23.2 percent versus 12.9 percent, respectively (U.S. Census Bureau, Population Division 2002, table 14.1). The poverty rate for Latinas is more than 2.5 times that of non-Latina white women. Among Latina subgroups, Puerto Rican women have the highest poverty rates in all age categories, at 27.8 percent, more than three times the poverty rate of non-Latina white women (U.S. Census Bureau, Population Division 2002, table 14.2).

On a daily basis, then, many Latinas face tremendous barriers to meeting their and their children's daily needs. At the same time, they are an integral part of the U.S. economy in key sectors that rely on low-wage labor to maintain a competitive edge in the market. Latinas are thus poised demographically as an important yet underutilized resource in the United States. Unfortunately, their demographic and economic position correlates with greater risks for adverse health outcomes resulting from diseases and lack of medical treatment.

Latinas' Health Status: What We Know and What Hides Beneath

Dolor de Cabeza

Dolor de cabeza es algo muy frecuente principalmente entre el sexo femenino.

Por lo general provienen del estómago, siendo acompañantes de enfermedades de este último órgano y síntoma a vez de que el aparato digestivo no trabaja correctamente ... es importante abstenerse de grasas y carnes en los días en que se sufren dolores de cabeza. (Wagner 1952, 54, 55)

Headache

Headache is a frequent illness, particularly among the female sex.

In general, it comes from the stomach, accompanied by illnesses of the latter organ and symptomatic, at times, of a digestive system that is not working properly. . . . [I]t is important to abstain from grease and meat on the days when one suffers from headaches.

Within the folklore of Mexican indigenous medicine, the idea that some diseases are linked to gender is well established. Thus, it is not surprising that illnesses such as dolor de cabeza require treatments that consider gendered aspects of the disease. Moreover, traditional healers frame their diagnosis and treatment of an illness within the context of the whole individual, so diet, clinical treatments that include physical observation and touch, and social networks to support the ill person become part of the comprehensive treatment of a disease.

Many empirical observations about Latinas ignore the important and complex intersections that frame how indigenous healers (curanderas/os) throughout Latin America approach illness. They, like Western medical practitioners, observe illnesses that can be categorized by age, gender, and preexisting conditions, such as susto (fear that shakes the soul from the body). Indeed, in some regions, such as Oaxaca, Mexico, many curanderas attribute a significant number of illnesses to susto because it is an illness that requires the curandera to play an important mediating role in helping the patient identify the external forces that created the observed illness. Once this external problem is identified, both the spiritual and material treatments become obvious. Looking beyond the observed illness, the curanderas treat their patients holistically and, some would argue, provide a system of care for their patients that is more accessible physically, emotionally, and spiritually (Trotter and Chavira 1997).

As U.S. Latinas have become better situated economically and socially, our illnesses have become characterized within the dominant U.S. medical model. We have less access to our indigenous rubrics for disease and healing, and our illnesses and symptoms are now compared to those of the dominant non-Latina general population. Our health data are collected primarily at clinics and hospitals and through various government agencies. These bland inventories of data do provide important information for pinpointing potential areas of risk for our population, but they give no insight into the meaning of these diseases for our families and communities.

Latinas are burdened by many of the same major causes of death as non-Latina women. The three leading causes of death among Latinas are cardiovascular disease (heart disease and stroke), cancer, and diabetes. For older Latinas, infectious diseases, such as influenza and pneumonia, and neurological diseases, such as Alzheimer's, are also among the top ten causes of death. With the exception of diabetes and chronic liver disease and cirrhosis, the age-adjusted mortality rates for Latinas from the top ten diseases are lower than the average for all U.S. women.

Although much of the attention on Latina health focuses on the major causes of illness, other diseases are also of increasing concern for this community, including sexually transmitted diseases such as HIV/AIDS; autoimmune diseases such as lupus, Graves' disease, and rheumatoid arthritis; neurological diseases such as Parkinson's and dementia; and chronic health conditions such as arthritis. In addition, a growing body of research suggests that mental illness, which is not captured in aggregate mortality data, is also of increasing concern within the Latina/o community (Torres and Rollock 2007).

Therefore, it is important to understand how the medical community describes the risk factors associated with these diseases. These identified risks can then become important information for developing culturally competent interventions for prevention and treatment.

Latinas and Heart Disease

Arterioescleriosis

Un remedio popular muy eficaz para combatir esta enfermedad es el ajo o el jugo del mismo en cantidades suficientes. La arteriosclerosis aparece por lo general en la vejez y es un síntoma de que el cuerpo está muy gastado. . . . Una dieta vegetariana es muy importante para el tratamiento de esta enfermedad. (Wagner 1952, 49)

Arteriosclerosis

A common and very effective remedy to combat this illness is garlic or the juice thereof in a sufficient quantity. Arteriosclerosis generally appears with old age and is an indicator that the body is worn out. A vegetarian diet is very important for the treatment of this illness.

Heart disease ranks as the primary cause of mortality among all Latina subgroups in the United States. Together with stroke, heart disease accounts for one-third of all Latina deaths (Hertz, Unger, and Ferrario 2006). Key heart disease risk factors for Latinas include a high rate of reported diabetes, being overweight or obese, reports of limited physical activity, and smoking (Sundaram et al. 2001).

Although multiple risk factors are associated with heart disease, the rapid growth of obesity within Latino communities, particularly among women and children, has become a central concern. Mexican American women have one of the highest rates of being overweight and obese (71.7 percent). This percentage is dramatically higher than for U.S. women as a whole (46.9 percent), non-Latina white women (43.3 percent), and non-Latina black women (65.2 percent) (Hedley et al. 2004). Thus, the current mortality rates for heart disease do not capture this dangerous health trend that is directly correlated to heart disease.

Mexican American women have lower rates of hypertension than the general U.S. female population, non-Latina white women, and non-Latina black women, but those Latinas with hypertension are significantly less likely than any of these other populations to report awareness of or current treatment for their condition. They also are less likely to indicate that their condition is under control (Glover et al. 2005). As is true for the Latina obesity epidemic, there is little awareness within Latina subpopulations of the importance of these underlying risk factors to the quality of their lives and health outcomes. Thus, preventive measures such as healthful diet and physical activity are not often in the forefront of their daily life choices.

Latinas and Cancer

Galio (*Galicium verum*)

Esta planta proporciona en forma de té, un buen remedio para el cáncer, y es usada también contra los barros. Además se emplea en la epilepsia. (Wagner 1952, 28)

Galio (*Galicium verum*)

This plant is used as a tea, a good remedy for cancer; it is also used for pimples [and acne]. In addition, it is used to treat epilepsy.

Cancer victimizes many within our Latino communities. Cancer mortality rates alone do not capture the significance of this disease for Latinas because their cancer outcomes appear relatively better than for other groups in the United States. At the same time, however, emerging research suggests that lack of adequate screening, outreach, and prevention as well as emerging resilient types of cancers are making both breast and cervical cancers important cancers to monitor within Latina groups.

Although breast cancer is diagnosed approximately 40 percent less often in Latinas than in non-Latina white women, it is more frequently diagnosed at a later stage (Bauer et al. 2007). A recent study has also found that an aggressive and hard-to-treat type of breast cancer is disproportionately affecting Latinas (Bauer et al. 2007). Known as triple-negative or "basal-like" carcinomas, these tumors do not respond to the newer target therapies. The findings are alarming not only because of the deadly nature of these carcinomas, but also because many Latinas face multiple barriers to obtaining comprehensive health care. Based on this study, Latinas are more likely to face later diagnosis—thus more widespread disease—and experience a cancer that does not respond to standard levels of care (Bauer et al. 2007).

In 2003, the incidence of cervical cancer among Latinas (14.9 cases per 100,000) was more than twice as high as among non-Latina white women (6.7 cases per 100,000) (CDC NCHS 2004a, table 53). Cervical cancer is easily treatable with early screening. Yet many Latinas are not adequately screened, placing them at greater risk of adverse health outcomes. Moreover, recent biomedical research has resulted in an important tool to combat cervical cancer further: the human papilloma virus vaccine. Further research is needed to determine the importance of both the vaccine and outreach efforts to reduce cervical cancer among Latinas (Tiro et al. 2007).

Latinas and Diabetes

Tronadora (*Tecoma mollis*)

La Tronadora es un remedio importante y conocido contra la diabetes.

Es una de las pocas plantas con las que se puede alcanzar la curación de este terrible enfermedad siguiendo lineamientos determinados. La tronadora debería hacerse conocer de todo el mundo. Para el cocimiento se toman unos diez gramos por litro de agua, debiendo tomarse este cantidad en el curso de un día.

La tronadora estimula el apetito e influye favorablemente en la digestión. (Wagner 1952, 117)

Tronadora *(Tecoma mollis)*

Tronadora is a very important and well-known treatment for diabetes.
It is one of the few plants that can come close to a cure for this horrible disease if it is used following specific guidelines. Tronadora should be known throughout the world. For the infusion, one takes ten grams per liter of water, drinking this quantity throughout the day.
Tronadora stimulates the appetite and positively influences the digestion.

As of 2004, two million Latino adults eighteen years and older, approximately 10.4 percent of this population group, had diabetes. On average, Latinos are 1.7 times more likely to have diabetes than are whites (Geiss et al. 2006). Diabetes is more than a growing chronic health condition for this population; it is becoming increasingly significant as a source of disability and death.

Today, the Latina death rate from diabetes is higher than that for non-Latina women and second only to that for African American women. Type 2 diabetes is largely preventable, but prevention efforts have thus far failed to stem the increasing incidence of this disease. Like cardiovascular disease, diabetes, especially type 2, is associated with how Latinas live their daily lives. The growing obesity epidemic within Latino families has positioned diabetes as one of the top four causes of death for Latinas.

For Latinas of childbearing age, gestational diabetes—a form of glucose intolerance that develops in some women during pregnancy—is also of great concern (Xiang et al. 2006). Gestational diabetes occurs relatively more frequently among African American, Hispanic/Latina, and American Indian women (Kjos et al. 1998). It is more common among obese women and among women with a family history of diabetes.

Screening for gestational diabetes is critical for the health of Latina mothers and their babies. However, many Latina women do not receive adequate and timely prenatal care. More than twice as many Latinas as white women had either late (third-trimester) or no prenatal care (5.3 versus 2.2 percent) (Xiang et al. 2006).[2] Because Latina women are less likely to have private health insurance or to use federal health-insurance systems such as Medicaid, they are especially vulnerable to falling out of the health-care delivery system (Frisbie, Echevarria, and Hummer 2001).

Latinas and Sexually Transmitted Diseases

Gonorrea

Un té excelente que se debe tomar durante el tratamiento llevado a cabo por algún especialista con un éxito satisfactorio, es el que se prepara de una mezcla de Folia uvae ursi y herbae herniariae (obtenibles de la botica). Una condición esencial es la dieta. Alimentación ligera y vegetariana, aun mejor una alimentación cruda durante algunas semanas. . . . Secreciones purulentas serán eliminadas con más facilidad si se vive durante algunas semanas de alimentación cruda. (Wagner 1952, 60)

Gonorrhea

An excellent tea that provides good results and that should be consumed for the duration of the illness as prescribed by a specialist is a mixture of *Folia uvae ursi* and *Herbae herniariae* (obtainable in a pharmacy). An essential element is diet. The diet should be light and vegetarian, and even better is a diet of raw foods for weeks. . . . Purulent secretions are more easily eliminated if the person lives several weeks on raw foods.

Latinas experience disproportionate rates of morbidity and mortality from HIV/AIDS. An estimated 361,000 persons in the United States are currently living with HIV, approximately 29 percent of whom are women. Although the rate of HIV diagnosis in adult and adolescent women overall decreased significantly from 2001 to 2004, the rate for Hispanic women still remains disproportionately high. In 2004, the rate for Hispanic women was five times that for non-Hispanic white women. Among the cases reported, heterosexual contact with an HIV-infected male was the most common means of infection (McDavid, Jianmin, and Leet 2006). Other research has found that women, including those who suspect their partners are at risk for HIV infection, may be reluctant to discuss condom use with their partners because they fear emotional and physical abuse as well as loss of financial support (CDC 2004a).

Latinas and the Rising Threat of Autoimmune and Neurological Diseases

Fríjol (*Phaseolus vulgaris*)

De la cáscara de fríjol se prepara un té que es un remedio magnífico contra el reumatismo, gota, diabetes y enfermedades de los riñones.

El sílice contenido en el fríjol elimina el ácido úrico que se acumula en el cuerpo, e influye favorablemente el sistema linfático. El té de cáscara de ejote revuelto con cola de caballo (*Aquistum arvense*) se emplea con buenos resultados para enfermedades del cutis. (Wagner 1952, page unknown)

Bean (*Phaseolus vulgaris*)

From the husk of the bean is prepared a tea that is a wonderful treatment for rheumatism, gout, diabetes, and kidney illnesses. The silica in the bean eliminates uric acid that accumulates in the body and has a positive influence on the lymphatic system. The tea from the husk of the bean with horsehair herb gives good results for illnesses that affect the skin.

Chuchupaxtle

Se utilice esta planta por los indígenas para la diabetes, para nervios, para el cerebro y contra insomnio. (Wagner 1952, 99)

Chuchupaxtle

This plant is used by the indigenous people for diabetes, for nerves, for the brain, and to combat insomnia.

Although widely different in their symptoms, lupus and Graves' disease fall within the broad category of autoimmune diseases. Although data and studies are limited for these two diseases, the diseases clearly have an impact on the growing numbers within the Latino community.

Lupus affects an estimated 239,000 people in the United States, about 9 out of 10 of whom are women. Approximately one-third of deaths due to lupus occur in those younger than forty-five. Lupus is also relatively more common in women of Hispanic descent, and they tend to develop symptoms at an earlier age than other women (Bastian et al. 2002).

Graves' disease is most commonly seen as a form of hyperthyroidism. It affects women five to ten times more frequently than men, a fact that has been attributed to the influence of estrogens on the immune system, specifically the B cell repertoire (Allahabadia et al. 2000). One study found that Mexican mestizos had a genetic susceptibility to autoimmune thyroid diseases due to a strong genetic influence of Amerindian genes (González-Trevino et al. 2002).

Parkinson's disease, although less visible than diseases such as heart disease and diabetes, is also making inroads within the Latino community. Stephen K. Van Den Eeden and colleagues (2003) found that the overall incidence rate for Parkinson's disease among Latinos was the highest for any racial/ethnic group, estimated at 16.6 per 100,000, compared with 13.6 per 100,000 for non-Hispanic whites, 11.3 per 100,000 for Asians, and 10.2 per 100,000 for blacks. In general, data on risk factors for Parkinson's disease are scarce as a result of difficulties in identifying affected individuals and the low frequency of diagnosed cases. In recent years, however, Parkinson's disease has been associated with both genetic and environmental factors. Two studies suggest that both the prevalence and the incidence rates for Parkinson's disease increase with age for blacks, Latinos, and whites (Mayeux et al. 1995; Van Den Eeden et al. 2003).

Latinas' Mental Health: Growing Concerns and Unmet Needs

Valeriana (*Valeriana procera*)

La valeriana mexicana da los mismos resultados que la europea. Los indios la emplean para neviosidad, falta de sueño, y debilidad del corazón. (Wagner 1952, 118)

Valerian (*Valeriana procera*)

Mexican valerian gives the same results as the European variety. The Indians use this for nervousness, sleeplessness, and weakness of the heart.

Mental health problems are increasingly surfacing as an important indicator of overall health for Latina women. For example, the prevalence of depressive symptoms in Mexican American women, both adolescents and adults, is reportedly higher than for non-Latina white women (Cuellar and Roberts 1997). The National Comorbidity Survey, which used a national probability sample of adults, found that the lifetime and thirty-day prevalence rates of major depressive episodes were highest among Hispanics, in particular Hispanic women (Torres and Rollock 2007). And depression is not the only mental health problem that poses greater health risks for the Latina community. Through their life cycle, Latinas face various challenges to their mental health as physical and mental stressors enter their lives. According to recent evidence, twice as many females as males suffer from these types of disorders (Torres and Rollock 2007). Unfortunately, very limited ethnic-specific research exists on such problems. Ataques de nervios and other anxiety disorders have been viewed within the Latino community as a part of the overall repertoire of disorders to be diagnosed and treated by indigenous healers. Given the proclivity for academic scholarly work to focus on narrow medical diagnostic tools, it may be opportune to revisit how traditional healers diagnose and treat these types of diseases and to integrate elders' knowledge into our mental health diagnostic tool set. As indicated earlier, diseases such as susto or mal de ojo[3] are rooted in traditional medicine within the context of Latinas' broader lived environment. This is one reason for the high rates of this type of diagnosis and treatment by curanderas. The way that curanderas view their patients within their extended social networks—both familial and communal—allows them to integrate effectively those diagnostic techniques that capture their patients' emotional, spiritual, and physical needs.

Access to high-quality mental health services geared to Latinas' needs is a documented problem, and a recent surgeon general's report on mental health indicates significant disparities in access to and quality of mental health care received by members of U.S. racial and ethnic minority groups. Moreover, Latinos are less likely than their white non-Latino counterparts to obtain treatment for depression and other mental health conditions (Schraufnagel et al. 2006). Clearly, then, it is time to consider both more resources for providing mental health-care services and the addition of services that include the knowledge of our traditional healers.

Latinas and the Golden Years: Aging in Body and Mind

Reumatismo

Contra el reumatismo hay muchos tés de hierbas que tienen la particularidad de limpiar la sangre y eliminar el ácido úrico que es la causa de la enfermedad. Un cocimiento de grama (hervido por espacio de una hora) es algo magnífico para estimular la eliminación de ácido úrico . . . para el reuma se aconseja también un tratamiento de limón . . . de un mes más o menos. Son saludables los baños de aguas sulfurosas y de aguas pantanosas. (Wagner 1952, 65)

Rheumatism

To combat rheumatism there are many herbal teas that help clean the blood and eliminate uric acid, which is the cause of the illness. An infusion of grama (boiled for one hour) is wonderful for stimulating the elimination of uric acid . . . for rheumatism also recommended is a lemon treatment for approximately a month. Sulfur water and pantanosas baths are very healthy as well.

Latinos are among the most rapidly growing ethnic groups of seniors in the United States. Yet most medical research has focused on younger populations. Several illnesses that impact our elders need to be considered with regard to health education, outreach, and new treatment models.

Chronic health conditions such as diabetes, heart disease, and arthritis are compounded as Latinas age. Elder Latinas frequently must cope with an array of illnesses that further debilitate their bodies, creating a host of problems for themselves and their families. As the Latina population ages, the social structures that traditionally have supported them are simultaneously weakening with the increase in dual-income working families, changing cultural expectations, and greater geographic distances separating family members. The traditional multigenerational caregiver model begins to fail as elders' expectations grow and families' ability to meet those expectations become stretched both financially and emotionally.

Our narratives provide a glimpse of the daily challenges in caring for our aging parents, yet we need still more information about how Latinas age and what illnesses most affect us. There is some evidence, for example, that elderly Latinos are particularly vulnerable to dementia. Data on neuropsychiatric and behavioral symptoms associated with dementia suggest that Latino populations experience higher levels of symptoms (Ortiz et al. 2006). We need to understand why these symptoms emerge and what types of pharmacological and behavioral treatments will assist Latinas in living with this disease and maintaining a higher quality of life through the aging process.

A particular form of severe dementia impacting our aging Latino community and creating increasing alarm within Latino families is Alzheimer's disease. On average, Latinos experience Alzheimer's symptoms 6.8 years earlier than non-Hispanic whites do, at an average age of 67.6 (Clark 2004). According to Christopher Clark (2004), the implication of the overall growth of the Latino aging population combined with the earlier onset of the disease in this population is that 1.3 million Latinos will develop and be affected by Alzheimer's within forty years. Given that women live longer than men and that the incidence of dementia increases with age, women are likely to be particularly affected.

Mind and body intersect throughout the aging process. When Latinas age, so do our bodies and our need to address la reuma, or rheumatism, as we colloquially refer to the age-related aches in our bones, joints, and bodies. Like most aging Americans, Latinos suffer from an array of health problems directly associated with arthritis. In addition, arthritis is the most common reported cause of disability. A higher proportion of Latinos with doctor-diagnosed arthritis report severe joint pain, compared with whites (32.5 percent versus 22.6 percent [CDC 2002a]), a dynamic we need to understand better. In addition, more clinical trials are needed to understand how Latinas express their pain and treat la reuma. For example, given that arthritis is not life threatening, to what extent do Latinas self-medicate using popular remedies or over-the-counter prescriptions? We also need a better sense of Latinas' pain threshold because women, in particular Latina women, are culturally socialized to place their personal needs behind those of other family members. Are elderly Latinas aguantando (putting up with) pain unnecessarily? If so, how do we support families and health-care providers in beginning pláticas with aging Latinas about their pain in order to develop culturally innovative interventions that increase both their comfort levels and their physical mobility?

The narratives in this volume and empirical observations of health status provide a window on some of our challenges and an important entry point for us to observe, diagnose, and work within our social networks to improve our own health outcomes. But we also need to explore how the structure of the U.S. health-care system creates and perpetuates the health-care disparities that we continue to observe throughout the Latina life cycle. Access to health care that is both culturally sensitive and financially viable is an important final element in our plática about Latina health.

Latinas: Challenges in Access to Health Care

Many of the health problems Latinas face throughout the life cycle are linked to the broader health-policy issue of access to adequate health care. As the demographic profile illustrates, Latinas are disproportionately underemployed, dependent on their spouses, or employed in low-wage sectors that do not provide health insurance. In 2003, 29.6 percent of Latinas did not have health-insurance coverage at any time during the year, more than double the percentage for all U.S. women (14.4 percent) and almost three times that for non-Hispanic white women (10.4 percent) (U.S. Census Bureau, Housing 2004). Lack of insurance prevents Latinas from accessing the primary health care necessary to screen for preventable diseases and obtain continuous treatment that might prevent the progression of existing health conditions and diseases. For instance, between 1987–94 and 1998–2000, Latinas forty years and older were significantly less likely than non-Latina white women to report having had a mammogram within the previous two years; and for 1998–2000, Latinas eighteen years and older were significantly less likely than either non-Latina white or black women to report having had a pap smear within the previous three years (CDC NCHS 2004a, table 81).

It should be noted, however, that fewer Latinas than Latino males lacked health-insurance coverage during 2003 (35.7 versus 29.6 percent) and that more Latinas than Latinos were covered by a government health plan (29.5 versus 23.7 percent) (U.S. Census Bureau, Housing 2004). In addition, Latinas of childbearing age are relatively better off with respect to health-insurance coverage due to the fact that the U.S. public health-insurance system, Medicaid, predominantly targets women of childbearing age and children. Unfortunately, this means that Latinas past their child-bearing years but too young to be eligible for Medicare are at greatest risk for underinsurance. This is the time frame when many face the onset of severe chronic health problems such as hypertension, diabetes, and heart disease. Without adequate insurance coverage, Latinas have a disproportionate risk of complications and death from otherwise preventable or treatable conditions.

Another important policy consideration relates to how we construct and deliver health care. In the past, many Latinas relied on traditional healers within their families or communities for their health care. Moreover, in the context of their class position and cultural interpretation of illnesses, many Latina women wait until the illness manifests clear clinical symptoms, such as pain or visible inflammation, before entering the U.S. medical system. This places them at risk for not receiving treatment until a late stage of the disease, when treatment may be more difficult and the likelihood of a good health outcome is reduced. In addition, in some communities in the Southwest, traditional healers have become an alternative system of health care (Trotter and Chavira 1997). Although we do not suggest that this traditional system should replace mainstream medical care for these women, we still need to build on Latinos' cultural knowledge of complementary systems of care that include traditional remedies that encompass mind, body, and soul. Such cultural sensitivity will help Latinas feel more comfortable within and willing to access the mainstream health-care system. Traditional healing practices and customs can help them understand and cope with their illnesses. Complementary therapies may include medicinal herbs, touch therapy, social networks, and spiritual beliefs that augment the diagnostic and healing process. We may very well find that rather than being a hindrance to care, our culturally based alternative therapies and beliefs may enhance the effectiveness of mainstream medical practices.

Latinas, in espíritu and salud, are clearly at risk given the trajectory of diseases within the overall population and the lack of access to affordable and culturally sensitive screening and preventive treatment. Nevertheless, Latinas have enormous capacity to develop healing strategies and gain power over their illnesses, as can be seen from the narratives in this book. We need only reflect on Gloria Anzaldúa's powerful words, "I have to open myself up to the belief system that I *can* heal myself, that my body can heal itself with the help of the spirit," to recognize that our familial social support systems, our shared pláticas, our strategies for self-healing, our deep spirituality, and our collective wisdom can broaden the scope of how we view and treat illness. Health professionals need to begin listening to and reflecting on these narratives in order to create a more just and humane system of health care.

Notes

Introduction

1. As Debbie Lupton explains, "The mass media are important in portraying medicine, health care, disease, illness and health risks in certain ways, from the soap opera's kindly doctor to the news bulletin's account of medical miracles, contributing to people's understandings of these phenomena, especially when they have little or no direct experience of them. . . . The linguistic and visual representations of medicine, illness, disease, and the body in elite and popular culture and medico-scientific texts are influential in the construction of both lay and medical knowledges and experiences of these phenomena" (2003, 19, 83).

2. For a classic, foundational narrative inquiry that focuses on the doctor-patient relationship and incorporates the case study and the idea of "empathetic witnessing," see Arthur Kleinman's oft-cited *The Illness Narratives: Suffering, Healing, and the Human Condition* (1988). Although his insights that "we must inquire into the structure of illness meanings: the manner in which illness is made meaningful" and that "illness is transactional, communicative and profoundly social" (85–86) are important, his common generic constructions of patients and "the human condition" contrast with our focus on the unique experiences of Latina subjects, as does his method of incorporating patients' voices as brief quotations bolstering his argument. Also see Frank 1995. Other more recent works are authored by women (see Charon 2006) or are the products of collaborations between women scholars (see Mattingly and Garro 2000) or between women scholars and physicians (see DasGupta and Hurst 2007). In *Latina Realities* (1997), Olivia M. Espín also argues that the narrative approach is important for women's lives.

3. Gloria Anzaldúa passed away during the week of May 15, 2004. In "Remembering Gloria Anzaldúa (1942–2004)," AnaLouise Keating describes Gloria's legacy and struggles with health:

One of the boldest feminist thinkers and social justice activists of our time, Anzaldúa and her writings give courage and inspiration to many. . . . Although Anzaldúa had been living with diabetes for over a decade, many of her readers were unaware of the disease's ongoing, debilitating effects on her life. Even those of us who knew her well were shocked by her sudden death. . . . It is impossible to fully describe the complex, multidimensional nature of Anzaldúa and her writings. A versatile author, she published poetry, theoretical essays, short stories, autobiographical narratives, interviews, children's books, and anthologies. As one of the first openly queer Chicana writers, she played a major role in defining Chicana/o, queer, and female identities. And as editor or coeditor of three multicultural, multigenre feminist anthologies, she helped to develop new, inclusionary movements for social justice. Although she chose to work outside the university system (except for carefully selected teaching engagements and conference speaking gigs), her impact on many disciplines—including American studies, composition studies, cultural studies, ethnic studies, feminism/feminist theory, literary studies, and women's studies—was immense. She also played a leading, though seldom acknowledged role in developing queer theory. (2004)

Not only were health narratives a part of the memorials that celebrated Anzaldúa's life, but she herself left a chronicle of her life with diabetes in *this bridge we call home*, published in 2002, where she describes the frightening outcomes associated with the disease: "Three weeks after the doctor confirms your diagnosis you cross the trestle bridge near the wharf, our short-cut to downtown Santa Cruz. As you listen to your footsteps echoing on the timber, the reality of having a disease that could cost you your feet . . . your eyes . . . your creativity . . . penetrates, arresting you in the middle del Puente [bridge]. You're furious with your body for limiting your artistic activities, for its slow crawl toward the grave" (Anzaldúa 2002, 55).

Another important inspiration for this book was Lata Mani. Her seminal online article "What Makes a Life Worth Living" was instrumental for my conceptualization of Latina health "work." In regard to people who are bedridden from disability, Mani says, "The challenge of their situation often demands more of them cognitively and physically than [of] people around them, but their efforts fall beyond the bounds of a narrow definition of action or doing. Their work to process, confront and live creatively with their situation remains invisible, unclassifiable" (2001).

4. Adela de la Torre and Antonio Estrada suggest, "The shortage of Hispanic health care professionals limits access to health care for the Mexican American population because minority health care professionals overwhelmingly serve in their respective communities. Most of these communities are poor and underserved because of a low ratio of health professionals to this population. According to a Council on Graduate Medical Education report, . . . Hispanic health care professionals are important because they bridge the

gap between the culture of the minority group and that of heath care service providers" (2001, 90).

5. These barriers are significant given that "despite notable progress in the overall health of the nation, there are continuing disparities in the burden of illness and death experienced by Latinas/os and other groups compared to the U.S. population as a whole" (CDC OMH 2007, n.p.).

6. De la Torre and Estrada (2001) describe cultural competency as a process that requires individuals and systems to expand their ability to know about, be sensitive to, and have respect for cultural diversity.

7. I use the term *Americans* not only to refer to those who have been born in the United States, but also to highlight an affiliation with the hemispheric region of the Americas.

8. Lupton notes that "the lay perspective on the illness experience, hospitalization and the cause of illness and disease has often been neglected" (2003, 111).

9. In Exhibit 1.2, Aguirre Molina and Molina state that "compared to other women, Latinas reported higher levels of difficulty when communicating with their providers and faced considerable access barriers to healthcare" (quoted in Aguirre-Molina and Molina 2003, 16).

10. In some clinical settings, Latinas' expressive health-oriented discourses may be undervalued as unnecessary and excessive. Medical practitioners may view Latinas' discursive style as a cultural manifestation of a hyperexpressive temperament that must be reined in to facilitate "really meaningful" health communication (i.e., established Western formulaic discursive practices). Yet "medicalese" is no less culturally mediated than Latina discourses are. Cultural mediations can be found in clinical discourses and settings, medical textbooks and records, exchanges with health-care practitioners, and self-help books written for the general public.

11. "Latinas make up approximately half of the Latino community and 6 per cent of the total U.S. population. By the year 2050 they will make up 25 per cent of the total female population; one in four women will be a Latina" (Aguirre Molina and Molina 2003, 4).

12. We are inspired here by Vicki Ruiz's description of Latina legacies (Ruiz and Sánchez Korrol 2005, 16).

1. Of Breasts and Baldness

1. For confirming data, see statistics compiled and published by the National Cancer Institute (2006). In 2003, per 100,000 women, 126 white women, 119 African American women, 87 Asian American women, and 80 Hispanic women had breast cancer.

2. On lymph node involvement and general breast cancer workup protocols, see National Comprehensive Cancer Network 2005, 8–15, 17–18.

3. On DCIS, see National Comprehensive Cancer Network 2005, 13, 32–37. See also http://www.cancer.gov/cancertopics/types/breast.

4. "BRACA 1" and "BRACA 2" stand for Breast Cancer Gene 1 and Breast Cancer Gene 2. Tests for these genes are done to determine potential for inherited abnormalities that predispose one to breast or ovarian cancer. For more information on this gene testing and how to determine whether to get tested, see U.S. Preventive Services Task Force 2005.

5. On lymph node dissection, see National Comprehensive Cancer Network 2005, 17–18. For general information on staging breast cancer, see pp. 13–15.

6. An excellent source on lymphedema and lifelong management of it is American Cancer Society 2006.

7. The Community Breast Health Project provides support, information, and education for women at any stage of breast cancer, as well as for their families and caregivers. It can be contacted at 390 Cambridge Ave., Palo Alto, CA 94306, (650) 326-6299, http://www.cbhp.org. WomanCARE offers women's cancer advocacy, resources, and education for women with any type of cancer, as well as for their families, friends, and caregivers. Contact Woman-CARE at P.O. Box 944, Santa Cruz, CA 95060, (831) 457-CARE, office@ womencaresantacruz.org.

8. *Ganas* is a complex term for which there is no English equivalent. It roughly means "determination" and "desire," and carries connotations derived from its root verb *ganar*, "to win, to attain, to get ahead of."

9. Premenopausal cancer patients face a dizzying array of options for preserving fertility. For further information, consult the Fertile Hope Project, a nonprofit organization based in New York that provides reproductive information and support to cancer patients: http://www.fertilehope.org. For current information on cancer and in-vitro fertilization procedures, see Oktay et al. 2005.

10. Physician treatment protocols are standardized by the National Comprehensive Cancer Network, which publishes guidelines and even decision trees (i.e., "if x condition exists, then y options should be considered") that help to inform oncologists in their decision making about patient treatment (see National Comprehensive Cancer Network 2007).

11. Locks of Love is a public nonprofit organization that provides human-hair wigs to financially disadvantaged children under age eighteen suffering from long-term medical hair loss from any diagnosis (see http://www.locksof love.org).

12. The term *chismiando* literally means "gossiping," but it connotes serious information exchange and tale-telling among women.

13. For more information on chemotherapy side effects and how to manage them, see http://www.cancer.gov/cancertopics/chemotherapy-and-you/page4.

14. Taxol, like other chemotherapy drugs, works against cancer by interfering with the growth of cancer cells while slowing their spread in the body. Taxol is used in the treatment of breast, ovarian, and lung cancers, as well as of AIDS-related Kaposi's sarcoma (see http://www.drugs.com/taxol.html).

15. For information on supplements that may make a difference in lymphedema during radiation, see Gothard et al. 2004.

16. For more on upper-extremity DVT, see Joffe and Goldhaber 2002 and Martinelli et al. 2004.

17. For information on various chemotherapy drugs, see http://www.clinical pharmacology.com. Some very new research indicates the potential benefits of immunotherapy in treating cancer in the future. See "Next Generation" 2005.

18. For information on AIs, see, for example, Buzdar et al. 2006.

2. Embodying Dementia

1. Gloria Anzaldúa (2003) uses this metaphor to describe women who will no longer be silenced.

2. A poem I wrote for my mother:

Aura

I think of you, Viejita
And you call my name
You leave the gray cloud
Of your dementia
And respond to my soul's
Silent call

I will miss you when you leave
I will long for your caresses
The ones you also could not give me
When I was a child

Because I no longer miss
The intelligence you lost
I have become accustomed to your obsessions
Your old fears
The vacant look in your eyes

You are no longer who you were
But your maternal instinct
Cannot be extinguished
You still perceive
What I do not tell you
You still foresee
The dangers blind to me
You still read the desires
Invisible even to me

I will miss you, Viejita
When you are finally gone

3. *Viejita* literally means "old lady"; it is a term of endearment used for elderly women, in particular mothers.

4. Traditional Panamanian dish of rice, chickpeas, and well-seasoned flank steak.

3. *Countering the Pain That Never Heals*

1. In Latina culture, pláticas are discussions among women within the context of their personal values, family, and culture (Avila 1999). Charlas are get-togethers (parties). Chisme is gossip, usually discussions regarding education, community events, politics, jobs, and children (see http://www.cafecon chisme.com).

2. Descartes describes the pain pathways as follows: "If, for example, fire comes near the foot, the minute particles of this fire, which as you know move with great velocity, have the power to set in motion the spot of the skin of the foot which they touch, and by this means pulling upon the delicate thread which is attached to the spot of the skin, they open up at the same instant the pore against which the delicate thread ends, just as by pulling at one end of a rope one makes to strike at the same instant a bell which hangs at the other end" (1644, quoted in Morris and Goli 1994, 11).

4. *Letters to Ceci*

1. For this chapter, I have edited the letters in order to focus on the interweaving of a professional life with health issues. Moreover, what began as communication with Ceci through handwritten letters eventually became e-mail correspondence.

2. According to the New York Thyroid Center Web site (2005), in hyperthyroidism the thyroid produces excess thyroid hormone. This condition affects more than twenty million Americans, mostly women. The symptoms can range from mild nervousness, weight loss, and insomnia to a dangerously fast heartbeat that can be life threatening. The most common of the several types of hyperthyroidism is Graves' disease (or diffuse toxic goiter), a disease caused by antibodies in the blood that stimulate the thyroid to grow and produce excess hormone. Other symptoms associated with hyperthyroidism are hypertension (high blood pressure); sudden paralysis; thyroid enlargement (lump in the neck); pretibial myxdemia: thick redness on the front of the legs (specific to Graves' disease); thin, delicate skin and irregular fingernail and hair growth; menstrual disturbance (decreased flow); impaired fertility; mental disturbances; and significant protrusion of the eyes due to swelling of the tissue behind them (with Graves' disease).

3. In 1989, Lawrence I. Ross McDougall wrote, "Barbara Bush's recent disclosure that her thyroid gland 'just went wacko' focused attention on the serious problems that can result when something disturbs the production of hormones by the thyroid."

4. I was to find out much later that for those who have had long-term Graves' disease, the problems with uptake of calcium become unavoidable.

5. See Balch and Balch 1990.

6. For updated information, see http://www.mayoclinic.com, http://www.endocrineweb.com, http://www.endo-society.org, and http://www.thyroidmanager.com.

7. To the original list I sent out to my siblings, I have added the findings of the Lermann and Murray studies reported in Wiersinga and DeGroot 2004. These findings are of particular interest because all of us eventually were affected by all of these symptoms. The insidious and nonspecific nature of hypothyroidism (as you can see from the long list) means that it may be undiagnosed for years. A high degree of suspicion on the part of the patient and physician is required for its early diagnosis. The following symptoms and signs of moderate to severe hypothyroidism are listed in order of decreasing significance according to the majority of studies (see, e.g., Khurram et al. 2003); the italicized items are considered most specific to its detection: weakness, dry skin, *coarse skin, lethargy, slow speech, edema of the eyelids (buildup of fluid between tissue cells), sensation of cold, decreased sweating,* cold skin, thick tongue, edema of the face (buildup of fluid between tissue cells), coarseness of hair, cardiac enlargement (revealed by X ray), pallor of skin, impaired memory, constipation, weight gain, hair loss, pallid lips, dyspnea (difficulty in breathing), peripheral edema, *hoarseness,* anorexia, nervousness, menorrhagia, deafness, palpitations, poor heart sounds, precordial pain, poor vision, rundus oculi changes (i.e., in the retina of the eye opposite the pupil), dysmenorrhea (severe pain or cramps in the lower abdomen during menstruation), weight loss, atrophic tongue, emotional instability, choking sensation, fineness of hair, cyanosis (bluish color of the skin and mucous membranes due to lack of oxygen in the blood), dysphagia (difficulty in swallowing), brittle nails, depression, muscle weakness, muscle pain, joint pain, *paresthesia (abnormal or unexplained tingling, pricking, or burning sensation on the skin),* slow cerebration (ability to think or reason), and *slow movements.*

8. It is quite common for patients to take a few months to regain thyroid hormone balance after they initiate thyroid-replacement therapy. Notwithstanding laboratory test results within normal ranges, a minority of patients continue to suffer from hypothyroid symptoms, which may or may not worsen. Sparse attention has been given to these cases until very recently. Kaplan, Sarne, and Schneider comment, "We tell our patients, 'It's really quite simple, your thyroid is not working (or has been removed or destroyed by our treatment). The tablet contains the natural hormone that your body cannot make. Don't worry, you'll be fine.' For many of our patients, T4 therapy resolves their symptoms and they are fine. For some, however, this therapy remains unsatisfactory, with the persistence of specific symptoms or a failure to regain a normal sense of well-being" (2003, 4540–42). Also see Romijn, Smit, and Lamberts 2003.

9. With this project, I published an English translation of Leonor Villegas de Magnón's *The Rebel* (1994).

10. Hashimoto's disease is a chronic inflammation of the thyroid wherein white blood cells attack the thyroid, leading to hypothyroidism.

11. Common triggers for thyroid disease listed in the literature are major surgery, contraceptives, pregnancy, and stress. In April 1995, the Environmental Protection Agency sponsored a workshop to establish the research needs for risk assessment of health and environmental effects of endocrine disruptors (U.S. Environmental Protection Agency, Endocrine Disruptor Research Initiative, at http://epa.gov/endocrine/pubs.html). As I began to learn of these studies, I kept a close watch for information on the endocrine disruptors found in agricultural pesticides. Recent books and reports have brought more public attention to the issue; see Colborn, Dumanoski, and Peterson Myers 1996; Kegley, Neumeister, and Martin 1999; Reeves et al. 1999; Krimsky 2000; *Global Pesticide Campaigner* 2001; and Madsen, Kucher, and Olle 2004. To this day, the topic of pesticide effects is quite sensitive, as Lintelmann and colleagues indicate: "The possibility that some chemicals may disrupt the endocrine systems in humans and animals has received considerable attention in the scientific and public community. Endocrine disruption is on the agenda of many experts' groups, steering committees and panels of governmental organizations, industry, and academia throughout the world. Because the disturbance of the endocrine system is a very sensitive topic, scientific findings or observations are often controversially discussed among scientists, environmentalists, and authorities" (2003, 631).

12. *Telling to Live: Latina Feminist Testimonios* (Latina Feminist Group 2001) received the Myers Outstanding Book Award for 2002 from the Gustavus Myers Center for the Study of Bigotry and Human Rights in North America, located in Boston.

13. Correlations between thyroid hormone-replacement therapy and both bone loss and cognitive changes are discussed in Bennett et al. 1989; Stepán and Límanová 1992; Mennemeier, Garner, and Heilman 1993; Leentjens and Kappers 1995; and Wekking et al. 2005.

14. *One Wound for Another / Una herida por otra: Testimonios de Latinas in the U.S. (11 septiembre 2001–11 enero 2002)* (Joysmith and Lomas 2005).

15. Since the late 1980s, several studies have probed the neurocognitive effects of hyperthyroidism, even after treatment. In one study, "54 percent of the treated individuals manifested cognitive dysfunction at 10 years posttreatment, and in half of these persons, the dysfunction was described as marked to severe in range. Weaknesses were identified in the areas of attention, concentration, conceptual reasoning, visual-spatial processing, and long-term memory" (Erlanger, Kutner, and Jacobs 1999, 188). Researchers continue working on issues of patient assessment and appropriate treatment

(see McMillan et al. 2006). However, as Romijin, Smit, and Lamberts point out, the medical field cannot yet adequately resolve the many issues surrounding endocrine-replacement therapy. With regard to thyroid hormone, they state, "[I]t is highly likely that, in patients treated with L-thyroxine, subtle derangements at the tissue level are present with respect to thyroid hormone availability, and probably also thyroid hormone action. Unfortunately, we lack sensitive signs and symptoms to evaluate this in clinical practice. In addition, we do not have sensitive biochemical markers of thyroid hormone action at the tissue level other than TSH [thyroid-stimulating hormone]" (2003, 93).

5. Fat in America

1. I am using a pseudonym that provides me with much-needed anonymity. To the overweight and obese Latinas among us: ¡Adelante: Sí se puede! The title for this paper was inspired by Luis Rodríguez's poem "Fat in America" (in Rodríguez 2005).

2. According to the Minority Women's Health Web page (http://www.4woman.gov/minority/hispanicamerican/obesity.com), "Women with a BMI of 25 to 29.9 are considered overweight, while women with a BMI of 30 or more are considered obese. All adults (aged 18 years or older) who have a BMI of 25 or more are considered at risk for early death and disability from being overweight or obese. These health risks increase as the BMI rises." You can calculate your BMI on this site. The article also suggests that where you carry your fat makes a difference. For instance, if you carry it around your waist or middle and have a waist larger than thirty-five inches, you have higher health risks.

3. Gallstones are clusters of solid material, mostly cholesterol, that form in the gallbladder. They sometimes can cause abdominal or back pain. According to the Weight-Control Information Network, an information service of the National Institute of Diabetes and Digestive and Kidney Diseases, type 2 diabetes, heart disease and stroke, cancer, sleep apnea, osteoarthritis, and fatty liver disease are other health problems that those who are overweight or obese may develop (2004, 2).

4. According to the National Diabetes Information Clearinghouse Web page, "54 million people in the United States had pre-diabetes in 2002" (2006). The Palo Alto Medical Foundation reports that "about 11 percent of people with pre-diabetes in the Diabetes Prevention Program standard or control group developed type 2 diabetes each year during the average 3 years of follow-up. Other studies show that most people with pre-diabetes develop type 2 diabetes in 10 years" (2003). There is hope that I can turn my condition around because for "some people with pre-diabetes, intervening early care can actually turn back the clock and return elevated blood glucose levels to the

normal range." Yet "recent research has shown that some long-term damage to the body, especially the heart and circulatory system, may already be occurring during pre-diabetes" (American Diabetes Association n.d.e.).

5. The National Diabetes Information Clearinghouse refers to fatty liver as "the silent liver disease" (2006). According to an American Liver Foundation fact sheet, in fatty liver, fat accounts for 5 to 10 percent or more of the liver's weight. In terms of health consequences, fatty liver may cause no damage or may lead to inflammation of the liver (steatohepatitis), which does damage the liver and can lead to cirrhosis. People with fatty livers are encouraged to lose weight, exercise regularly, and lower their triglyceride levels through diet or medication or both (American Liver Foundation n.d.).

6. On its "Dietary Fats: Know Which Ones to Choose" (2003) Web page, the Mayo Clinic urges readers to choose unsaturated fats (monounsaturated and polyunsaturated) over saturated or trans fats. "These fats, if used in place of others, can lower your risk of heart disease by reducing the total and low-density lipoprotein (LDL) ['bad'] cholesterol levels in your blood."

7. I am also learning how specific types of foods affect blood sugar. Part of this education has come from the American Diabetes Association's Diabetes Learning Center. The center has a useful interactive tool called "Rate Your Plate," which recommends that your plate contain one-quarter protein, one-half vegetables, and one-quarter carbohydrates.

7. *Debe ser la reuma*

1. An immigrant woman's culture, acculturation level, and legal status may increase her vulnerability to intimate-partner violence (Raj 2002). However, studies addressing ethnic differences in intimate-partner violence have produced mixed results for the Mexican American and Mexican migrant population. Some studies find that Mexican Americans have lower levels of intimate partner violence than do African Americans and non-Mexican whites (Rouse 1988; Sorenson, Upchurch, and Shen 1996; Benson et al. 2000). Yet others find that Mexican Americans are more violent than non-Hispanic whites (Straus and Smith 1990; Sorenson and Telles 1991) or find no differences between Mexican Americans and non-Mexican whites (Kantor, Jasinski, and Aldarondo 1994).

2. Although almost no longitudinal studies address the effect of intimate-partner violence on women's health, Plichta (2004) states that such violence is associated with increased levels of injury and disability, chronic pain, substance abuse, reproductive disorders, poorer pregnancy outcomes, and worse general health among the women who are its victims.

3. The sun was rising when I said good-bye / in the breeze, there you came to my mind / arriving at the bridge, from the bridge I went back / covered in tears, tears that I shed for you.

4. Although osteoarthritis cannot be cured, some interventions are effective

in reducing pain and stiffness and in slowing the progression of the disease. The treatment protocol specifies a hierarchy of progressive treatments depending on each patient's attitude and response. Weight loss and exercise are always recommended and are usually the first treatment. They are combined with application of heat and cold over the joint and topical pain relievers. Medication is the next step (analgesics, nonsteroidal anti-inflammatory drugs, and corticosteroids). Surgery is the last recourse and may consist of joint immobilization, osteotomy (removal of bone spurs), or arthroscopy (surgery to the joint).

5. Abusers are often extremely possessive and jealous. They tend to have the attitude that they own their victims and, in order to control them, prohibit them from talking to other people and break any sources of social support they might have. Abusers thus maintain the power of violence by insulating their victims from people who might encourage them to leave (Rokach 2006). At the same time, the victims are frequently very committed to the relationship, lack self-confidence, believe the myths about domestic violence (including the argument that they are responsible for the abuse), have nowhere else to go, truly believe the abuser will change, and, in most cases, are very conscious of the dangers in leaving and are economically dependent on the abuser. Therefore, victims rarely leave their abusers.

6. There are five main types of depression; the least severe, dysthymia, places the patient at risk for major depression. Major depression is a mood disturbance that may include overwhelming feelings of sadness and grief, loss of interest or pleasure in activities the person usually enjoys, and feelings of worthlessness or guilt. An adjustment disorder, in contrast, is a state of feeling tense, sad, overwhelmed, or angry because of a traumatic event, such as the loss of a loved one, which severely affects the individual's life activities. Bipolar disorder and seasonal affective disorder are the other two main types of depression.

A person with depression may lose interest in normal daily activities; feel sad, helpless, or hopeless; have crying spells; and experience sleep disturbances (sleeping too much or having difficulty sleeping). The person may also have trouble concentrating, making decisions, and remembering information (Constantino et al. 2002). She may experience increased or reduced appetite and may seem restless, agitated, irritable, and easily annoyed. Fatigue or slowing of body movements are other possible signs. Feelings of worthlessness and excessive guilt, decreased interest in sexual relations, thoughts of death, gastrointestinal problems (indigestion, constipation, or diarrhea), headache, and backache can be manifestations of concealed depression.

7. Psychotherapy plays an important role in treating mild to moderate depression, but major depression almost always requires treatment with antidepressant medications. Among these medications are selective serotonin reuptake inhibitors, tricyclics, and monoamine oxidase inhibitors. It is some-

times necessary to try a variety of antidepressants before finding the most effective medication or combination for a particular individual, and the dosage must be progressively increased until it reaches an effective level. Thus, a doctor must carefully monitor patients on antidepressant medications and must choose the medication most likely to be effective based on each patient's family history and the match between his or her symptoms and the medication's expected action and side effects. Antidepressant medications must be taken regularly for three to four weeks (or even up to nine weeks) before any therapeutic effect is noticed.

9. "I Wake Up and Go to Bed with Pills"

1. For a discussion of Latina hypertension by California regions, see Baezconde-Garbanati, Portillo, and Garbanati 2003, 44.

2. The American Heart Association reports that "African-American and Hispanic women have higher prevalence rates of high blood pressure, obesity, physical inactivity, diabetes and metabolic syndrome than white women. Yet they are less likely than white women to know that being overweight, smoking, physical inactivity, high cholesterol and a family history of heart disease increase their heart disease risk" (2004b). This lack of awareness has increased in recent years: "The percentage of Hispanic women who reported seeing, hearing or reading information on heart disease in the past 12 months dropped from 68 percent in the 2000 survey to 61 percent in 2003. That was significantly behind the 82 percent and 74 percent reported for white and African-American women [respectively]. . . . Also, fewer Hispanic women (30 percent) said their doctors have discussed heart disease with them, compared to 38 percent of African-American and 40 percent of white women." Moreover, their doctors have never discussed the fact that these women are in a high-risk group for heart disease (American Heart Association 2004a).

3. Tapering caffeine consumption can be an important tool for lowering hypertension. "Caffeine can . . . possibly increase your blood pressure. . . . Caffeine's influence on blood pressure is a topic of debate. . . . Exactly what causes this spike in blood pressure is uncertain. . . . As a precaution, many doctors advise people with high blood pressure to limit daily caffeine intake to no more than two cups of coffee, three or four cups of tea or two to four cans of caffeinated soda" (Sheps 2002, 128–29).

4. The major classes of blood pressure medicine are diuretics, beta blockers, angiotensin-converting enzyme inhibitors, angiotensin II receptor blockers, calcium antagonists (calcium channel blockers), alpha blockers, central-acting agents, and direct vasodilators. For descriptions of these medications, see Sheps 2002, 158–72.

5. Taking hypertension medications on a regular schedule is particularly important to keep blood pressure levels stable and to limit side effects. For this

reason, Sheldon Sheps (for the Mayo Clinic) recommends strategies such as tying medications to daily events, using alarms, or organizing pills in pillboxes (2002, 147–48).

6. The ability to afford expensive medications is an important issue in patient compliance with medication regimens (Sheps 2002, 171).

7. Although the cause of high blood pressure in a specific case may be undeterminable, common causes are family history, obesity, high intake of salt or alcohol, sedentary lifestyle, and, alas, normal aging. Typically, if no organ damage has occurred, physicians initially recommend weight loss, dietary restrictions, and lifestyle changes. These steps may be supplemented, when necessary, with medications (Yahoo Health 2004).

8. Blood pressure rises steeply in women after age forty. By the fifty-five to sixty-four age range, some 30 to 40 percent of menopausal women will have hypertension ("Manage Menopause" 2006).

9. In *Your Guide to Lowering Your Blood Pressure with DASH*, the U.S. Department of Health (2006) recommends reducing sodium intake, following the Dietary Approaches to Stop Hypertension (DASH) plan, reading food labels carefully, and cooking with spices other than salt. This publication also includes many recipes for healthy living and lowering blood pressure.

10. For a video demonstration of home monitoring, visit the High Blood Pressure Center at the Mayo Clinic Web site, http://www.mayoclinic.com.

11. For possible synergistic effects of combining certain blood pressure medications and other medications that are often prescribed together, see Sheps 2002, 170, 186.

12. A University of California, Irvine, analysis of more than twenty-four thousand respondents to the 2001 California Health Interview Survey revealed that working more than a forty-hour week is one risk factor for developing high blood pressure ("Working" 2006).

13. For a full description of breathing techniques and other relaxation methods, see Sheps 2002, 138–39. One of the treatments for hypertension not mentioned in this narrative is exercise. Lourdes Baezconde-Garbanati, Carmen Portillo, and James Garbanati (citing Grassi et al. 1999) point to various barriers that commonly limit Latinas' activity levels, including "(1) not having a nearby location to exercise, (2) living in unsafe neighborhoods, (3) lacking transportation, (4) unaffordable programs, (5) not knowing where to go, (6) not knowing how to start a physical activity program, (7) family responsibilities, and (8) work schedules" (2003, 50).

14. "While it's hardly surprising that arguing with your spouse or fighting with the boss can make blood pressure soar, research has shown that virtually any communication can put blood pressure on the rise." Researchers at the University of Maryland discovered that speaking can cause blood pressure to increase by 10 to 50 percent, with hypertensive individuals showing the greatest increase (Tkac 1990, 79).

10. A Tapestry of Illness

1. "Retinopathy is a serious complication of diabetes that results from damage to the blood vessels of the light-sensitive tissue at the back of the eye (retina). Retinopathy can progress and cause vision loss. Laser surgery and surgical removal of the vitreous gel (vitrectomy) are the only two effective treatments for advanced stages of diabetic retinopathy. Although vitrectomy does not cure the disease, it may improve vision, especially in people who have developed bleeding into the vitreous gel (vitreous hemorrhage), retinal detachment, or severe scar tissue formation" (from the Mayo Clinic Web site at http://www.mayoclinic.com).

11. "Working toward Wholeness"

Author's Note: I dedicate this essay to the spirit and memory of Gloria Anzaldúa. Thanks to Eddy Lynton and Kit Quan for reading and commenting on earlier drafts of this essay.

1. Anzaldúa's writings have been included in *The Norton Anthology of American Literature; The Heath Anthology of American Literature; The Norton Anthology of Literature by Women; The Norton Anthology of Theory and Criticism; Infinite Divisions: An Anthology of Chicana Literature; The Latino/a Condition; Living Chicana Theory; Border Texts; Feminism and "Race";* and other leading anthologies.

2. For additional information on Anzaldúa's concept of autohistoria-teoría, see my article "Shifting Worlds, una entrada" (Keating 2005b).

3. See, for instance, Anzaldúa's discussion of El Mundo Zurdo in "La Prieta" (1983) and "Now let us shift" (2002).

4. The interview transcript is copyrighted by AnaLouise Keating and the Gloria E. Anzaldúa Literary Estate. An edited version of this dialogue was published in Anzaldúa's *Interviews / Entrevistas* (2000).

5. For additional information on Anzaldúa's holistic worldview, see Amala Levine's "Champion of the Spirit: Anzaldúa's Critique of Rationalist Epistemology" (2005) and my "Shifting Perspectives: Spiritual Activism, Social Transformation, and the Politics of Spirit" (Keating 2005a).

6. Thanks to Kit Quan for suggesting that I include these details.

13. A Retrospective on the Narratives of Latina Health

1. As Debbie Lupton suggests, "Metaphor works by association, by comparing two non-associated entities with each other centering on the ways in which they resemble one another" (2003, 59).

14. Latina Health

1. All translations of Wagner 1952 are by Adela de la Torre.

2. Figures from the National Center for Health Statistics corroborate these statistics; in 2000, almost three times as many Latinas as white women had

late or no prenatal care. And whereas African American women in this year (as in 2002) had higher rates of late or no prenatal care than did Latinas as a whole, Mexican-origin Latinas had slightly higher rates than black women (U.S. DHHS HRSA 2004).

3. Adela de la Torre and Antonio Estrada define mal de ojo as "an illness caused by being stared at; usually perceived in children or babies who have been paid more attention than usual; the illness also has a supernatural component" (2001, 130).

References
and Further Reading

Aetna. 2006. *Plan for Your Health.* At http://www.womenshealth.aetna.com. Accessed November 2006.

Aguirre-Molina, Marilyn, and Carlos W. Molina. 2003. *Latina Health in the United States: A Public Health Reader.* San Francisco: Jossey-Bass.

Allahabadia, A., J. Daykin, R. Holder, M. Sheppard, S. Gough, and J. Franklyn. 2000. Age and gender predict the outcome of treatment for Graves' hyperthyroidism. *Journal of Clinical Endocrinology and Metabolism* 85 (3): 1038–42.

American Cancer Society. 2006. *Lymphedema: Understanding and Managing Lymphedema after Cancer Treatment.* Foreword by Sam Donaldson. Atlanta: American Cancer Society.

American College of Obstetricians and Gynecologists Practice Bulletin. 2001. Gestational diabetes: Number 30. *Obstetrics and Gynecology* 98:525–38.

American College of Rheumatology. 2004. Medscape Conference coverage of selected sessions at the American College of Rheumatology 68th Annual Scientific Meeting, October 16–21, 2004, San Antonio, Texas.

American Diabetes Association. n.d.a. All about diabetes. At http://www.diabetes.org/about-diabetes.jsp. Accessed January 2007.

———. n.d.b. Frequently asked questions about pre-diabetes. At http://www.diabetes.org/prediabetes/faq.jsp. Accessed February 2, 2007.

———. n.d.c. Gestational diabetes. At http://www.diabetes.org/gestational-diabetes.jsp. Accessed September 15, 2005.

————. n.d.d. How to prevent or delay diabetes. At http://www.diabetes
.org/diabetes-prevention/how-to-prevent-diabetes.jsp.   Accessed
July 30, 2008.

————. n.d.e. Pre-diabetes. At http://www.diabetes.org/diabetes-prevention/
pre-diabetes.jsp. Accessed March 3, 2007.

American Diabetes Association, Diabetes Learning Center. n.d. Rate your
plate. At http://www.diabetes.org/all-about-diabetes/chan_eng/i3/i3p4
.htm. Accessed March 4, 2007.

American Heart Association. 2004a. Latina/Hispanic women most at risk
group for cardiovascular disease. August 23. At http://www.american
heart.org/presenter.jhtml?identifier=3024293. Accessed March 10, 2007.

————. 2004b. Minority women unaware of higher heart risk. Journal
Report, February 4. At http://www.americanheart.org/presenter.jhtml
?identifier=3018809. Accessed March 10, 2007.

————. 2007. Hispanic women at higher risk for heart disease. March 2.
At http://www.americanheart.org/presenter.jhtml?identifier=3045794.
Accessed March 10, 2007.

American Institute for Cancer Research. n.d. The new American plate. At
http://www.aicr.org/site/PageServer?pagename=pub_nap_index_21.
Accessed March 4, 2007.

American Liver Foundation. n.d. Q & A series: Fatty liver. At http://www
.liverfoundation.org/images/articles/1105/Q&AFattyLiver.pdf. Accessed
March 3, 2007.

American Medical Association. 1998. *Essential Guide to Hypertension*. New
York: Pocket Books.

American Thyroid Association. 2006. Graves' disease. At http://www
.thyroid.org/patients/patient_brochures/graves.html#diagnosis.
Accessed December 10, 2005.

Anzaldúa, Gloria E. 1983. La prieta. In *This Bridge Called My Back: Writings by
Radical Women of Color*, edited by Cherríe Moraga and Gloria Anzaldúa,
198–209. New York: Kitchen Table, Women of Color Press.

————. 1987. *Borderlands / La frontera: The New Mestiza*. San Francisco: Spin-
sters, Aunt Lute.

————, ed. 1990. *Making Face, Making Soul / Haciendo caras: Creative and Critical
Perspectives by Feminists of Color*. San Francisco: Aunt Lute.

————. 1999. S.I.C. Spiritual identity crisis. Unpublished manuscript.

————. 2000. *Interviews / Entrevistas*. Edited by AnaLouise Keating. New
York: Routledge.

————. 2002. Now let us shift: . . . the path of conocimiento . . . inner
work, public acts. In *this bridge we call home: radical visions for transformation*,

edited by Gloria E. Anzaldúa and AnaLouise Keating, 540–78. New York: Routledge.

————. 2003. Speaking in tongues: Letter to third world women writers. In *Women Writing Resistance: Essays on Latina America and the Caribbean*, edited by Jennifer Browdy de Hernandez, 79–90. Cambridge, Mass.: South End Press.

————. 2005. Let us be the healing of the wound: The Coyolxauhqui imperative—la sombra y el sueño. In *One Wound for Another / Una herida por otra: Testimonios de Latinas in the U.S. (11 septiembre de 2001–11 enero de 2002)*, edited by Claire Joysmith and Clara Lomas, 92–103. Mexico City: Centro de Investigación de América del Norte, Universidad Nacional Autónoma de México.

Anzaldúa, Gloria E., and AnaLouise Keating, eds. 2002. *this bridge we call home: radical visions for transformation*. New York: Routledge.

Arias, E., M. F. MacDorman, D. M. Strobino, and B. Guver. 2003. Annual summary of vital statistics—2002. *Pediatrics* 112 (6, Part 1): 1915–30.

Arrien, Angeles. 1992. *Signs of Life: The Five Universal Shapes and How to Use Them*. Sonoma, Calif.: Arcus.

Arthritis Society. 2005. Rheumatoid arthritis. Last updated March 29, 2005. At http://www.arthritis.ca/types%20of%20arthritis/ra/default.asp?s = 1. Accessed August 8, 2005.

Avila, Elena. 1999. *Woman Who Glows in the Dark: A Curandera Reveals Traditional Aztec Secrets of Physical and Spiritual Health*. New York: J. P. Tarcher, Putnam.

Bachman, Linda. 2006. *Another Morning: Voices of Truth and Hope from Mothers with Cancer*. Emeryville, Calif.: Seal Press.

Baezconde-Garbanati, Lourdes, Carmen J. Portillo, and James A. Garbanati. 2003. Disparities in health indicators for Latinas in California. In *Latina Health in the United States: A Public Health Reader*, edited by Marilyn Aguirre-Molina and Carlos W. Molina, 37–62. San Francisco: Jossey-Bass.

Balch, Phyllis A., and James F. Balch. 1990. *Dietary Prescription for Cooking and Dietary Wellness*. Greenfield, Ind.: P.A.B.

Bastian, H., J. Roseman, G. McGwin, G. Alarco, A. Friedman, B. Fessler, B. Baethges, and J. Reveille. 2002. Systemic lupus erythematosus in three ethnic groups. XII. Risk factors for lupus nephritis after diagnosis. *Lupus* 11 (3): 152–60.

Bateson, Catherine Mary. 1990. *Composing a Life*. New York: Plume Books.

Bauer, K. R., M. Brown, R. D. Cress, C. Parise, and V. Caggiano. 2007. Descriptive analysis of estrogen receptor (ER)–negative, progesterone receptor (PR)–negative, and HER2-negative invasive breast cancer, the so-called triple-negative phenotype. *Cancer* 109 (9): 1721–28.

Behar, Ruth. 1993. *Translated Woman: Crossing the Border with Esperanza's Story.* Boston: Beacon Press.

——. 1997. *The Vulnerable Observer: Anthropology That Breaks Your Heart.* Boston: Beacon Press.

Bender, Sue. 1996. *Everyday Sacred: A Woman's Journey Home.* San Francisco: Harper San Francisco.

Bennett, G. W., C. A. Marsden, K. C. P. Fone, F. V. Johnson, and D. J. Heal. 1989. TRH-catecholamine interactions in brain and spinal cord. *Annals of the New York Academy of Sciences* 553:106–20.

Benson, M. L., G. Fox, A. DeMaris, and J. Van Wyk. 2000. Violence in families: The intersection of race, poverty, and community context. In *Contemporary Perspectives in Family Research,* vol. 2, edited by G. L. Fox and M. L. Benson, 91–109. New York: Elsevier Science.

Berkow, Robert, ed. 1997. *Merck Manual of Medical Information.* Whitehouse Station, N.J.: Merck Research Laboratories.

Bookwala, J., T. L. Harralson, and P. A. Parmelle. 2003. Effects of pain on functioning and well-being in older adults with osteoarthritis of the knee. *Psychology of Aging* 18 (4): 844–50.

Buzdar, Aman, Rowan Cheblowski, Jack Cuzick, Sean Duffy, John Forbes, Walter Jonat, and Peter Ravdin. 2006. Defining the role of aromatase inhibitors in the adjuvant endocrine treatment of early breast cancer. *Current Medical Research and Opinion* 22 (8): 1575–85.

Campo, Rafael. 2003. *The Healing Art: A Doctor's Black Bag of Poetry.* New York: W. W. Norton.

Casey, B. M., M. J. Lucas, D. D. McIntire, and K. J. Leveno. 1997. Pregnancy outcomes in women with gestational diabetes compared with the general obstetric population. *Obstetrics and Gynecology* 90 (6): 869–73.

Centers for Disease Control and Prevention (CDC). 2002a. A demographic and health snapshot of the U.S. Hispanic/Latino population. At http://www.cdc.gov/NCHS/ data/hpdata2010/chcsummit.pdf. Accessed June 21, 2005.

——. 2002b. *Racial/Ethnic Differences in the Prevalence and Impact of Doctor-Diagnosed Arthritis—United States, 2005 MMWR.* Atlanta: Centers for Disease Control and Prevention.

——. 2004a. HIV/AIDS among Hispanics. At http://www.cdc.gov/hiv/resources/factsheets/PDF/hispanic.pdf. Accessed June 13, 2007.

——. 2004b. *National Diabetes Fact Sheet: General Information and National Estimates on Diabetes in the United States, 2003.* Rev. ed. Atlanta, Ga.: U.S.

Department of Health and Human Services. At http://www.cdc.gov/diabetes/pubs/pdf/ndfs_2003.pdf. Accessed August 8, 2004.

Centers for Disease Control, National Center for Health Statistics (CDC NCHS). 2004a. *Health, United States, 2004, with Chartbook on Trends in the Health of Americans.* Hyattsville, Md.: CDC NCHS. Also available at http://www.cdc.gov/nchs/data/hus/hus04trend.pdf.

————. 2004b. *National Health Interview Survey.* Ser. 10, no. 222, Summary Health Statistics for U.S. Adults. U.S. Department of Health and Human Services (DHHS) Publication no. 2004-1550. Atlanta, Ga.: U.S. DHHS.

Centers for Disease Control and Prevention, National Immunization Program (CDC NIP). 2001. How serious is chickenpox? At http://www.cdc.gov/nip/diseases/varicella. Accessed November 15, 2006.

Centers for Disease Control and Prevention, Office of Minority Health (CDC OMH). 2007. About minority health. At http://www.cdc.gov/omh/AMH/AMH .htm. Accessed January 13, 2007.

Charon, Rita. 2006. *Narrative Medicine: Honoring the Stories of Illness.* Oxford: Oxford University Press.

Chong, Jia-Rui. 2007. Virus may be cause of mad cow. *Los Angeles Times,* January 31.

Clark, Christopher M. 2004. Latino patients with Alzheimer's disease have an earlier age of symptom onset compared to Anglos. *Neurobiology of Aging* 25:s106.

Cohen, Deborah A., and Robert M. Gelfand. 2002. *Just Get Me through This: A Practical Guide to Coping with Breast Cancer.* New York: Kensington Books.

Cohen, Lawrence. 2006. Introduction: Thinking about dementia. In *Thinking about Dementia: Culture, Loss, and the Anthropology of Senility,* edited by Annette Leibing and Lawrence Cohen, 1–22. New Brunswick, N.J.: Rutgers University Press.

Colborn, Theo, Diane Dumanoski, and John Peterson Myers. 1996. *Our Stolen Future: Are We Threatening Our Fertility, Intelligence, and Survival?* New York: Dutton.

Colenda, C., J. Wilk, and J. West. 2002. The geriatric psychiatry workforce in 2002: Analysis from the 2002 National Survey of Psychiatric Practice. *American Journal of Geriatric Psychiatry* 13 (9): 756–65.

Constantino, R. E., L. K. Sekula, J. Lebish, and E. Buehner. 2002. Depression and behavioral manifestations of depression in female survivors of the suicide of their significant other and female survivors of abuse. *Journal of the American Psychiatric Nurses Association* 8 (1): 27–32.

Conway, Jill Kerr. 1998. *When Memory Speaks: Reflections on Autobiography.* New York: Alfred A. Knopf.

Cook, Marshall. 1996. *Slow Down and Get More Done.* Cincinnati: S&W.

Corpi, Lucha. 1995. *Cactus Blood: A Mystery Novel.* Houston: Arte Público Press.

Council on Graduate Medical Education. 1998. *Twelfth Report: Minorities in Medicine.* Rockville, Md.: Council on Graduate Medical Education.

County of Los Angeles Public Health Office. 2004. Diabetes. *L.A. Health* (August). At http://search.lapublichealth.org/wwwfiles/ph/hae/ha/la_health_diabetes_82004.pdf. Accessed February 1, 2007.

A Course in Miracles. 1975. New York: Foundation for Inner Peace.

Coustan, D. R. 1995. Management of gestational diabetes. In *Diabetes Mellitus in Pregnancy*, edited by E. Albert Reece and Donald R. Coustan, 277–86. New York: Churchill Livingstone.

Cox, C., and A. Monk. 1993. Hispanic culture and family care of Alzheimer's patients. *Health Social Work* 28:92–100.

Cuellar, I., and R. E. Roberts. 1997. Relations of depression, acculturation, and socioeconomic status in a Latino sample. *Hispanic Journal of Behavioral Sciences* 19 (2): 230–38.

Dabelea D., J. K. Snell-Bergeon, C. L. Hartsfield, K. J. Bischoff, R. F. Hamman, and R. S. McDuffie. 2005. Increasing prevalence of gestational diabetes mellitus (GDM) over time and by birth cohort: Kaiser Permanente of Colorado GDM Screening Program. *Diabetes Care* 28 (3): 579–84.

DasGupta, Sayantani, and Marsha Hurst, eds. 2007. *Stories of Illness and Healing: Women Write Their Bodies.* Kent, Ohio: Kent State University Press.

Defining dementia. 2008. *Medline Medical Encyclopedia.* Last updated February 4, 2008. At http://www.nlm.nih.gov/ medlineplus/ency/article/000739 .htm#Definition. Accessed April 23, 2008.

De la Torre, Adela. 2002. *Moving from the Margins: A Chicana Voice on Public Policy.* Tucson: University of Arizona Press.

De la Torre, Adela, and Antonio Estrada. 2001. *Mexican Americans and Health: ¡Sana! ¡Sana!* Tucson: University of Arizona Press.

Delgado, Jane. 2002. *¡Salud! A Latina's Guide to Total Health—Body, Mind, and Spirit.* New York: HarperCollins.

Denzin, Norman K., and Yvonna S. Lincoln, eds. 2005. Part IV. Methods of collecting and analyzing empirical materials. In *The Sage Handbook of Qualitative Research*, 641. Thousand Oaks, Calif.: Sage Publications.

Dequeker, J., and P. A. Dieppe. 1998. Disorders of bone cartilage and connective tissue. In *Rheumatology*, 2d ed., edited by J. H. Klippel and P. A. Dieppe, 8.1.1–8.1.2. London: Mosby.

Dibner, Robin. 1994. *Lupus Handbook for Women*. New York: Fireside.

Donald, Anna. 1998. The worlds we live in. In *Narrative-Based Medicine*, edited by Trisha Greenhalgh and Brian Hurwitz, 17–26. London: BMJ Books.

Dooley, S. L., B. E. Metzger, N. Cho, and K. Liu. 1991. The influence of demographic and phenotypic heterogeneity on the prevalence of gestational diabetes mellitus. *International Journal of Gynecology and Obstetrics* 35 (1): 13–18.

Dossey, Larry. 1993. *Healing Words*. San Francisco: Harper San Francisco.

Duff, Kat. 1993. *The Alchemy of Illness*. New York: Bell Tower.

Elwyn, Glyn, and Richard Gwyn. 1998. Stories we hear and stories we tell . . . analyzing talk in clinical practice. In *Narrative-Based Medicine*, edited by Trisha Greenhalgh and Brian Hurwitz, 165–75. London: BMJ Books.

Erlanger, D. M., K. C. Kutner, and A. R. Jacobs. 1999. Hormones and cognition: Current concepts and issues in neuropsychology. *Neuropsychology Review* 9 (4): 188.

Espín, Olivia M. 1997. *Latina Realities: Essays on Healing, Migration, and Sexuality*. Boulder, Colo.: Westview Press.

———. 2003. *Latina Healers: Lives of Power and Tradition*. Encino, Calif.: Floricanto Press.

Estés, Clarissa Pinkola. 1992. *Women Who Run with the Wolves*. New York: Ballantine Books.

———. 1995. *The Faithful Gardener: A Wise Tale about That Which Can Never Die*. San Francisco: Harper San Francisco.

Evenson, K. R., O. L. Sarmiento, K. W. Tawney, M. L. Macon, and A. S. Ammerman. 2003. Personal, social, and environmental correlates of physical activity in North Carolina Latina immigrants. *American Journal of Preventive Medicine* 25 (3): 77–85.

Expert Committee on the Diagnosis and Classification of Diabetes Mellitus. 2003. Report of the Expert Committee on the Diagnosis and Classification of Diabetes Mellitus. *Diabetes Care* 26 (1): S5–S20.

Ferrara, A., M. M. Hedderson, C. P. Quesenberry, and J. V. Selby. 2002. Prevalence of gestational diabetes mellitus detected by the National Diabetes Data Group or the Carpenter and Coustan plasma glucose thresholds. *Diabetes Care* 25 (9): 1625–30.

Ferrara, A., H. S. Kahn, C. P. Quesenberry, C. Riley, and M. M. Hedderson. 2004. An increase in the incidence of gestational diabetes mellitus: Northern California, 1991–2000. *Obstetrics and Gynecology* 103 (3): 526–33.

Flores, Yvette, Ladson Hinton, Carol E. Franz, and Judith L. Baker. 2008. Between love and obligation: Latina daughters of elderly with dementia. Unpublished manuscript.

Frank, Arthur W. 1995. *The Wounded Storyteller: Body, Illness, and Ethics.* Chicago: University of Chicago Press.

Fregoso, Rosa Linda, and Angie Chabram. 1990. Chicana/o cultural representations: Reframing alternative critical discourses. *Cultural Studies* 4 (3): 203–12.

Frisbie, W. P., S. Echevarria, and R. A. Hummer. 2001. Prenatal care utilization among non-Hispanic whites, African Americans, and Mexican Americans. *Maternal and Child Health* 5 (1): 21–33.

Geiss, L., L. Pan, B. Cadwell, E. Gregg, S. Benjamin, and M. Engelgau. 2006. Changes in incidence of diabetes in U.S. adults, 1997–2003. *American Journal of Preventive Medicine* 30 (5): 371–77.

Georgiou, Archelle. 2006. Cardiovascular disease. *Latina Style* 12 (3). At http://www.latinastyle.com/currentissue/v12-3/cardio.html. Accessed October 25, 2007.

Girard, Vickie. 2004. *There's No Place Like Hope: A Guide to Beating Cancer in Mind-Sized Bites.* Seattle: Compendium.

Global Pesticide Campaigner. 2001. Vol. 11, no. 2 (August). At http://www.panna.org/resources/gpc.html. Accessed December 15, 2005.

Glover, M. J., K. J. Greenlund, C. Ayala, and J. Croft. 2005. Racial/ethnic disparities in prevalence, treatment, and control of hypertension—United States, 1999–2002. *Morbidity and Mortality Weekly Report* 54 (1): 7–9.

González, Adela. 2006. Latinas: A call to action. ¡Punto Final! column. *Latina Style* 12 (3). At http://www.latinastyle.com/currentissue/v12-3/punto.html. Accessed July 30, 2008.

González-Trevino, O., J. Yamamota-Furusho, T. Cutido-Moguel, B. Hernandez-Martinez, T. S. Rodríguez-Reyna, R. Ruiz-Moralez, G. Vargas-Alarcon, and J. Granados. 2002. HLA study on two Mexican mestizo families with autoimmune thyroid disease. *Autoimmunity* 35 (4): 265–69.

Gothard, L., P. Comes, J. Earl, E. Hall, J. MacLaren, P. Mortimer, J. Peacock, C. Peckitt, M. Woods, and J. Yarnold. 2004. Double-blind placebo-controlled randomized trial of vitamin E and pentoxifylline in patients with chronic arm lymphoedema and fibrosis after surgery and radiotherapy for breast cancer. *Radiotherapy and Oncology* 73:133–39.

Graham, Janice. E. 2006. Diagnosing dementia: Epidemiological and clinical data as cultural text. In *Thinking about Dementia: Culture, Loss, and the Anthropology of Senility*, edited by Annette Leibing and Lawrence Cohen, 80–105. New Brunswick, N.J.: Rutgers University Press.

Grassi, K., M. G. Gonzalez, P. Tello, and G. He. 1999. La Vida Caminando: A community-based physical activity program designed for rural Latino Families. *Journal of Health Education* 30 (2, Suppl.): 13–17.

Groopman, Jerome. 2004. *The Anatomy of Hope: How People Prevail in the Face of Illness.* New York: Random House.

Harpham, Wendy Schlessel. 2004. *When a Patient Has Cancer: A Guide to Caring for Your Children.* New York: HarperCollins.

Harwood, D. G., W. W. Barker, R. L. Ownby, M. Bravo, H. Aguero, and R. Duara. 2000. Predictors of positive and negative appraisal among Cuban American caregivers of Alzheimer's disease patients. *International Journal of Geriatric Psychiatry* 15:481–87.

Hedderson, M. M., A. Ferrara, and D. A. Sacks. 2003. Gestational diabetes mellitus and lesser degrees of pregnancy hyperglycemia: Association with increased risk of spontaneous preterm birth. *Obstetrics and Gynecology* 102 (4): 850–56.

Hedley, A. A., C. L. Ogden, C. L. Johnson, M. D. Carroll, L. R. Curtin, and K. M. Flegal. 2004. Prevalence of overweight and obesity among U.S. children, adolescents, and adults, 1999–2002. *Journal of the American Medical Association* 291 (23): 2847–50.

Hertz, R., A. Unger, and C. Ferrario. 2006. Diabetes, hypertension, and dyslipidemia in Mexican Americans and non-Hispanic whites. *American Journal of Preventive Medicine* 30 (2): 103–10.

Hinton, Ladson, Carol E. Franz, and Yvette G. Flores. 2000. *National Institute of Aging–Funded Study of Anglo and Latino Caregivers of Elderly with Dementia.* Washington, D.C.: National Institutes of Health.

Hinton, Ladson, Mary Haan, Sue Geller, and Dan Mungas. 2003. Neuropsychiatric symptoms in Latino elders with dementia or cognitive impairment without dementia and factors that modify their association with caregiver depression. *The Gerontologist* 43:669–77.

Hispanic community needs increased awareness of hypertension treatment options according to national survey. 2007. HispanicBusiness.com, February 14. At http://www.hispanicbusiness.com/news/newsbyid.asp?id=20965. Accessed June 10, 2007.

Hollingsworth D., Y. Vaucher, and T. R. Yamamoto. 1991. Diabetes in pregnancy in Mexican Americans. *Diabetes Care* 14 (7): 695–705.

Hugher, Ghram. 2000. *Lupus: The Facts.* Cambridge: Oxford University Press.

Jaffe, Eric. 2006. Health column. *Los Angeles Times,* November 26.

Joffe, G. M., J. R. Esterlitz, R. J. Levine, J. D. Clemens, M. G. Ewell, B. M. Sibai, and P. M. Catalano. 1998. The relationship between abnormal glucose tolerance and hypertensive disorders of pregnancy in healthy nulliparous women. Calcium for Preeclampsia Prevention Study Group. *American Journal of Obstetrics and Gynecology* 179 (4): 1032–37.

Joffe, Hylton V., and Samuel Z. Goldhaber. 2002. Upper-extremity deep vein thrombosis. *Circulation* 106: 1874–80. At http://www.circulationaha .org. Accessed October 29, 2007.

Johnson, Carla A. 2007. U.S. docs tough on blood pressure. *CBS News Healthwatch,* January 22. At http://www.cbsnews.com/stories/2007/01/22/ap/ health/mainD8MQJO1O2.shtml_. Accessed June 10, 2007.

Joysmith, Claire, and Clara Lomas. 2005. *One Wound for Another / Una herida por otra: Testimonios de Latinas in the U.S. (11 septiembre de 2001–11 enero de 2002).* Mexico City: Centro de Investigación de América del Norte, Universidad Nacional Autónoma de México.

Kantor, G. K., J. L. Jasinski, and E. Aldarondo. 1994. Socioeconomic status and incidence of marital violence in Hispanic families. *Violence and Victims* 9:207–22.

Kaplan, Michael M., David H. Sarne, and Arthur B. Schneider. 2003. In search of the impossible dream? Thyroid hormone replacement therapy that treats all symptoms in all hypothyroid patients. *Journal of Clinical Endocrinology and Metabolism* 88 (10): 4540–42.

Katerndahl, D., and J. Realini. 1998. Panic disorder in Hispanic patients. *Family Medicine* 30 (3): 210–14.

Kaufman, Sharon R. 2006. Dementia "near death" and life itself. In *Thinking about Dementia: Culture, Loss, and the Anthropology of Senility,* edited by Annette Leibing and Lawrence Cohen, 23–42. New Brunswick, N.J.: Rutgers University Press.

Keating, AnaLouise. 2004. Remembering Gloria Anzaldúa (1942–2004). *Women's Review* (October). At http://www.wellesley.edu/WomensReview/ archive/2004/ 10/highlt.html. Accessed January 13, 2007.

———. 2005a. Shifting perspectives: Spiritual activism, social transformation, and the politics of spirit. In *EntreMundos / AmongWorlds: New Perspectives on Gloria E. Anzaldúa,* edited by AnaLouise Keating, 241–54. New York: Palgrave Macmillan.

———. 2005b. Shifting worlds, una entrada. In *EntreMundos / AmongWorlds:*

New Perspectives on Gloria E. Anzaldúa, edited by AnaLouise Keating, 1–12. New York: Palgrave Macmillan.

Kegley, Susan, Lars Neumeister, and Timothy Martin. 1999. *Disrupting the Balance: Ecological Impacts of Pesticides in California.* San Francisco: Pesticide Action Network North America and Californians for Pesticide Reform. At http://www.panna.org/resources/documents/disruptingAvail.dv .html. Accessed January 15, 2007.

Khurram, Irfan M., Kiran S. Choudhry, Khan Muhammad, and Najmul Islam. 2003. Clinical presentation of hypothyroidism: A case control analysis. *Journal of Ayub Medical College Abbottabad* 15 (1). At http://www .ayubmed.edu.pk/JAMC/PAST/15-1/Irfan%20Hypothyroidism.htm. Accessed December 10, 2005.

Kieffer, E. C., W. J. Carman, B. W. Gillespie, G. H. Nolan, S. E. Worley, and J. R. Guzman. 2001. Obesity and gestational diabetes among African-American women and Latinas in Detroit: Implications for disparities in women's health. *Journal of the American Medical Women's Association* 56 (4): 181–87, 196.

Kjos, S. L., R. K. Peters, A. Xiang, D. Thomas, U. Schaefer, and T. A. Buchanan. 1998. Contraception and the risk of type 2 diabetes mellitus in Latina women with prior gestational diabetes mellitus. *Journal of the American Medical Association* 280 (6): 533–38.

Kleinman, Arthur. 1988. *The Illness Narratives: Suffering, Healing, and the Human Condition.* New York: Basic Books.

Krimsky, Sheldon. 2000. *Hormonal Chaos: The Scientific and Social Origins of the Environmental Endocrine Hypothesis.* Baltimore: Johns Hopkins University Press.

Lang, Anthony E. 2005. Parkinson's disease: Selected basic and clinical research developments over the past decade. At the National Parkinson Foundation Web site, http://www.parkinson.org/NETCOMMUNITY/ Page .aspx?&pid=390&srcid=198. Accessed March 2, 2007.

Lara, Irene. 2005. Daughter of Coatlicue: An interview with Gloria Anzaldúa. In *EntreMundos / AmongWorlds: New Perspectives on Gloria Anzaldúa*, edited by AnaLouise Keating, 41–55. New York: Palgrave Macmillan.

Latina Feminist Group. 2001. *Telling to Live: Latina Feminist Testimonios.* Durham, N.C.: Duke University Press.

Lawrence, R. C., C. G. Helmick, F. C. Arnett, R. A. Deyo, D. T. Felson, E. H. Giannini, S. P. Heyse, R. Hirsch, M. C. Hochberg, G. G. Hunder, M. H. Liang, S. R. Pillemer, V. D. Steen, and F. Wolfe. 1998. Estimates of the prevalence of arthritis and selected musculoskeletal disorders in the United States. *Arthritis and Rheumatism* 41 (5): 778–99.

Leentjens, A. F. G., and E. F. Kappers. 1995. Persistent cognitive defects after corrected hypothyroidism. *Psychopathology* 28:235–37.

Lefers, Mark. 2004. Arthritis. *Hedgehog Signaling Glossary.* Last updated July 26, 2004. At http://www.biochem.northwestern.edu./holmgren/ Glossary/ Definitions/Def-A/arthritis.html. Accessed August 8, 2005.

Levine, Amala. 2005. Champion of the spirit: Anzaldúa's critique of rationalist epistemology. In *EntreMundos / AmongWorlds: New Perspectives on Gloria Anzaldúa,* edited by AnaLouise Keating, 171–84. New York: Palgrave Macmillan.

Levins Morales, Aurora. 1998. *Medicine Stories: History, Culture, and the Politics of Integrity.* Cambridge, Mass.: South End Press.

Lévy, Bernard-Henri. 2006. *American Vertigo,* New York: Random House.

Lieberman, Abraham N., Govindan Gopinathan, Andreas Neophytides, and Menek Goldstein. n.d. *Parkinson's Disease Handbook.* Brochure. New York: American Parkinson Disease Association.

Lintelmann, J., A. Katayama, N. Kurihara, L. Shore, and A. Wenzel. 2003. Endocrine disruptors in the environment. International Union of Pure and Applied Chemistry Technical Report. *Pure and Applied Chemistry* 75 (5): 631.

Lucas, María Elena. 1993. *Forged under the Sun: The Life of María Elena Lucas.* Ann Arbor: University of Michigan Press.

Lupton, Debbie. 2003. *Medicine as Culture: Illness, Disease, and the Body in Western Societies.* Thousand Oaks, Calif.: Sage.

Lupus Foundation of America. 1995. *Living Well with Lupus.* Washington, D.C.: Lupus Foundation of America.

Madsen, Travis, Yana Kucher, and Teri Olle. 2004. *Growing Up Toxic: Chemical Exposures and Increases in Developmental Diseases.* Los Angeles: Environment California Research and Policy Center. At http://www .environmentcalifornia.org/center/improving-environmental-health/ growing-up-toxic. Accessed December 15, 2005.

Manage menopause without pressure. 2006. *The Star Online,* November 28. At http://thestar.com.my/health/story.asp?file=/2006/11/26/ health/16103419&sec=health. Accessed June 10, 2007.

Mani, Lata. 2001. What makes a life worth living? *The Hindu,* September 16.

Marsa, Linda. 2006. Health column. *Los Angeles Times,* August 28.

Martinelli, Ida, Tullia Battaglioli, Paolo Bucciarelli, Serena Maria Passamonti, and Pier Mannuccio Mannucci. 2004. Risk factors and recurrence rate of primary deep vein thrombosis of the upper extremities. *Circulation* 110:566–70. Also at http://www.circulationaha .org.

Mattingly, Cheryl, and Linda C. Garro, eds. 2000. *Narrative and the Cultural*

Construction of Illness and Healing. Berkeley and Los Angeles: University of California Press.

Max, D. T. 2006. *The Family That Couldn't Sleep: A Medical Mystery.* New York: Random House.

Mayeux, R., K. Marder, L. Cote, J. Denaro, N. Hemenegildo, H. Mejia, M. X. Tang, R. Lantigue, D. Wilder, B. Gurland, and A. Hauser. 1995. The frequency of idiopathic Parkinson's disease by age, ethnic group, and sex in northern Manhattan, 1988–1993. *American Journal of Epidemiology* 142 (6): 820–27.

Mayo Clinic. 2003. Dietary fats: Know which ones to choose. At http://www .mayoclinic.com/health/fat/NU00262. Accessed March 3, 2007.

McCue, Kathleen. 1994. *How to Help Children through a Parent's Serious Illness: Supportive, Practical Advice from a Leading Child Life Specialist.* New York: St. Martin's, Griffin.

McDavid, K., L. Jianmin, and L. Leet. 2006. Racial and ethnic disparities in HIV diagnosis for women in the United States. *Journal of Acquired Immune Deficiency Syndrome* 42 (1): 101–7.

McDougall, Lawrence I. Ross. 1989. Thyroid disorders are common, but diagnosis is sometimes difficult. The Doctor's World. *New York Times,* April 25. At http://query.nytimes.com/gst/fullpage.html?sec=health&res= 950DE2DC1E3FF936A15757C0A96F948260. Accessed December 10, 2005.

McMillan, C., C. Bradley, S. Razvi, and J. Weaver. 2006. Psychometric evaluation of a new questionnaire measuring treatment satisfaction in hypothyroidism: The ThyTSQ. *Value in Health* 9 (2): 132–39.

Medlineplus National Library of Medicine, John Hopkins Vasculitis Center. 2006. Prednisone. At http://vasculitis.med.jhu.edu/treatments/ prednisone .html. Accessed November 15, 2006.

Mennemeier, M., R. D. Garner, and K. M. Heilman. 1993. Memory, mood, and measurement in hypothyroidism. *Journal of Clinical and Experimental Neuropsychology* 15:822–31.

Miller, Benjamin Frank, and Claire Brackman Keane. 1983. *Encyclopedia and Dictionary of Medicine, Nursing, and Allied Health.* 3rd ed. Philadelphia: W. B. Saunders.

Moraga, Cherríe L., and Gloria E. Anzaldúa, eds. 2002. *This Bridge Called My Back: Writings by Radical Women of Color.* 1981. Exp. and rev. 3rd ed. Berkeley, Calif.: Third Woman Press.

Morris, C. E., and V. Goli. 1994. The physiology and bio-medical aspects of chronic pain in later life. In *Older Women with Chronic Pain,* edited by Karen A. Roberto, 9–24. Binghamton, N.Y.: Haworth Press.

Murphy, Robert F. 1987. *The Body Silent*. New York: W. W. Norton.

Myers, H. F., I. Lesser, N. Rodriguez, C. B. Mira, W. C. Hwang, C. Camp, D. Anderson, L. Erickson, and M. Wohl. 2002. Ethnic differences in clinical presentation of depression in adult women. *Cultural Diversity and Ethnic Minority Psychology* 8 (2): 138–56.

Myss, Carolyn. 1997. *Why People Don't Heal and How They Can*. New York: Three Rivers Press.

Nalick, Jon. 2002. No Parkinson's zone. *USC Health Magazine* (spring). At the University of Southern California Health Sciences Center Web site, http://www.usc.edu/hsc/info/pr/hmm/02spring/parkinsons.html. Accessed March 2, 2007.

National Cancer Institute. 2006. U.S. National Institutes of Health Surveillance, Epidemiology, and End Results (SEER) Program. At http://www.seer.cancer.gov. Accessed October 25, 2007.

————. n.d. Breast cancer home page. At http://www.cancer.gov/cancer topics/types/breast. Accessed October 25, 2007.

National Comprehensive Cancer Network. 2005. *Breast Cancer: Treatment Guidelines for Patients*. Version VII, August. Jenicktown, Pa.: National Comprehensive Cancer Network.

————. 2007. NCCN clinical practice guidelines in oncology. At http://www.nccn.org/professionals/physician_gls/default.asp. Accessed October 27, 2007.

National Diabetes Information Clearinghouse. 2006. *Insulin Resistance and Pre-diabetes*. National Institutes of Health (NIH) Publication no. 06-4893, August. Bethesda, Md.: NIH. At http://diabetes.niddk.nih .gov/dm/pubs/insulinresistance/index.htm. Accessed March 3, 2007.

National Digestive Diseases Information Clearinghouse. 2006. Non-alcoholic steatohepatitis. National Institutes of Health (NIH) Publication no. 07-4921, November. Bethesda, Md.: NIH. At http://digestive .niddk.nih.gov/ddiseases/pubs/nash/. Accessed March 3, 2007.

National Institute of Diabetes and Digestive and Kidney Diseases. 2006. Diabetes overview. September. At http://diabetes.niddk.nih.gov/dm/pubs/overview/index.htm. Accessed February 2, 2007.

National Institutes of Health. 1996. *Platillos Latinos ¡Sabrosos y saludables! Delicious Heart-Healthy Latino Recipes*. National Institutes of Health (NIH) Publication no. 96-4049. Bethesda, Md.: NIH. At http://www.nhlbi.nih .gov/health/public/heart/other/sp_recip.pdf. Accessed March 4, 2007.

Neumann, Anna, and Penelope Peterson, eds. 1997. *Lessons from Our Lives*. New York: Teachers College, Columbia University.

The New Good Housekeeping Family Health and Medical Guide. 1989. New York: Hearst Corp.

New York Thyroid Center. 2005. Hyperthyroidism. At http://cpmcnet .columbia.edu/dept/thyroid/HyperthyroidismHP.html. Accessed December 10, 2005.

Next generation: Cancer immunotherapies: New approaches promise to change the face of cancer. 2005. *StartUp* (Windhover Information, Inc.) (October): 31–39.

Obesity swells into a mega-epidemic. 2006. Director's Column. *National Center on Physical Activity and Disability (NCPAD) Newsletter* (February 16). At http://www.ncpad.org/director/fact_sheet .php?sheet=391. Accessed March 3, 2007.

Oktay, Kutluk, Erkan Buyuk, Natalie Libertella, Munire Akar, and Zev Rosenwaks. 2005. Fertility preservation in breast cancer patients: A prospective controlled comparison of ovarian stimulation with Tamoxifen and Letrozole for embryo cryopreservation. *Journal of Clinical Oncology* 23:4347–53.

Ortiz, F., J. Fitten, J. L. Cummings, S. Hwang, and M. Fonseca. 2006. Neuropsychiatric and behavioral symptoms in a community sample of Hispanics with Alzheimer's disease. *American Journal of Alzheimer's Disease and Other Dementias* 21:263–73.

Palo Alto Medical Foundation. 2003. Q & A on pre-diabetes. November. At http://www.pamf.org/diabetes/qa_pre-diabetes.html. Accessed March 3, 2007.

Piscatella, Joseph C., and Barry A. Franklin. 2003. *Take a Load off Your Heart.* New York: Workman.

Plichta, S. B. 2004. Intimate partner violence and physical health consequences. *Journal of Interpersonal Violence* 19 (11): 1296–323.

Radziuna, Eileen. 1989. *Lupus: My Search for a Diagnosis.* Alameda, Calif.: Hunter House.

Raj, A. 2002. Violence against immigrant women: The roles of culture, context, and legal immigrant status on intimate partner violence. *Violence Against Women* 8 (3): 367–98.

Reeves, Margaret, Kristin Schafer, Kate Hallward, and Anne Katten. 1999. *Fields of Poison: California Farmworkers and Pesticides.* San Francisco: Pesticide Action Network North America and Californians for Pesticide Reform. At http://www.panna.org/resources/documents/disrupting Avail.dv.html. Accessed January 15, 2007.

Rinpoche, Sogyal. 1994. *The Tibetan Book of Living and Dying.* San Francisco: Harper San Francisco.

Rodríguez, Luis J. 2005. *My Nature Is Hunger: New and Selected Poems, 1989–2004*. Willimantic, Conn.: Curbstone.

Rokach, A. 2006. Loneliness in domestically abused women. *Psychological Reports* 98 (2): 367–73.

Romero, Elaine. 1999. *The Fat-Free Chicana and the Snow Cap Queen.* In *Puro teatro: A Latina Anthology*, edited by Alberto Sandoval-Sánchez and Nancy Saporta Sternbach, 89–145. Tucson: University of Arizona Press.

Romijn, J. A., J. W. A. Smit, and S. W. J. Lamberts. 2003. Intrinsic imperfections of endocrine replacement therapy. *European Journal of Endocrinology* 149:91–97.

Rouse, L. P. 1988. Abuse in dating relationships: A comparison of blacks, whites, and Hispanics. *Journal of College Student Development* 29:312–19.

Ruiz, Vicki L., and Virginia Sánchez Korrol. 2005. *Latina Legacies: Identity, Biography, and Community.* New York: Oxford University Press.

Sacks, Oliver. 1995. *An Anthropologist on Mars.* New York: Alfred A. Knopf.

Schraufnagel, T., A. W. Wagner, J. Miranda, and P. Roy-Byrne. 2006. Treating minority patients with depression and anxiety: What does the evidence tell us? *General Hospital Psychiatry* 28:27–36.

Serros, Michele. 1999. Planned parenthood: Age sixteen. In *Chicana Falsa and Other Stories of Death, Identity, and Oxnard*, 70. New York: Riverhead Trade.

Setji, T. L., A. J. Brown, and M. N. Feinglos. 2005. Gestational diabetes mellitus. *Clinical Diabetes* 23 (1): 17–24.

Sheps, Sheldon G. 2002. *Mayo Clinic on High Blood Pressure.* Rochester, Minn.: Mayo Clinic.

Sorenson, S. B., and C. A. Telles. 1991. Self-reports of spousal violence in a Mexican American and non-Hispanic white population. *Violence and Victims* 6:3–15.

Sorenson, S. B., D. M. Upchurch, and H. Shen. 1996. Violence and injury in marital arguments. *American Journal of Public Health* 6:35–40.

Stanley, Patricia B. 2007. The female voice in illness: An antidote to alienation, a call for connection. In *Stories of Illness and Healing: Women Write Their Bodies*, edited by Sayantani DasGupta and Marsha Hurst, 22–30. Kent, Ohio: Kent State University Press.

Stepán, J. J., and Z. Límanová. 1992. Biochemical assessment of bone loss in patients on long-term thyroid hormone treatment. *Bone and Mineral* (the Netherlands) 17 (3): 377–88.

Straus, M. A., and C. Smith. 1990. Violence in Hispanic families in the United States: Incidence rates and structural interpretations. In *Physical Violence in American Families: Risk Factors and Adaptations to Violence in 8,145*

Families, edited by M. A. Straus and R. J. Gelles, 341–68. New Brunswick, N.J.: Transaction.

Sundaram, A., C. Ayala, K. Greenlund, and N. Keenan. 2001. Differences in the prevalence of self-reported risk factors for coronary heart disease among American women by race/ethnicity and age. *American Journal of Preventive Medicine* 29 (5, supp. 1): 25–30.

Talman, Donna Hamil. 1991. *Heartsearch: Toward Healing Lupus*. Berkeley, Calif.: North Atlantic Books.

Tiro, J., H. Meissner, S. Kobrin, and V. Chollette. 2007. What do women in the U.S. know about human papillomavirus and cervical cancer? *Cancer Epidemiological Biomarkers* 16 (2): 288–94.

Tkac, Debora. 1990. *The Doctor's Book of Home Remedies*. Emmaus, Penn.: Rodale.

Torres, L., and D. Rollock. 2007. Acculturation and depression among Hispanics: The moderating effect of intercultural competence. *Cultural Diversity and Ethnic Minority Psychology* 13 (1): 10–17.

Trotter, Robert T., II, and Juan Antonio Chavira. 1997. *Curanderismo: Mexican American Folk Healing*. 2d ed. Athens: University of Georgia Press.

Turok, D. K., S. D. Ratcliffe, and E. G. Baxley. 2003. Management of gestational diabetes mellitus. *American Family Physician* 68 (9): 1767–72. Review and erratum in *American Family Physician* 69 (6) (2004): 1362.

U.S. Census Bureau, Housing and Household Economic Statistics Division. 2004. Table HI01: Health insurance coverage status and type of coverage by selected characteristics, 2003. In *Current Population Survey, 1988 to 2004 Annual Social and Economic Supplements*. Washington, D.C.: U.S. Census Bureau. At http://pubdb3.census.gov/macro/032004/health/h01_016.htm. Accessed June 21, 2005.

U.S. Census Bureau, Population Division, Ethnic and Hispanic Statistics Branch. 2002. *The Hispanic Population in the United States: March 2002 Detailed Tables (PPL-165)*. Washington, D.C.: U.S. Census Bureau. At http://www.census.gov/population/socdemo/hispanic/ppl-165. Accessed June 22, 2005.

U.S. Department of Health and Human Services (DHHS). 2005. The heart truth for Latinas: An action plan. At the Magellan Health Services Web site, http://www.magellanassist.com/mem/library/default.asp?TopicId = 140&CategoryId=0&ArticleId=94. Accessed October 23, 2007.

———. 2006. *Your Guide to Lowering Your Blood Pressure with DASH*. National Institutes of Health (NIH) Publication no. 06-4082. Bethesda, Md.: NIH. At http://www.nhlbi.nih.gov/health/public/ heart/hbp/dash/new_dash.pdf. Accessed October 23, 2007.

U.S. Department of Health and Human Services, Health Resources and Services Administration (DHHS HRSA). 2004. Prenatal care. In *Women's Health, USA, 2004.* Washington, D.C.: U.S. DHHS. At http://www.mchb .hrsa/gov/whusa04/pages/ch2.htm#prenatal. Accessed June 22, 2005.

U.S. Department of Health and Human Services (DHHS), Minority Women's Health. 2006a. Hispanic American/Latinas. At the Women's Health Web site, http://womenshealth.gov/minority/hispanicamerican. Accessed June 10, 2007.

———. 2006b. Overweight and obesity. At the Women's Health Web site, http://www.womenshealth.gov/minority/hispanicamerican/obesity .cfm. Accessed March 3, 2007.

U.S. Preventive Services Task Force. 2005. Genetic risk assessment and BRCA mutation testing for breast and ovarian cancer susceptibility: U.S. Preventive Services Task Force recommendations (clinical guidelines). *Annals of Internal Medicine* 143 (September 6): 355–61.

Valle, Ramon. 1998. *Caregiving across Cultures: Working with Dementing Illness and Ethnically Diverse Populations.* Washington, D.C.: Taylor and Francis.

Van Den Eeden, S., C. Tanner, A. Bernstein, R. Fross, A. Leimpeter, D. Bloch, and L. Nelson. 2003. Incidence of Parkinson's disease: Variation by age, gender, and race/ethnicity. *American Journal of Epidemiology* 157 (11): 1015–22.

Velez-Ibañez, Carlos G. 1996. *Border Visions: Mexican Cultures of the Southwest United States.* Tucson: University of Arizona Press.

Villegas de Magnón, Leonor. 1994. *The Rebel.* Edited and introduced by Clara Lomas. Houston: Arte Público Press.

Wagner, Federico. 1952. *Plantas medicinales y remedios caseros.* 1936. Reprint. Mexico City: Aurora Editorial.

Wallis, Velma. 1993. *Two Old Women: An Alaska Legend of Betrayal, Courage, and Survival.* San Francisco: Harper San Francisco.

Waters, Michelle. 2003. *Dancing with the Diagnosis: Steps for Taking the Lead when Facing Cancer.* Scotts Valley, Calif.: Rising Star Press.

Weight-Control Information Network. 2004. Do you know the health risks of being overweight? At http://win.niddk.nih.gov/publications/health _ risks.htm. Accessed March 3, 2007.

Weiss, Rick. 2002. The stem cell divide. *National Geographic* (July): 3–27.

Wekking, E. M., B. C. Appelhof, E. Fliers, A. H. Schene, J. Huyser, J. G. P. Jijssen, and W. M. Wiersinga. 2005. Cognitive function and well-being in euthyroid patients on Thyroxine replacement therapy for primary hypothyroidism. *European Journal of Endocrinology* 153:747–53.

Wells, H. G. 1910. *In the Country of the Blind.* London: Nelson.

Wendler, M. Cecilia. 2005. Frida Kahlo: Wounded woman—A nursing perspective. At http://www.k-state.edu/english/janette/installations/Cecilia/kahlo. Accessed December 16, 2006.

Wiersinga, W. M., and L. J. DeGroot. 2004. Adult hypothyroidism. In *Thyroid Disease Manager*, edited by L. J. DeGroot and G. Hennemann, 33–35. Chicago: University of Chicago Pritzker School of Medicine, Endocrine Education. Also at http://www.thyroidmanager.org. Accessed December 10, 2005.

Williamson, Marianne. 1992. *A Return to Love*. San Francisco: Harper-Collins.

Woods, Michael. 2004. Weight gain in a pill: Some common prescription drugs can make patients put on pounds. *Toledo Blade*, May 24. At http://www.toledoblade.com/apps/pbcs.dll/article?AID=/20040531/NEWS32/405290303/-1/NEWS. Accessed March 10, 2007.

Working more than 40 hours a week raises blood pressure, research discovers. 2006. NewsTarget.com, August 30. At http://www.newstarget.com/ 020234.html. Accessed June 10, 2007.

Xiang, A. H., R. K. Peters, S. L. Kjos, A. Marroquin, J. Goico, C. Ochoa, M. Kawakubo, and T. A. Buchanan. 2006. Effect of pioglitazone on pancreatic {beta}-cell function and diabetes risk in Hispanic women with prior gestational diabetes. *Diabetes* 55 (2): 517–22.

Yahoo Health. 2004. *Healthwise Encyclopedia*. At http://health.yahoo.com/ency/ healthwise/hw62787.2004. Accessed June 10, 2006.

Youdim, Moussa B. H., and Peter Riederer. 1997. Understanding Parkinson's disease. *Scientific American* (January 1997): 52–59.

Zohar, Danah. 1990. *The Quantum Self: Human Nature and Consciousness Defined by the New Physics*. New York: Quill/William Morrow.

About the Editors

ANGIE CHABRAM-DERNERSESIAN is a professor of Chicana/o studies at the University of California, Davis, with a specialization in cultural studies and Chicana feminism. She has coedited two special issues of the *International Journal of Cultural Studies* and has recently edited *The Chicana/o Cultural Studies Reader* (2006) and *The Chicana/o Cultural Studies Forum* (2007). Her published work is also featured in the anthologies *Displacing Whiteness, Between Woman and Nation, Cultural Studies,* and *The Chicana/o Studies Reader.*

ADELA DE LA TORRE is a health-policy economist and professor of Chicana/o studies at the University of California, Davis, and an adjunct professor in the Department of Family and Community Medicine at the university's School of Medicine. She is the director of Chicana/o studies at Davis, and currently serves as the director of the Center of Public Policy, Race, Ethnicity, and Gender. In her current research, Dr. de la Torre is coprincipal investigator on a longitudinal study funded by the National Institutes of Health that examines the impact of targeted HIV-prevention education on health behaviors of high-risk sex workers on the U.S.–Mexico border. In this capacity, she helped develop the first culturally sensitive Spanish-based training manual for sex-worker interventionists and community-based outreach workers. She has also served as principal investigator for the California Department of Public Health's LabAspire Program and has spearheaded two study-abroad programs that create opportunities for undergraduate Chicana/o and Latina/o studies students to study health, economics, and policy issues in Argentina and Oaxaca, Mexico. She is the mother of two daughters, Adelita and Gaby, and lives with her husband, Stephen Bartlett, in Sacramento.

About the Contributors

GABRIELA F. ARREDONDO is associate professor of Latin American and Latina/o studies at the University of California, Santa Cruz. She received her Ph.D. from the University of Chicago. She is coauthor of *Chicana Feminisms: A Critical Reader* (2008) and *Mexican Chicago: Race, Identity, and Nation, 1916–1939* (2008). Dr. Arredondo is currently a faculty research fellow at the Center for Comparative Study of Race and Ethnicity at Stanford University. Her teaching and research interests include comparative Latina/o histories, gender and racial formations, U.S.–Mexico transnationalisms, comparative immigration, postcolonial Mexico, and U.S. social history, as well as Chicana/o history. Her current research project explores a variety of historical interracial contacts between Mexicans and non-Mexicans to understand how such experiences contributed to contemporary conceptions of race and gender. This comparative project, grounded in the 1920s and 1930s, includes sites such as Chicago, San Francisco, Mexico City, and the Mexican state of Michoacán.

CONCHA DELGADO GAITAN is an award-winning ethnographic researcher and writer of oral and written traditions in immigrant communities, including family and community empowerment through literacy. She has worked with Latino, Southeast Asian, Russian refugee, and Alaskan Native communities in the United States. She describes the empowerment of families, communities, and schools in her many publications, including seven books: *Building Culturally Responsive Classrooms* (2006), *Involving Latino Families in the Schools* (2004), *The Power of Community* (2001), *Crossing Cultural Borders* (1991), *Literacy for Empowerment* (1990), and *School and Society* (1988). Dr. Gaitan brings to her scholarly work a broad experience as an elementary school teacher, elementary school principal, ethnographic researcher, and professor of anthropology and education at the University of California, Santa Barbara and Davis. She has recently been invited to be a visiting professor at the University of Texas, El Paso. When she is not lecturing or researching in other parts of the country, she is a writer in the San Francisco Bay Area, where she lives with her husband, Dudley Thompson, and their tabby cat, Sofia.

YVETTE G. FLORES is a licensed clinical psychologist (California) with more than twenty years' experience in the treatment of substance abuse, trauma depression, family and intimate partner violence, and adjustment problems related to migration and acculturation. With a doctorate in clinical psychology from the University of California, Berkeley, she is a professor of psychology in Chicana/o studies at the University of California, Davis. She has also taught in Argentina, Costa Rica, Panama, and Mexico. Dr. Flores has published extensively in the area of Latina/o mental health. Her current research interests include HIV prevention along the U.S.–Mexico border, health promotion among rural Mexicans, and caregivers of elderly Latinos with dementia. Dr. Flores lectures nationally and internationally on the treatment of intimate partner violence and addiction and is a cultural competency trainer. She is also the mother of two young adults and the grandmother of two wonderful baby girls.

LORENA GARCÍA, an epidemiologist, is an assistant professor in Chicana/o studies at the University of California, Davis. She received a master's in epidemiology/biostatistics and public health from Boston University in 1996 and a doctorate in public health from the Department of Epidemiology at the University of California, Los Angeles, in 2002. Dr. García has been engaged in Latino health research since the early 1990s, with a special interest in injury and violence prevention in the Latino community. She has participated in various projects dealing with Latino health, such as injury, acculturation, diabetes, HIV/AIDS prevention among sex workers along the U.S.–Mexico border, intimate partner violence among Latinas in the United States and Latin America, health-insurance status of Latinas, Latino health-care access and utilization, inhalant abuse among Latino youth, community-based HIV-prevention and intervention programs for pregnant women at high risk, U.S.–Mexico border health, community-based health initiatives to address Latino communities, and ethnic and cultural differences in health behavior and health problems.

ANALOUISE KEATING, professor of women's studies at Texas Woman's University, worked with Gloria Anzaldúa for more than ten years. She is the editor of *EntreMundos / AmongWorlds: New Perspectives on Gloria Anzaldúa* (2005) and of Anzaldúa's *Interviews / Entrevistas* (2000); she and Anzaldúa edited *this bridge we call home: radical visions for transformation* (2002) and were working on several projects at the time of Anzaldúa's death in 2004. Keating is also the author of *Teaching Transformation: Transcultural Classroom Dialogues* (2007) and *Women Reading, Women Writing: Self-Invention in Paula Gunn Allen, Gloria Anzaldúa, and Audre Lorde* (1996), as well as of articles on Latina authors, African American literature, queer studies, multiculturalism, eighteenth- and nineteenth-century American writers, feminist theory, and pedagogy.

CLARA LOMAS is professor in the Department of Romance Languages at the Colorado College. She has published in *Women's Studies International Forum* (London), *Dictionary of Literary Biography*, *FEM: Revista feminista* (Mexico), and *Revista Chicano-Riqueña*; has contributed chapters to *Oxford Encyclopedia of Latinos and Latinas in the United States* (2006), *Cultures D'Amérique Latine aux Etats-Unis: Confrontations et métissages* (1995), *Chicana Voices: Intersections of Class, Race, and Gender* (1993), *Longman Anthology of World Literature by Women, 1895–1975* (1989), *Estudios Chicanos and the Politics of Community* (1989), and the journal *Multi-Ethnic Literature of the United States*; and coedited *One Wound for Another / Una herida por otra: Testimonios de Latinas in the U.S. (11 de septiembre de 2001–11 de marzo de 2002)* (with Claire Joysmith, 2005) and *Chicano Politics after the 80s* (with Juan García and Julia Curry, 1987). She also coauthored *Telling to Live: Latina Feminist Testimonios* (2001) and edited and introduced Leonor Villegas de Magnón's autobiographies *The Rebel* (1994) and *La rebelde* (2004). A Fulbright scholar during the 2001–2002 academic year, Dr. Lomas conducted research and prepared her current manuscript, "The Alchemy of Erasure: On Mapping Women's Intellectual History of the Borderlands," while in Mexico City at the Dirección de Estudios Históricos at the Instituto Nacional de Antropología e Historia.

JESSICA NÚÑEZ DE YBARRA currently works at the State of California Department of Public Health in the Division of Communicable Disease Control, Office of Workforce Development, as a public-health medical officer coordinating public-health training and emergency preparedness activities. She previously served as a deputy public-health officer in the Kern County Department of Public Health and as director of its Office of Public Health Preparedness. She is presently a volunteer assistant clinical professor in the School of Medicine's Department of Public Health Sciences at the University of California, Davis. She has also served as a lecturer in the university's Chicano/a Studies Program. Jessica has an M.D. from Davis and an MS in public health and health services administration from the University of California, Los Angeles. She is board certified in public health and general preventive medicine and lives in Sacramento, California, with her husband, Steven J. Ybarra.

ADALJIZA SOSA-RIDDELL is a professor emeritus and former director of Chicana/o studies at the University of California, Davis. An esteemed activist, writer, and scholar of Chicana feminism, she was instrumental in founding Mujeres Activas en Letras y Cambio Social (MALCS), an organization of Chicanas, Latinas, and Native American women working within academia and communities to promote and support work on Chicana, Latina, and Native women's issues. She has been published in the proceedings of the National Association for Chicana/o Studies, as well as in the anthology *The Chicana/o Studies Reader.* She is also a published poet whose work has focused on Chicana themes.

ENRIQUETA VALDEZ-CURIEL is a medical doctor, radio producer, and professor of research in the Medical School at the University of Guadalajara (Guzmán City campus) in Mexico. Born in Ameca, Jalisco, to Mexican migrant worker parents, Dr. Valdez-Curiel earned a medical degree from the University of Guadalajara and later earned a master's degree in community development at the University of California, Davis, where she focused on rural women's health. During this period, she began conducting qualitative research on entertainment-education radio programs and later worked as a consultant to Radio Bilingüe (Bilingual Radio) in Salinas, California. Since 1998, she has worked on a variety of projects involving medical anthropology and entertainment education. She currently directs the project Radio ADO, an entertainment-education radio program developed and produced for youth by youth to promote sexual education in Mexico.